Feb/90

To Aunt Florence
Take a joke with each
pill and another for
each pain!
Love, Deb
XO

GUARANTEED TO MAKE YOU
Laugh!

Joey Adams

GUARANTEED TO MAKE YOU Laugh!

WYNWOOD™ Press
New York, New York

Library of Congress Cataloging-in-Publication Data

Adams, Joey, 1911–
    Guaranteed to make you laugh.

    1. American wit and humor.   I. Title.
PN6162.A279   1989   818'.5402   89-5400
ISBN 0-922066-04-3

Copyright © 1989 by Joey Adams
Published by WYNWOOD™ Press
New York, New York
Printed in the United States of America

Encyclopedia of Humor

I have collected jokes, gags, funny stories, and roast lines for you for any and all occasions. If you're making a speech, answering a summons, writing a creditor, roasting a friend, or getting in or out of any problem, use these punch lines instead of punches.

If you're out in public, you must be prepared. The encyclopedia will prepare you for everything but failure.

CONTENTS

8 Contents

FOREWORD AND BACKWORD

When President John F. Kennedy sent me around the world as America's Goodwill Ambassador, he told me, "Use a joke instead of a stick, use a gag instead of a rock, use a laugh instead of a bomb." That's why I wrote this book: to prepare you in case you run into a bad audience, a tough opponent, or a rough customer. . . .

I'll get you ready if you're going to make a speech or roast a friend, or if you're a salesman looking for business. *Guaranteed to Make You Laugh* will give you the ammunition to bring out the joy in any situation. As my great friend Dr. Martin Luther King explained when I asked him how he handled his enemies: "Love the hell out of them—and do it with a laugh . . . ."

My godfather, the late, great mayor of the city of New York, Fiorello La Guardia, always solved his problems with a bit of wit. He once appointed a man to public office who took a $20,000 bribe. The mayor went on the air and took full responsibility: "I very seldom make a mistake—but when I do it's a beaut"—and it was all over . . . .

I will best remember him for reading the funnies to the kids every day on the radio during a newspaper strike in New York. I can still hear his high-pitched voice telling the youngsters about what was happening to Dick Tracy, "And remember, kids, dirty money never did anybody any good."

In love or hate, his sense of humor always came through. When Congressman La Guardia married his longtime secretary, Marie Fischer, she gave up the job to run his home. He never stopped complaining, "I lost a great secretary and found a lousy cook."

La Guardia hated bookies, gamblers, lawyers, royalty, big brass, male ballet dancers, and abstract art—in that order. But when he loved—especially children—he did it with a passion. When I opened at Loew's State Theatre, my best big chance on Broadway, he invited all his cronies to come and see "my boy."

If he had been a plumber, his pals would probably have been plumbers. But since he was the mayor, his gang was the city chiefs—the police commissioner, fire chief, and all the big wheels of our town. They were to meet in the lobby of the theater at two o'clock Saturday afternoon. When the manager of the theater saw all the city fathers gathered together with their uniformed drivers, it looked like a raid.

"What's wrong, Mr. Mayor?" the manager begged. The mayor grasped the humor of the situation immediately. "Guard the exits," he roared at the police commissioner. "Check the aisles," he barked at the license commissioner . . . . "Oh Mr. Mayor," the manager said, now out of his mind, "can't we do something about this?" "There's only one thing you can do," La Guardia shouted at the frightened theater man. "Anything—anything," the manager pleaded. "We'll do anything—just don't close us up." "Well," the mayor smiled, "give Joey Adams a raise and top billing."

JFK threw one-liners better than any stand-up comic. Whenever he had a problem, I would supply him with the jokes to get out of it. When they said his father was buying his election, he announced at a White House dinner: "I have this wire from my very generous Daddy: 'I don't mind paying for your election—but I refuse to pay for a landslide.' "

Another time, when he appointed his kid brother Bobby as attorney general, just out of law school (I think he was eleven years old at the time), the reporters asked, "Mr. President, how could you appoint your young brother attorney general of the greatest country in the world—and him just out of law school?" The prez had my joke ready: "Well, he *is* my kid brother, and I wanted to give him *some* experience before he opened up his own law office."

A good joke will get you out of any tough spot.

Ronald Reagan is the greatest: "What do you mean I'm too old to be president? In this country about the only job a seventy-seven-year-old man can get is president of the United States."

When I said on the air, "Why do you say he's too old? Just because his social security number is *two*?" he called the next day. "What kind of a lousy joke is that—'my social security number is two?' " I said, "You got a better one?" He said, "Yes, my social security number is in Roman numerals."

Ron's sense of humor saved his life after the assassination attempt, say his doctors. The prez wanted to make sure that his surgeons were all qualified: "I hope you're all Republicans." When he came out of ether, he offered a simple apology to Nancy: "Honey, I forgot to duck." He said to the reporters, "If I'd gotten this much attention in Hollywood—I never would have left."

Reagan handles it all with laughs: "Considering the problems facing this country—we probably should open an embassy in Lourdes."

Talking about age, George Burns is always ready with gag lines to destroy his age lines: "The big thing is to think young—I feel fortunate that at ninety-two I can do anything I could do when I was ninety-one."

George tells the big joke going the rounds: Adam said to Eve, "Let's go out tonight." Eve asked, "Where?" Adam replied, "The Garden Club—they're featuring a comic called George Burns."

George always has a young girl with him: "It's better than leaning on a cane. . . ." He lectures, "Sex can be fun after 80, after 90, after 100, and after lunch." George admits he loves to go with young girls—"But now I forget what for!"

Johnny Carson really needs jokes to handle all those alimony payments: "Marriage is the most expensive way of discovering your faults," he lectures. "The difference between divorce and separation is that a legal separation gives a husband time to hide his money."

Johnny is always going through a change of wife and he pays a lot of alimony—but it pays off in joke lines: "In Hollywood, a faithful husband is one whose alimony check is always on time."

"Alimony is giving comfort to the enemy—a husband's cash-surrender value."

"Paying alimony is like having the TV set on after you've fallen asleep."

"It is better to have loved and lost—providing no alimony is involved."

John V. Lindsay was the handsomest mayor in New York's history, but he would have rather handled jokes than handle the city. When he had to make a speech or a personal appearance or a press conference, I gave him the gag lines to fit the situation.

At one big show business dinner, I was the toastmaster and he was the guest of honor. He insisted I give him my best jokes, and I did—I gave him eight great one-liners. I also rehearsed him.

The night of the dinner, he was waiting for me in the lobby of the hotel. "Let's go to the men's room," he said, "and rehearse the lines—I want to do great here." Sure. How do you refuse your mayor? I sat there while he went over every line twenty times, with all the gestures and inflections. Then we went in to sit on the dais.

After the dinner, I went to the microphone to do my job. At the end, just before I introduced Lindsay, I did all the eight jokes I had given and rehearsed with him. The mayor then walked to the mike slowly: "I met Joey Adams in the men's room," he started, "and he was crying because he didn't have any jokes for tonight. He said this was a show business audience and he had to make good with his peers. I felt sorry for him, so I gave him all my jokes—you just heard them—so good night!"

New York has a great spiritual leader: Cardinal John J. O'Connor. He comes to us with a great sense of humor: "The Lord created the world in six days; on the seventh day he rested. On the eighth day he started to answer complaints."

His Eminence notes, "It makes me nervous to hear people say they found God—I didn't know he was lost."

The cardinal also says, "They haven't really taken prayers out of the schools: You should hear the teachers just before they open the doors."

Cardinal O'Connor's wit covers a lot of sins: "Different people look for different things in the Bible. Some are looking for divine guidance, some for a code of living—most are looking for loopholes."

"I do benefits for all religions," I told the cardinal. "I'd hate to blow the hereafter on a technicality." His Eminence agreed: "Just remember you must pay for your sins. If you already paid, forget I told you."

As Cardinal O'Connor told the IRS guy, "The law may be on your side, sir, but the Lord is on mine."

His Eminence will not discuss the TV evangelists—but *I* will: "Reverend" Bakker says the new bible in his church will only have nine commandments. That annoying one about adultery is definitely out, but he is going heavy on the love thy neighbor bit.

Religion must be important in every election and the jokes that go with it: Gary Hart could have won the 1988 presidential election if he'd campaigned through the Sunbelt and the Bible belt—while wearing a chastity belt.

The cardinal told me about Gregory, who keeps praying and beseeching God to let him win the lottery. Every time somebody wins, he pleads, "Why not me, Lord? I'm so much more pious." This goes on for weeks and months. Finally, God responds, "Give me a break, Gregory. Buy a ticket."

I'm for religion all the way: Now take His Holiness the Pope. He draws huge crowds wherever he goes. It's kind of amazing when you consider the man has never had a hit record.

New York City has Donald Trump and Mayor Ed Koch— the greatest team since Abbot and Costello: They're always prepared to throw punch lines—especially at each other . . . .

Donald says he would contribute to Ed's campaign, if he would run again for mayor—of any city in South America . . . .

Ed says, "What can you say about Donald Trump that hasn't been said about warts?"

Says Donald, "That Koch really likes you to come out and say what you think . . . when you agree with him."

Every year, Christmas is great at the Trumps. Santa comes down the chimney and Donald gives *him* a present. This year he may give him Ed Koch.

Ed says, "Donald Trump's a great guy in my book—and in his too."

Donald says, "Ed Koch has done a lot for the people—so has Kaopectate."

President Sukarno of Indonesia was one of the all-time great leaders of the world. His sense of humor and his wit got him in and out of trouble constantly. Cindy and I were with him in Russia when his wit really saved his life.

Sukarno was *the* ladies' man. He had four wives, six concubines, and a broad behind every bush. Of course, the Reds knew all about this. So, when he checked in, they gave him a five-room suite and planted five beautiful Russian gals as hors d'oeuvres for his personal pleasure.

The next morning, when we all went to the Kremlin for the real business, one of the Reds told him, "We'd like to talk to you personally, sir." Sukarno said, "Cindy is writing my life story and Joey is my best pal. You can talk in front of them."

"Well," the man started, "we gave you those beautiful Russian ladies in your room—and we took pictures of you in every possible position and act. Our leaders say, unless you do what they need from you, they will send these pictures to your country."

Sukarno didn't blink or stop to think: He said, "I hope they're in color—my countrymen will be very proud of me."

GUARANTEED
TO MAKE YOU
Laugh!

Absentminded People

I once suffered from senility—but I forgot about it.

The executive was so absentminded he had his mail sent to the golf course and played with his secretary all day.

A man I know was traveling by train. The conductor came and asked for the ticket. The man searched his pockets but couldn't find it. The conductor, who knew him, saw that he was upset and said, "Don't worry, please. You send it to me when you find it." The man replied, "Oh, that's not the matter—I want to know where I'm going!"

The TV star does all his shows by using teleprompters. He swears that at his wedding ceremony he had to use cue cards.

How absentminded can you get? The waitress kissed her boyfriend good-night and then said, "Is that all, sir?"

And how about the professor who kissed his students good-bye and then went home and gave his wife an examination?

This character was really absentminded: He parked his car in front of the loan company.

The secretary said to the boss's wife: "Your husband is so absentminded that last night I had to keep reminding him that he's married to you and not to me."

Listen, an elephant never forgets—but then, what has he got to remember?

Everyone in town knew Grandpa was getting a little forgetful, so Grandma wasn't surprised when he came home with the announcement that he had lost his umbrella. "When did you first miss it?" she asked. "Just this minute," he replied. "The rain stopped and when I reached up to close it, it was gone!"

Actors

You can always tell an actor by the faraway look that comes into his eyes when the conversation gets away from him.

I was crazy about this girl, but her father said, "I'll never let my daughter marry an actor." I said, "At least come and see my show." After the performance I ran to see her old man. "You can marry my daughter," he said. "You're not an actor."

One small-time producer was interviewing girls for the lead in an off-Broadway extravanonsense! This gorgeous fugitive from Hollywood caught his eye: "You're just right" he told her. "Right face, right voice, right coloring— just what the script calls for. By the way, what's your salary?" The girl said, "Twelve hundred a week!" He said, "Sorry—you're too tall!"

Actors aren't people, although there are plenty of people who are actors. I love them for their illusions just as much as I love them for their talents, their exaggerations, their persistency, their guts, and their faith in God and themselves. And I know in this case they'll forgive me for giving God top billing.

An actor is a man who tries to be everything but himself.

A true actor will never find anyone who can give him the love and devotion that he gives himself. That's why fan clubs are formed. A fan club is a group of people who tell an actor he's not alone in the way he feels about himself.

Actors never give up: Two old thespians in their mid-eighties were sitting at the Actor's Retirement Home and were naturally hallucinating about their next starring roles. In a break in their bragging, one turned to the other and said, "Hey, I forgot, was it you or your brother who died last year?"

Ed Wynn decided to leave home at the age of fifteen and join a theater company. His father was furious: "A son of mine on the stage? " he cried. "It's a disgrace. What if the neighbors find out?" The comic-to-be said, "I'll change my name." The old man yelled, "Change your name? What if you're a success—how will the neighbors know it's my son?"

This ham was bragging that his fan mail kept five secretaries busy. "It sure does," said his press pal. "They're busy writing it."

The only thing an actor fears more than losing his mind is regaining it.

A celebrity works all his life to become famous—then goes around in dark glasses so nobody will know who he is.

She was the wife of a third-rate actor. When she announced she was going to have his baby, her agent said, "I hope you have a better delivery than your husband."

"I can't leave the theater," he told his wife. "I'm married to it." She said, "Then why not sue it for nonsupport?"

A reporter once asked the aging actor-lothario who was playing Hamlet at the Barrymore Theater: "In your opinion, did Shakespeare intend that Hamlet was making it with Ophelia?" The actor answered, "I'm not sure—but I frequently do."

The actor was sitting with the playwright on the opening night of his show. "What's with all the booing?" the actor asked the writer. "There's some clapping," the author noted. "Don't fool yourself," the actor said. "That's for the booing."

The best actors at the Tony Award ceremonies are the good losers.

The overweight actress claimed all her weight was just water. One critic wrote, "It's true. On the right side she's got the Atlantic Ocean, on the left, the Pacific, and in the rear, the Dead Sea."

I'm going to watch the Academy Awards whether I need the sleep or not. It's what they call escapist entertainment: Before it's over, you want to escape.

I don't know why they hold the Academy Awards in Hollywood. The best acting is done in Washington.

I know one actor with such an ego he brings his makeup man when he goes for his passport photos.

One star had an alias, an unlisted phone, a cable address, and a Swiss bank account. When his agent finally got a job for him, he couldn't find him to book him.

Scientists have just constructed a new clock that will lose only one second per 5 million years—and the Academy Awards will still run two hours overtime.

Advice

We would all be more willing to accept good advice if it didn't always interfere with our plans.

Listen, if you can't tell the difference between good and bad advice, then you sure don't need advice.

It's always more blessed to give than receive—especially if you're a professional boxer.

Never buy an evening gown from a vending machine.

There's an old proverb that goes something like this: "If one man calleth thee a donkey, pay him no mind. If more than one man calleth thee a donkey—get thee a saddle."

One reader wrote me, "I was on Eighth Avenue and a girl asked me, 'Do you want to have some fun?' I said, 'Yes.' So she sold me a joke book."

My niece cried, "I set out to reform my fiancé. I got him to give up smoking, drinking, swearing, and gambling. When I finished with him, he decided I wasn't good enough for him—so he got rid of me."

Don't play in the street—you may get that run-down feeling. Don't drop out of school—especially if you're on the third floor. Don't kiss a girl under the mistletoe—it's more fun under the nose.

The difference between virtue and vice is that the former is usually learned at Mother's knee, while the latter is learned at some other joint.

Airlines

I'm fascinated with those no-frill airlines: The stewardess announced, "In case of emergency, your oxygen mask will drop down—if not, open the window." On no-frills they charge you for everything—it's the first time I ever saw an oxygen mask with a meter . . . Comfort, safety, relaxation? Fly no-frills and get away from all that.

I like to watch the searching parties at the airlines. You ought to see this old maid. It's amazing—she's been three days out at the airport, getting frisked. What makes it amazing, she doesn't even have a ticket. Eighty-seven passengers were in transit—this old gal was in heaven. I'll tell you how intimate the airline search is: One airline got five complaints—two from passengers and three from massage parlors.

Where might you find atheists at prayer? In an airport baggage claim area.

Does all lost baggage go to Columbus, Ohio? Columbus is Central Losing. Your misplaced luggage will go there unless Columbus is where you are going. What if you're traveling on an airline that doesn't have any flights to Columbus? Don't worry—it will get there anyway.

What is the best way to avoid having your baggage lost when traveling by air? Go by bus.

Last week the airline luggage handlers were going on strike but decided against it—somebody lost the picket signs.

Why do they tell you to check in at the gate an hour before departure time? It's for your own good: The sooner you check in, the sooner you will find out about the delay.

When can you be reasonably certain of a delay in departure time? When you make your reservations.

How can you tell a plane is about to hit turbulence? The stewardess is serving coffee.

The last time I flew on one of those no-frill airlines I didn't feel too safe—especially when during the middle of the flight, our pilot came back to the tourist section and proudly showed everybody his new learner's permit.

Some airlines are real nasty: They're slashing their fares but figure to get even with passengers by serving larger portions of food!

Boy, talk about a small airline—during an emergency, a little compartment over my seat popped open and a rabbit's foot came out. The stewardess was a midget, and she was offering condensed milk. During a flight to Europe, they handed out fishing poles at dinner time and flew real low.

My brother walked up to the ticket counter and said, "I'd like two chances on your three o'clock flight to Miami."

The pilot was talking to his passengers: "Sit back and relax and enjoy the trip. You will know immediately if anything goes wrong: Our co-pilot will become hysterical."

On a no-frill airline: "Ladies and Gentlemen," the pilot announced, "the cabin attendants will now begin our food service. Since this is a low-cost, no-frill flight, you are to take only one bite before passing the sandwich along."

Alaska

Nobody was happier than I when Alaska become our forty-ninth state—but I don't intend to go there again until it melts.

I love God's frozen people, but I get a chill when I open the refrigerator.

It was so freezing—I was cold in places I didn't even know I had.

I didn't have to go to Florida last winter. I came home from Alaska with some color—blue. Would you believe the penguins were bringing babies instead of the stork? One Eskimo advertised in the local snow-sheet that she was looking for a man with a high fever for a roommate.

I worked in a nightclub in Anchorage and I must admit I was a big hit. The only trouble was the audience was a little old. I talked to one guy for an hour before I found out he was a snowman. Everybody came formal, sporting tuxedos with built-in parkas and patent leather snow-shoes. The ringside was reserved for eight—the mayor, his missus, and six huskies.

Many young couples are shoving off to Alaska on their honeymoons. They want to have a long first night—and six months is a long night.

Just a word or two of warning: Make sure there's Prestone in your waterbed. And remember, it's a little tough to start your car in the morning and your wife at night, but you can make a little extra money renting out your bedroom as a meat locker.

Everybody talks about the weather—which isn't easy when your teeth are chattering.

It was so cold I sneezed and broke my Kleenex.

It was so cold Superman froze his *S* off.

The man in Alaska was arrested for bigamy: He had a wife in Nome, another in Fairbanks, and still another in Anchorage. The judge screamed at the culprit: "How could you do such a thing?" The guy shrugged: "Fast dog team."

Animals

The sweet young female oyster had just returned from her first date and was telling her experience to several of her oyster girlfriends. As she was recounting how striking her oyster date was, and how soulfully he looked into her eyes, she suddenly clutched her throat and screamed, "My God—my pearls!"

We no longer believe that people can change themselves into animals, yet the world is full of men who make hogs and asses of themselves.

A theatrical agent wouldn't listen to the actor who claimed he could do any kind of bird imitation. "At least listen to my act," he begged. The agent said, "Haven't got time— bird imitators died with vaudeville." "Okay," the artist said. "If that's how you feel, nuts to you!"—and he flew out the window.

A lobster strolled into a restaurant and sat down at a table by the window. "What would you like, sir?" the waiter asked. The lobster answered, "A little mayonnaise."

An elephant lumbered into a saloon. "We're not allowed

to serve intoxicating liquids to pachyderms," the bartender said. "Who wants intoxicating liquids?" the elephant said. "I just came in for the peanuts!"

I had a long talk with the elephant at the circus and cleared up a lot of things: "Why do elephants have trunks?" "Because they don't have glove compartments."

"Why do elephants live in the jungle?" "Because it's out of the high-rent district."

"Why don't many elephants go to college?" "Few finish high school."

"Why aren't elephants allowed on beaches?" "Because they can't keep their trunks up."

The actor walked into the restaurant with his pet terrier. The maitre d' gave them a corner table for two and handed the actor the menu. "Does it look like I'm eating alone?" the star yelled. "Service for two." After coffee and brandy, the waiter brought the check and placed it in front of the actor. "Are you nuts?" he yelled again, throwing the check in front of the dog. "Don't you understand anything? I'm his guest."

I was in the card room at the club and was surprised to see three men and a dog playing bridge. I stopped to watch and then remarked on the extraordinary performance of the dog. "He's not so smart," the partner said. "Every time he gets a good hand he wags his tail and gives it away."

If any animal tells you he can talk, he's lying.

I found a donkey with an IQ of 138—hasn't got a friend in the world because nobody likes a smart ass.

My neighbor has a dog: "In some ways he's better than a wife. The license is cheaper, he doesn't have in-laws—and he already comes with a fur coat."

The rock 'n roller's dog got loose and ran away from the jam session. He noticed a parking meter by the curb and was about to approach it, when a motorist slipped a quarter into the slot. "Man," said the rocker's dog as he flipped. "Dig that crazy pay toilet!"

Why does the hummingbird hum? He can't remember the words.

My cousin and his dog entered the talent agency. Before my cousin could finish his sales pitch, the agent cut him short. "Dog acts are out!" he shouted as he slammed the door on the pair. A moment later the dog burst back in and said indignantly, "At least you gotta admit, you couldn't see my lips move."

I used to have a turtle but it passed away: It fell in love with a souvenir German helmet and died of a broken heart.

How can you tell when an elephant is about to charge? He takes out his American Express card.

Animals are very valuable, especially in a woman's life. She needs four animals: a Jaguar in her garage, a tiger in her bed, a mink in her closet, and a jackass to pay for it all.

A father mosquito who supervised a trial flight of his two young sons over the beach in Atlantic City was lecturing: "What a wonderful age we live in. When I was young, the only places you could sting those girls was on the hands and face."

My nephew told me, "I don't think animals are so smart. I took my dog to obedience school and I learned to sit and speak two hours before he did."

My neighbor rushed into the hospital emergency room: "Dog took a bite out of my leg!" he cried. The nurse said, "Did you put anything on it?" He said, "No—he liked it just the way it was."

Two mosquitos were cruising down the street one day when one said to the other, "Look down there—that drunk's an easy target." The other answered, "You bite him—I'm driving."

A dog has so many friends because he wags his tail instead of his tongue.

A dog is the only friend you can buy for money.

You never realize a dog is man's best friend until you start betting on the horses.

Don't misunderstand, animals can talk to each other—you just have to learn their language.

A movie producer tossed an old can of film into a lot. A goat that was passing by found it and ate it. While he was eating, another goat passed by and asked, "How does it taste?" The feasting goat replied, "I liked the book much better."

Some buffalo were grazing on the open range when a cowboy rode up. He stared at them for a few minutes and then screamed out, "You are such ugly creatures! Your hind legs are longer than your front ones, you have humps on your backs, shaggy hair, beady eyes, and tails with bushes. Ugly! Disgusting!" Then he rode away. "Gee," one buffalo remarked to the others, "I think we just heard a discouraging word!"

How much did the psychiatrist charge the elephant? Thirty-five dollars for the visit and $350 for the couch.

What do you get when you cross an elephant and a prostitute? A three-quarter-ton pickup.

Do animals talk? All I know is, I bought a parrot guaranteed to talk. My phone bill tripled.

I wanted to teach my parrot to talk. I stood in front of the cage and said, "Hello, pretty boy." But he just looked at me and said, "No hablo inglés"—so now he's teaching me Spanish.

Animals are not as dumb as people think—For instance, they have no lawyers.

A well-known actor comes into a bar with a gorilla and orders two martinis. The bartender says to the actor,

"Okay, what can he do, sing? Tell jokes? Dance? Act? What?" The actor replied, "Nothing." The bartender said, "Then why did you bring him into this bar?" The actor said, "He's my agent."

The salesman dropped in to see a customer. No one was in the office except a big dog emptying wastebaskets. The salesman thought he was imagining it until the dog looked up and said, "Don't be surprised, Buddy, this is part of my job." The man muttered, "Incredible. I can't believe it. I'm gonna tell the boss what a prize he has in you—an animal that can talk." The dog pleaded, "Please—no— don't. If that bum finds out I can talk, he'll make me answer the phones!"

A cowboy fell off his horse and broke his leg way out in the prairie. The faithful animal grabbed his master's belt in his teeth and carried him to a safe place under a tree. Then he went for the doctor. A friend praised the horse's intelligence. The cowboy said, "Hell—what's so smart about him? He came back with the veterinarian."

The cowboy asked the vet, "My horse walks normally sometimes and sometimes he limps. What shall I do?" Said the vet, "The next time he walks normally—sell him."

The sheriff of a small town upstate also happens to be the veterinarian. One night the telephone rang and his wife picked up the phone. The hysterical voice pleaded, "Is Doctor Dixie there?" She asked, "Do you want my hus- band as a veterinarian or sheriff?" The nervous reply came, "Both—we can't get our bulldog to open his mouth, and there's a burglar in it."

I walked by a pet shop the other day, and a sign in the window read, 100 RABBITS FOR SALE. A few days later I walked by the same pet shop, and the sign read, 1,500 RABBITS FOR SALE.

If you're thinking of having an animal over for dinner, a cow eats seven times as much as a sheep.

My friend brought his sick parrot to the ASPCA. The

doctor asked him, "What seems to be wrong?" My friend started to tell him, when the parrot interrupted, saying, "Hold on, Buster, I'm not like your stupid cat. I can talk for myself!"

A woman went to a pet store to buy a dog. The manager showed her a dachshund. "He's cute," she said, "but his legs are too short." "What do you mean, too short?" exclaimed the manager. "All four of them touch the floor!"

Two dogs met on the street and struck up a conversation. "I'm a mess," said one. "I think I'm headed for a nervous breakdown." "Why don't you see a psychiatrist?" said the other. "I can't, I'm not allowed on the couch."

Answering Machines

If somebody says, "This is Charlie—I'm not home now—leave a message when you hear the *beep*," I say, "I know you're not home—I prefer it. I'd rather talk to your machine than to you!" *CLICK!*

One woman left this message: "This is Sylvia. I'm not home. If it's important leave your name and a short message when you hear the *beep*." I said, "Just tell *your* machine to talk to *my* machine." *CLICK!*

The man on the phone cried hysterically: "What do you mean this is a recording? *You* phoned *me!*"

One secretary answered the phone: "Hello, this is 444-5555. Our answering machine is out of order. This is a real person talking."

Great Messages to Leave on Answering Machines

"Hello. This is Jane. The girl you met at that wild surprise party eight months ago. Well, in about a month, I'll have another surprise for you." *Click.*

"This is the city zoo. We know where you're hiding out. Are you going to come quietly—or do we bring a net?" *Click.*

"This is the National Charities Advertising Division. Congratulations! You've been named the poster boy for athlete's foot." *Click.*

"Hello—and congratulations! You've been selected to be a member of the city beautification committee. Your job is to keep out of sight!" *Click.*

"Hello! This is the Darwin Foundation. We're currently running tests to prove conclusively that man evolved from apes. Several people volunteered your name as a research subject!" *Click.*

"Hi! You've reached Fred and Ruth. We're gonna be out of town for a few days. We found that getting away once in a while helps our relationship—so I went to Acapulco and she went to Miami." *Beep.*

"Hello, this is Marvin. You won't be able to reach me all weekend because I have a tremendous sex drive—my girl lives 100 miles away." *Beep.*

"Hi! This is Charlie. I'm busy. . . . This is tax time and I'm one of those unlucky guys who got audited. I don't know when I'll be able to return your call. I asked the judge. He said, 'Ten-to-twenty.' " *Beep.*

"Hello! I've gone to visit a friend. I feel sorry for her— she's homely and lonely and has trouble getting dates. The last time I went to see her, she was playing strip solitaire!" *Beep.*

"This is your lawyer's office. Sorry I can't come to the phone—I've got a tough case going. This couple had a big fight. When she threatened to leave him, he brought up their wedding vow, 'Until death do us part'—so she shot him." *Beep.*

"Hi! The Constitution guarantees free speech, but it doesn't guarantee listeners—so keep it short!" *Beep.*

"This is Doctor Dick. I'm out now. Go get an apple." *Beep.*

"Sorry I can't talk now—I'm going for a beauty treatment. If I were a building I'd be condemned!" *Beep.*

"I'm as forlorn and neglected as Whistler's father. Call me when you hear the . . ." *Beep.*

"It's nice to hear from friends—even if you're not mine." *Beep.*

"Excuse me if I sound depressed, but I haven't been able to score with any women lately. Even my inflatable doll had a headache." *Beep.*

"This is Cliff—if you're calling about the money I owe you, you've got a wrong number." *Beep.*

"Hello. You've reached Dial-a-Prayer. Leave your name and number and pray I call you back." *Beep.*

"Hello. This is John. I don't know about you, but I'm concerned about the fast-rising traffic statistics. My neighbors are calling me paranoid, but I say you can't be too careful! Anyway, I'm out installing seat belts on my bicycle." *Beep.*

Art

All I know about art is if it's on the wall, it's a painting, and if you have to walk around it, it's a sculpture.

Abstract art gives a beautiful meaning to the word *ugly*.

I bought a painting in Europe and showed it to a dealer on Madison Avenue. He said, "First the good news: Your painting is a genuine Palagrini, finished during the Renaissance. Now for the bad news: Palagrini was a plumber."

Modern art is when you buy a picture to cover a hole on the wall and then decide that the hole looked better.

Antique collecting has become so popular, people are buying them faster than dealers can make them.

The most complete museum I ever visited was the one in Italy where they had two skulls of Christopher Columbus— one when he was a boy and one when he was a man.

An antique is anything that's too old for the poor—but not too old for the rich.

Michelangelo spent seven years painting the ceiling of the Sistine Chapel—and they couldn't say anything because he was union. He didn't mind the seven years so much; what bugged him was when they asked for a second coat.

A visitor to the modern artist's studio found the great painter staring dejectedly at his latest creation and muttering, "It's a failure." "How can you say that?" protested the visitor. "I think it's a masterpiece." "No," said the artist, "the nose is wrong. It throws the picture out of perspective." "Then why not fix the nose?" asked the visitor. "That's not possible," said the artist. "I can't find it."

Trying to figure out abstract art is like trying to follow the plot in a plate of alphabet soup. It's very obvious what these guys are saying: They need cash.

In Greenwich Village, a couple stopped in front of a shop window of abstract sculpture which was labeled "art objects." The man turned to his wife and said, "I can't say I blame art for objecting."

No woman is ever satisfied with the way she looks in a painting. "I don't like this at all," the society lady said to the artist. "The last time you painted me, I was gorgeous."

He said, "Forgive me—but when I painted that picture I was ten years younger."

One lady screamed at the artist: "I look plump in this picture! I expect you to give me a slender appearance." He said, "Madam, I am a painter, not a masseur."

One street-corner artist in the Village was explaining, "The world doesn't make sense—so why should I paint pictures that do?" A lady from uptown who was looking at this sidewalk artist's wild modern painting remarked, "How frightful!" The artist said haughtily: "I only paint what I see." The lady said, "You shouldn't paint when you're in that condition."

Today everybody in New York is an art maven. In the old days, if there was an empty store, a gypsy moved in— today it's art. Rembrandt painted three hundred pictures and Americans have all seven hundred of them. You have to be careful these days. One guy tried to sell me an "original Rembrandt." He said it was the only picture Rembrandt ever did in ball-point.

The artist whose expressionistic paintings sell for $10,000 or more admits, "I need a lot of light to paint. It's so hard to see those little numbers." When I told the artist his stuff was great, but a little too expensive, he told me about his brother: "He's also a painter, but much cheaper—two rooms for $300."

Bachelors

Bachelor's Day on Leap Year is when the women propose to men—and you should hear what they propose.

My unmarried brother tells me, "It's wonderful to be a

bachelor: You eat home-cooked meals, but have your choice of cooks."

A man who refused to fight used to be called a coward. Now they call him a bachelor.

Show me a man who does what he wants, and I'll show you a bachelor.

As the widow said to the bachelor, "Take it from me—don't get married."

The married man said to the good-looking bachelor, "How did you manage to stay single so long?" "Easy," was the reply. "Every time I look at TV commercials I learn that women are anemic and overweight, with large pores, straggly hair, and rough hands."

A bachelor is someone who occasionally wonders who would make the best wife—a blonde, brunette, or redhead—but who comes to his senses in the end and remembers that it really doesn't matter what color the truck is if it's going to run him over anyway.

A bachelor is a careful man who does not get married until he has saved enough money, and then he doesn't get married so he can keep what he's saved.

This guy knows more about women than married men—why else would he stay single? "My girlfriend wants to creep into my gut," my friend told me. "She said, 'I want to be part of you.' I said, 'Thanks, but who wants to have another kidney?'"

A bachelor is a guy who likes to love as long as it's not followed by honor and obey.

Two women met and one said to the other, "Say, I haven't seen you around here for months. Are you still engaged to that sensible, thrifty young man you were telling me so much about?" Her friend replied, "No—I married the cheap bum."

Banks

In the typical neighborhood bank there are always four people standing behind the counter. One is called Sylvia Potkin—the rest are called NEXT WINDOW.

Today you can always tell when a bank is in trouble by little things—like they come and repossess your toaster and take back their calendar.

I always wanted to work in a bank. Banks have everything I love—money and holidays.

There's one bank in my neighborhood that's so anxious to do business they'll give you a gift even when you make a withdrawal. This bank is so classy, instead of a camera that takes pictures of bank robbers, they have a guy who does charcoal sketches.

My bank is offering premiums for new deposits. For $500 you get a blanket. For $1,000 you get a digital clock. And for $10,000 you get an audit by the IRS.

This woman talked to the manager of the bank, "I'd like to open a joint account with someone who has a lot of money."

I told my neighbor I couldn't loan him any money because everything I have is in a joint account. He said, "But you can draw money from a joint account." "Not this one," I replied. "Our joint account is in the name of my wife and her mother."

The janitor was mopping up in the bank one night, when the phone rang. He picked up the receiver and said, "Hello." The voice on the phone said, "Tell me, sir, what the Federal Reserve discount rate is, the rate of prime paper, and our balance of payments at this moment?" The janitor said, "Mister, when I said 'Hello' I was telling you all I know about the banking business."

If it's as easy to borrow money from a bank as the advertising claims, why should anyone want to rob it?

My neighbor went to the bank and applied for a loan, and to his surprise he got it immediately. The next day he went to the bank and withdrew all the money he had on deposit there. He explained, "I don't trust a bank that would lend money to such a poor risk."

The man shouted at the loan arranger: "Of course I don't have any security—that's why I want the money!"

FDR closed our banks on March 5, 1933, to save our economy. Today the banks are open, but only to save our money for the IRS.

The finance company is for the man who has everything—but can't afford to pay for it.

If interest rates go any higher, pretty soon the loan sharks will be suing the banks for unfair competition.

When a poor man has too much money he lends it to the bank. When a rich man doesn't have enough, the bank lends it to *him*.

Show me a man with a gold tooth—and I'll show you someone who puts his money where his mouth is.

What is a banker? A pawnbroker with a manicure.

Money is so tight, some banks may have to diversify. But how will it sound? First National Savings and Pizza.

The vice-president of the bank said to the businessman, "Eighty thousand dollars? That's a lot of money you want. I'll have to ask you for a statement." The man said, "And you can quote me: *I'm optimistic.*"

My neighbor asked me: "I have two brothers. One is a banker and the other was executed in the electric chair. My mother takes numbers and my father peddles drugs.

Recently I met a wonderful girl who was just released from the reformatory. I want to marry her. My problem is this: If I marry this girl, should I tell her about my brother who is a banker?"

I liked it better when we had folding money instead of folding banks.

Personally, I always like to put aside a little something for a rainy day. Yesterday, I stopped by the savings and loan and deposited my galoshes.

Interest rates are murder. I walked into a bank yesterday and the loan officer was wearing a stocking mask.

A holdup guy became slightly confused when he shoved a note at a bank teller that read: "I've got you covered; hand over all the dough in the cage," and the teller handed him a note back: "Kindly go to the next window. I'm on my lunch hour."

A new bank teller was told to count a bundle of singles and make sure he had $100. The teller counted fifty-eight, then threw the bundle down. "Why did you stop counting?" asked the bank manager. "If it's all right this far, it's probably right all the way," said the teller.

Remember the good old days when bank robbers didn't work in the bank?

At my bank they always try to interest me in an *IRA*. What I'm interested in is an *IOU*.

Beggars

These days there is more begging done through the mails than with tin cups.

Let's not forget the bums on the street. If you help a bum he'll never forget you—especially the next time he is looking for a handout.

Not only is it more blessed to give than to receive—it is a lot more expensive.

To enjoy a good reputation, give publicly and steal privately.

A true philanthropist is one who gives away what he should give back.

One well-dressed man, vest and all, in Atlantic City, was approached by a seedy looking character: "Can you lend me twenty-five dollars? I've got no place to sleep and I haven't eaten in two days." The "vest" said, "How do I know you're not going to take the money and gamble with it?" The bum said, "No way—gambling money I've got."

The street character told the overweight dowager, "Lady, help. I haven't eaten in three days." She said, "I wish I had your will power."

An elegant society matron was stopped by a bum just as she was leaving one of the season's biggest charity balls. "Lady," said the beggar, "can you spare a poor man a dollar?" The matron screamed, "You must be out of your mind—I spent $250 dollars for a ticket to the ball, $1,500 for my gown, and, on top of that, I'm completely exhausted from all that dancing! How dare you ask me for money when I did all that for you?"

"Unless you give me some aid," the bum said to Mrs. Vanderschwartz, "I'm afraid I will have to resort to something it shocks me to contemplate doing." Mrs. Vanderschwartz handed him a five-dollar bill and asked lovingly, "What is it, my poor man, that I saved you from?" He said, "Work, madam."

The lady asked the beggar, "Can't you find work?" He said, "Yes, but they want a reference from my last employer." "So can't you get one?" "No, madam—he's been dead twenty-eight years."

One bum approached me, "Mister, can I have $125 for a cup of coffee?" I said, "A hundred and twenty-five dollars?" He said, "Well, I wouldn't go into a nice restaurant dressed like this!"

One tramp knocked on the door and asked the lady of the house for something to eat. She said, "Yes, I'll feed you—if you'll chop a load of wood first." The bum said, "Madam, I asked for a donation—not a transaction."

Did you know the bums have formed a union? With very strict bylaws: No member can be more than 100 years old. No member can look for or accept work of any description—members found working will be expelled. No members can go begging on Sunday at any price.

I was in a hurry and told the beggar, "I'll take care of you on my way back." He cried, "Oh, no, you don't. Already this year I've lost too much on charge accounts."

A bum knocked on the door of an inn called George and the Dragon. A woman opened it and he asked for some money. She screamed "No!" and slammed the door. He knocked again and the woman opened the door. He said, "Now could I have a few words with George?"

Have you heard about that new welfare doll? You wind it up and it doesn't work.

A bum approached a man and asked for a dime. The man told him he didn't have a dime but he'd be glad to buy him breakfast. "Man," the bum said, "I've had three breakfasts now, trying to get a dime."

"Actually, I'm an author," one bum told me. "I once wrote a book entitled, *One Hundred Ways to Make Money*." I asked, "Then why are you begging?" He said, "It's one of the ways."

The bum asked for twenty dollars and twenty-five cents for a cup of coffee. I said, "But coffee only costs twenty-five cents." He said, "I know, but coffee always makes me sexy."

The ragged stranger went to see my uncle: "You did me a favor ten years ago," the bum said. "And I've never forgotten it." My uncle said, "Ah, and you've come back to repay me?" The stranger said, "Not exactly—I just got into town and I need another favor and I thought of you right away."

I asked the beggar if he had ever been offered work. He said, "Only once. Apart from that, sir, I've met with nothing but kindness."

My brother-in-law said, "Remember last year when I was broke, and you helped me out and I said I would never forget you?" I said, "Yes." He said, "Well, I'm broke again."

"Do you think it's right for you to go begging from door to door?" the lady asked. The panhandler said, "No—I don't. But they refuse to bring it to me."

Bloopers and Other Goof-ups

An Italian restaurant featured this on it's menu: "Melon and prostitute ham."

This sign in a laundry on Staten Island: LADIES—LEAVE YOUR CLOTHES HERE AND SPEND THE AFTERNOON HAVING A GOOD TIME.

Sign in the window of a restaurant: WANTED—MAN TO WASH DISHES AND TWO WAITRESSES.

Notice at the club, advising proper attire: A SPORTS JACKET MAY BE WORN TO DINNER—BUT NO TROUSERS.

I asked my uncle: "Is it true that you wear a toupee?" He answered, "No, the hair is real—it's the head that's fake."

The California paper put this story on the front page: "Her pretty face and slim figure were to be found at the best parties and on the floors of the smartest night clubs."

In a cemetery, there's a sign that says, PERSONS ARE PROHIBITED FROM PICKING FLOWERS FROM ANY BUT THEIR OWN GRAVES.

Headline in a Philadelphia paper: "Woman Kicked by Her Husband Said to Be Greatly Improved."

Front-page story in a newspaper: "Officer Convicted of Accepting Bride."

On a church bulletin board: "Greater love hath no man than this, that a man lay down his wife for his friends" (John 15:13). From the church magazine: "Sorry about that story on the bulletin board—that should have been *life*, not *wife*, but Mr. Myron, who wrote it, has been quite unwell owing to his recent death—and is taking a short holiday to convalesce."

I'm still not sure if this was a blooper: After my speech at the

YMHA, one woman said to me, "You're a blessing. For forty years I've been suffering from insomnia—went to doctor after doctor who couldn't help. As soon as you opened your mouth I was cured." Another woman told me, "I loved your talk—I woke up from it refreshed." Then, a man said, "Your speech was like water to a drowning person." One guy started to walk out on me. "Sorry," he shouted, "I'm going for a haircut." I said, "Why didn't you get it before my speech?" He said, "I didn't need it then!"

When a man is married to one woman it is called monotony. When a man has more than one wife, he is a pigamist.

The fashionable lady stepped into the elevator at Saks and asked the operator: "Where can I find silk covering for my settee?" The young man said, "Third floor—lingerie department."

A local coach ran this classified ad in a show business magazine: "Girls who have ambitions to sing with a band should take vice lessons."

I loved this story in the paper: "Doctor Is Eulogized" was the headline. The story began, "The New York obstetrician practiced more than sixty years and is responsible for most of the babies born in this community." (Practiced hell, the doc was perfect.)

The sign in the window of the jewelry store said WHY GO ELSEWHERE TO BE CHEATED WHEN YOU CAN COME HERE?

The store poster declared: WE EXCHANGE EVERYTHING. BICYCLES, WASHING MACHINES, ETC. BRING YOUR WIFE AND GET THE DEAL OF YOUR LIFE.

This notice was displayed in bold letters on the Xerox machine in an advertising office: THE TYPIST'S REPRODUCTION EQUIPMENT IS NOT TO BE INTERFERED WITH WITHOUT PRIOR PERMISSION.

In a large park there is a small bandstand, around which are many seats. A sign states: THE SEATS IN THIS VICINITY OF THE BANDSTAND ARE FOR THE USE OF LADIES. GENTLEMEN SHOULD MAKE USE OF THEM ONLY AFTER THE FORMER ARE SEATED.

"Owing to the fuel crisis, officials are advised to take advantage of their secretaries between the hours of 12 and 2."

There was an accident on Wall Street today—a streetwalker was hit by a car. She was hurt in the business section.

"The members of Congress," said the editorial, "meet in Washington to disgust the nation and its problems."

"Myron Dunleavy of this station is going to be married next Saturday, so I'm dedicating the next number to Myron and his expectant bride."

"The operator of the other car, charged with drunken driving, crashed into Mrs. Field's rear end, which was sticking out into the road."

I told the waiter at the restaurant, "My soup tastes funny." He said, "Well, go ahead and laugh."

I asked the waiter, "Will the spaghetti I ordered be long?" He said, "I don't know, sir, we never measure it!"

The evangelist introduced a choral group and said, "Okay, now sin you singers."

Bores

A bore never runs out of conversation—just listeners. The biggest bore in town: You ask him how he feels and he tells you.

I interrupted one dull fellow with, "Excuse me, my leg has gone to sleep—do you mind if I join it?"

One dullard said to my brother, "I passed by your place yesterday." My brother responded, "Thanks a lot."

A bore is a person who talks when you want him to listen.

This speaker, running for office, was really waxing dull. The restive audience began to argue among themselves. "There's so much interruption," the orator complained, "that I can hardly hear myself speak." A voice in the rear yelled out: "Cheer up, Gov, you ain't missing much."

I know a guy who has nothing to say, but you have to listen a long time to find out.

This lady's life was so dull that she looked forward to dental appointments. Even her dog got bored and left her . . . .

Everybody is now writing to me about their old hometowns—which is the dullest? My cousin tells me, "I had some bad news from my hometown. The symphony orchestra had to cancel its performance of Beethoven's Fifth. The fella who played first ukulele quit."

My nephew was telling me how backward his old hometown is: "They even voted for Calvin Coolidge." I said, "Lots of people voted for Calvin Coolidge." He said, "Last year?"

My old hometown is so dead, they don't even ring the curfew at 8 P.M. anymore—it kept waking everybody up.

I went to visit my in-laws in their small town. The doorbell rang and it was the welcome wagon lady. She brought some thrilling gifts—things you wanted all your life: a blotter, a photograph of the manager of the drugstore, a six-inch ruler from the bank, a free breakfast for one at the Dairy Queen, with a coin for the jukebox, and an invitation to visit the local porno bookstore run by the minister. If it wasn't for bowling, there would be no culture at all in the town.

The dullest? This town is so small, the telephone directory only lists first names. The directory has one yellow page. . . . And it's a poor town. You know how some communities have public washrooms? They have pay bushes. This town is so square, a playboy is anyone who stays up to see the eleven o'clock news. Their biggest excitement is to go down to the hospital and watch the nurses rip off Band-Aids. Small town? The zip code is a fraction.

Bosses

A businessman can't win nowadays: If he does something wrong, he's fined; if he does something right—he's taxed.

If you want to know how to run a business, ask a man who hasn't any.

One manufacturer cried to me, "Business is so bad, even the people who don't intend to pay aren't buying."

My nephew told me, "I told the boss he's got to pay me what I'm worth, but he says he refuses to pay below the minimum wage."

The businessman explained, "We pay every two weeks because you can't buy anything with one week's pay."

The young lady looking for a job in a Madison Avenue advertising firm was asked, "What are your aims and ambitions?" She said, "I want to go as far as my education and sex will allow."

When secretaries work late, they won't go home by themselves anymore. They wait for their bosses to take them. At least then if they get attacked, it could mean a raise.

My neighbors were talking about their bosses. "I think he's great," the bookkeeper said. "You can't help liking him. If you don't, he fires you." My neighbor's wife said, "My boss gave me a big raise." Her husband said,

"Really? How did you get it?" She said, "I can tell you—but I don't think it will help *you* much."

"Our company is just one big happy family," my neighbor told me. "The main reason for this is because I hire all my relatives."

My boss told me, "There are hundreds of ways of making a fortune, but only one honest way." I asked, "What's that?" He said, "How should I know?"

One of the models at a Seventh Avenue dress house spent a weekend at an Atlantic City hotel with her boss. When she got back to the showroom on Monday morning, her friend was waiting with questions. "Tell me," she asked, "how did the boss register at the hotel?" The model squealed, "Terrific."

My cousin's secretary resigned—she caught him being a little too friendly with his wife. He immediately hired three gorgeous stenographers, each more sexy than the other. His buyer asked, as he eyed the new beauties, "How the hell do you expect to accomplish anything?" My cousin replied, "Easy—I'll give two of them the day off!"

A very handsome young lady walked into a sporting goods store and ordered all the equipment necessary for a baseball game, including a baseball bat, a catcher's mitt, and a catcher's mask. The salesman asked, "Are you sure you want all these?" She said, "Yes, I do. My boss said if I'd play ball with him we'd get along fine."

The pretty little baby-faced secretary phoned her mother to inform her, "I'll be late again for dinner tonight, Mom. I made a mistake last night and the boss wants me to do it over again."

The secretary said to the nontypist, "You'll love working for the boss—lots of opportunity for advances."

I asked my secretary, "How long did your sister work for her last boss?" She said, "Until she got him."

One secretary got her job when the boss saw her résumé. It was very impressive—especially the centerfold. The boss dictated a very difficult letter to his centerfold secretary. When she brought it back for his signature, he read a garbled version of his carefully thought-out remarks. "Didn't you read this letter before you put it on my desk?" he yelled. She answered, "Oh, no—I thought it was confidential."

The salesman took his boss for dinner on his birthday and presented him with a stereo and solid gold cuff links. The boss was overwhelmed that an employee would spend so much money on him, until he found out the salesman put it on his expense account.

The boss introduced the newcomer to the office staff: "This is my son. He's going to start at the bottom for a few days."

The boss approached one of his ambitious and competent men and told him: "I've had my eye on you for a long time. You're a very hard worker and you've put in long hours. You're very ambitious." Before the employee could say, "Gee, thanks," the boss continued: "So, consequently, I'm going to fire you before you learn too much. It's men like you who start competing companies."

A big garment manufacturer became extremely fond of one of his models, a gorgeous blonde. One day, when she was returning from lunch, he gave her a peck on the cheek and suggested that they visit his beach house for the weekend. "We'll have lots of fun," he added. "Okay," she agreed. "And I'll bring my fiancé." He asked, "What for?" She said, "In case your wife wants to have some fun, too!"

The boss was telling his son, "I'm retiring—it's all yours. I've made a good living because of two principles: honesty and wisdom. Honesty is important. If you promise the goods by the first of the month, no matter what happens, you must deliver by the first." The kid said: "Sure, Pop, but what about wisdom?" The boss said, "Wisdom means: Dummy, who said you should promise?"

The big executive told his new secretary he wanted some old-fashioned loving—so she introduced him to her grandmother.

The little old man asked the boss for Monday off to celebrate his golden anniversary. The boss growled, "My God, will I have to put up with this chutzpa every fifty years?"

The secretary said to her boss: "Me marry you? Are you kidding? You'll do anything to get out of paying overtime, won't you?"

Business

Women in business present a problem: If you treat them like men they start complaining; if you treat them like women your wife may find out.

The high-priced call girl cried, "If my business was legitimate, I would deduct a substantial percentage for depreciation of my body."

A firm advertising its product stated: "Money returned if not satisfactory." When someone applied for the return of his money, the reply he received was, "Your money is quite satisfactory and therefore we decline to return it."

The clerk asked the paymaster in the big plant, "Where's my paycheck?" The cashier explained, "Well, after deducting withholding tax, state income tax, city tax, Social Security, retirement fund, unemployment insurance, hospitalization, dental insurance, group life insurance, and your donation to the company welfare fund—you owe us $14.25."

The guy said to his boss, "On the salary you pay me, I can't afford to get married." "That's true," the boss admitted, "and in twenty years, you'll thank me!"

The secretary said to the young man, "How did you get this big executive job—you've only been here three months?" He explained, "I ran into my father and he took a liking to me."

The owner of one garment manufacturing company was asked, "How's business?" He replied, "Not too good— I've had to lay off my son-in-law and two of my wife's nephews."

The contractor wanted to give this government official a sports car. The official objected, saying: "Sir, common decency and my basic sense of honor would never permit me to accept a gift like that." The contractor said, "I quite understand. Suppose we do this: I'll sell you the car for ten dollars." The official thought for a moment. "In that case, I'll take two."

Everybody is complaining about business. My neighbor told me, "It's so bad, even my bills come postage due."

Even in times of high unemployment, the junior exec is still in demand. My neighbor told me, "I have three companies after me: Visa, Master Card, and American Express."

One young man applied for the job of bookkeeper. "Can you do double entry?" he was asked. "Yes," he said, "and I can do triple entry." The boss asked, "Triple entry?" "Sure. One for the working partner, showing the true profits, another for the sleeping partner, showing small profits, and a third for the income tax authorities, showing a loss."

It's great to take a loan. At least you know somebody is going to call you.

One Queens shoe store ordered a large consignment of shoes from a manufacturer in Buffalo. A week later the manager received a letter saying, "Sorry, we cannot fill

your order until full payment is made on the last one."
The man wrote back, "Please cancel the new order—I
can't wait that long."

Another manufacturer said to a storekeeper, "Thank you,
Mr. Schwartz, for your patronage. I wish I had twenty
customers like you." Schwartz said, "Gee, it's good to
hear you talk like that. I'm surprised. You know that I
protest every bill and I'm late in paying." The manufacturer said, "I still would like twenty customers like you;
but the trouble is I have two hundred."

My neighbor went to see his best friend: "I badly need
some extra money in my business, and they told me at the
bank that if you endorse the note they will be glad to
advance it." His pal said, "I'm surprised at you. Why
bother strangers for money when you can get it from a
friend? You go to the bank and let them endorse the note
and I'll give you all the money you need."

Two clothing manufacturers are discussing their problems
of business. In the middle of the conversation, one bolts to
the window and says, "I'm going to end it all and jump
out the window." And he does. The other is very depressed, but five minutes later his partner comes walking
in. The first partner says, "What happened? I saw you
jump out the window?" The other replied, "Yes, but I
landed on the returns."

In these days of high finance, it's interesting to note that
Noah was the first financier: He was able to float a
company when the whole world was in liquidation.

Executive ability—that's the art of getting the credit for all
the hard work somebody else does.

He's the perfect businessman: When others look at a proj-
ect and say, "How?" he looks at it and says, "How much?"

You must have positive thinking in business. My uncle
kept thinking he'd never make it. Now he's positive he's
not going to make it.

The sharpest business deal in this country was the Dutch purchase of Manhattan from the Indians. Peter Minuit had just conned Manhattan Island out of the Canarsie Tribe and was standing with the sellers on the banks of the East River surveying the purchase. "Hold it," he hollered. "Isn't that Brooklyn over there?" The Canarsie chief said, "Listen, wise guy, for twenty-four bucks you expect the place to be perfect?"

Flipping through her morning newspaper, the woman was attracted by a headline in the financial section. She read it with mounting perplexity, then turned to her husband and said, "What makes the market go up and down?" "Oh, all kinds of things," he replied. "Commodity fluctuations. Inflationary pressures. International imbalances. Political tensions. Financial instability." She put down the paper and said, "Look, if you don't know, why don't you just say so?"

And how about the yuppie who married the corporate president's daughter and hung her nude picture over his desk? He didn't want people to think he had married her just for her money. "What's it like to be married to the boss's daughter?" he was asked. "Well," he said, "the morning after our wedding she made some greasy eggs, burnt toast, half-raw bacon, and crummy coffee. It was then I realized she couldn't cook either."

Tarzan came home in the afternoon and asked Jane for a triple Jack Daniels. He sat down and in a few moments finished off the drink. "Let me have another," ordered the ape-man. After a moment of hesitation, Jane blurted out, "Tarzan, I'm worried about your drinking. Every afternoon you come home and proceed to get totally sloshed." "Jane, I can't help myself," Tarzan protested. "It's a jungle out there."

"My son is a good businessman," my neighbor said proudly. "He's so dedicated that he keeps his secretary near his bed in case he should get an idea during the night."

It was my uncle who taught me the legal maxim that has guided me these many years: Every man is innocent until proven bankrupt.

My neighbor told me: "Since I've been in business myself, I've had quite a few sales. My house, my car, my furniture . . . ."

One customer asked the owner of the store: "How can you make money selling watches so cheap?" The owner said, "Easy—we make our profit repairing them!"

Another store owner explained to his customer: "We had to raise the prices on these antiques—the cost of labor and materials has gone up so much lately."

The parking lot owner was telling his attendants: "We haven't had one dented fender in a week. How can we make money leaving that much space?"

This guy married the boss's daughter. On their wedding day the boss made him a partner. The boss said, "I gotta find something for you to do—I'll start you in shipping." "What do I know about shipping?" the son-in-law replied. "That's not for me." "Okay, then marketing." "Marketing is not my style." "Okay, then design." "I'm not a designer." The boss said, "Then what do you want?" The son-in-law said, "I want you to buy me out."

Cannibals

The cannibal loves his fellow man—with gravy.

The chief ate his mother-in-law and found she still disagreed with him.

The cannibal takes you seriously—or with a grain of salt.

The cannibal shows his hospitality by constantly having people for dinner.

Then there's the chief's son who studies at the University of Miami. The professor asked him, "Don't tell me you still eat people—after all this education?" He said, "Sure. But now I use a knife and fork."

Cannibals are not vegetarians—they are humanitarians. One member of the tribe complained he was getting fed up with people. The king asked, "What's for lunch?" The cook said, "Two old maids." The king screamed, "Leftovers again?"

Did I tell you about the cannibal who bought his wife a Valentine's Day gift? A five-pound box of farmer's fannies.

The tribe had eaten the missionary and had thoroughly enjoyed him. Next day, one of the cannibals, poking through the dead man's belongings, found a magazine. He began tearing out pictures of men, women, and children, cramming them into his mouth and chewing them. The chief watched him for a while and then asked, "Say, is that dehydrated stuff any good?"

Then there's the chief who had hay fever—from eating too many grass widows.

The chief's wife on the phone to her best friend: "Be sure to drop in after work Friday night—we've having the Browns for dinner."

The husband came home after a hard day and asked, "Am I late for dinner?" Madam answered, "Yes—everyone's already eaten."

The cannibal said to his wife, "I've just brought a friend home for dinner." She said, "Fine—put him in the deep freeze and we'll have him next week."

This young cannibal chief noticed a particularly beautiful young lady about to be placed in the burning kettle. "Wait," he shouted to the chief, "I'll have my breakfast in bed."

Then there's the chief who asked the U.S. State Department to send him a comic, in cultural exchange, who tells dirty stories—he wanted to have some special ham for dinner.

The two sailors were shipwrecked on a desert island. "Don't be nervous," the first sailor said, looking at the dancing natives. "They're only singing a welcome." The other said, "Welcome my eye—they're saying grace."

The cannibal chief's daughter came home in good spirits from a holiday at the seashore. "Did you meet a handsome man on the beach?" a friend asked. "Did I? You don't have to take my word for it—I've got him right here in my suitcase."

Cars

I just paid $4,500 for a used car which cost $3,250 when it was new. It cost me a lot of money for a secondhand car, but at least it gets me where I'm going—to the bank for a loan. Those aren't dents in the fenders—they're old-age wrinkles. Why can't they make a car with fenders on the *inside*?

Now they make cars for every price range—except cheap.

If automakers want to increase sales, they ought to stop guaranteeing parts for the life of the car and start guaranteeing them for the life of the car payments.

Used-car principle: "It's hard to drive a real bargain."

Every part of my car makes a noise—except the horn.

One thing about my old car: Vandals don't bother with it

when I leave it on the street at night. They figure somebody's already beaten them to it.

My car is so dangerous to drive it comes with a combination warranty and will!

The garage mechanic took a look at my bargain car and said, "Let me put it this way. If your car were a horse it would have to be shot."

A used car is all right as far as it goes.

I don't want a cheaper car—I want an expensive car that costs less.

My neighbor told me, "I think I'm finally gonna have to trade in that old car of mine. This morning I got passed while going uphill—by some punk kid on a skateboard."

My uncle complains: "I've had nothing but problems on that used car—the motor won't start and the payments won't stop. I was almost late for work today. My car's in the shop getting a wallet job."

Last year I deducted my used car as a religious expense, because whenever I drive it—I pray it'll reach my destination.

My automobile repair bills may be an example of a lemon putting the squeeze on you.

My car has a lot of options. I have the option of pushing it, towing it, fixing it, or junking it.

The best time to buy a used car is when it's new.

There are two things I hate about my used car—parts and labor.

If you want to improve the desirability of your present car—check out the prices of the new ones.

So far I've paid off three cars: My doctor's, my dentist's, and my plumber's.

Nowadays if you want to buy a $10,000 car, it's easy. Just buy a $4,000 car on time.

New-car prices are so high one dealer has a showroom and a recovery room.

I don't know anything about cars, but luckily I've got a good mechanic—and he believes in preventive maintenance. I bring it in every 500 miles so he can rotate the ashtrays and change the air in the tires.

An auto mechanic: That's a guy who stands behind his work—with a tow truck.

Nowadays every family needs two cars—one to drive while the other one's being recalled.

A good year for the automakers is when they sell more cars than they recall.

The key words in the auto industry are *lighter* and *heavier*. The cars are lighter and the payments are heavier.

A new-car buyer called an auto manufacturer: "Was it your company that announced that you recently put a car together in seven minutes?" The executive answered proudly, "Yes, sir, it was." The caller said, "Well then, I'd just like to let you know that I've got the car."

A new-car dealer whose business was in a lot of trouble went down to the beach to drown himself, picked up a bottle, rubbed it, and lo and behold, a genie appeared and asked what he wished most. The poor man thought a moment and said, "I'd like an imported-car dealership in a major city." The genie snapped his fingers and the guy found himself in Tokyo with a Chrysler agency.

Foreign cars have invaded the U.S. The slogan is "Buy American"—but the practice is drive foreign.

It's a funny thing about those foreign sports cars: Most of the people who can afford them can't fit into them.

There are so many Japanese cars being sold in America, my mechanic is learning to change spark plugs with chopsticks.

My brother the lover likes the Ferrari: "It gets more gals to the mile." Some of these foreign cars run on gasahol. The luxury models run on champagne, and an economy model runs on cheap wine. They are now planning a garbage truck that runs on beer.

My neighbor bought an English-made automobile and after careful computation over a month concluded that he was not getting the phenomenally high mileage so often credited to such cars. So he took it to a local mechanic, who, after checking it thoroughly, pronounced it in perfect condition. "I love the car," my neighbor confessed, "but isn't there something I can do to increase its mileage?" "Well, yes," the mechanic said. "You can do the same as most foreign-car owners do." "What's that?" my neighbor asked. "Lie about it."

My dealer gave me the good news: "Your car is not one of those being recalled by Detroit. The bad news is, since it's Japanese, it's being recalled by Tokyo."

I don't know if it means anything, but I saw Santa Claus—and the reindeer were pulling a Toyota.

I like that new French car built along feminine lines. Everything's different: You don't put gas in a tank anymore—you just dab a little behind each headlight. And it's just loaded with features that appeal to women! Lavender wall tires; a low-cut grille; and padded bumpers. You'll love it. They brought one into Detroit and three Ramblers chased it into an alley!

With all due respect to these automotive aliens, America leads the world in the number of automobiles produced. That tells us something about American workmanship. Of course, we also lead the world in the production of tow trucks.

My neighbor surprised his wife with a gorgeous new car. "Beautiful," she gushed. "Let's go for a ride right now." He said, "We can't go anywhere in it for a while—I didn't have any money left for gas or insurance."

Auto mechanics really have it made. Name me any other business where they can nick you $1,500 to fix a leak and not even be afraid to leave fingerprints.

If gas prices and car prices continue to spiral, an optional accessory on cars will be a bus ticket.

The man brought his car to the mechanic for the sixth time. "We've done everything we could," the mechanic said. "All we can offer now is a brief memorial service for fifty dollars."

My neighbor was bragging about his new car: "It has front-wheel drive, turbocharging, computer-monitored fuel injection, X42 sport suspension, adjustable gas-filled shocks, an electronically tuned stereo system with a five-band graphic equalizer. But it won't start."

By means of laser beams scientists are now able to measure distances to the billionth of an inch. Big deal. Parking lot attendants have been doing it for years.

A fellow who had been in a coma since 1944 recovered and was wheeled out of the hospital. He took one look at the parking lot and said, "My God, Japan and Germany won the war!"

Earl Wilson said it: "If you think nobody cares if you're alive, try missing a couple of car payments."

The used-car salesman answered the potential buyer, "Of course I'm an honest man. It's one of the conditions of my parole."

The guy was trying to buy a car. The salesman said, "That's right, the motor is $1,200—everything else is optional."

My neighbor's car is so old, his car insurance policy covers theft, fire, and Indian raids.

I found a way to make my wife drive more carefully: I remind her that if she has an accident, the papers will print her age.

I bought a car with defective brakes. I told the dealer, "I don't want you to stand behind this car—I want you to stand in front of it."

Cheap People

I'm looking for the cheapest guy in town: First prize is ten dollars—which the winner pays *me*! And don't call me collect. And I will not accept postage-due mail.

You think *I'm* cheap? Just because I refuse to pass the buck? Well, how about my brother-in-law? He thinks he's treating when he pays his own check. The last time I had dinner with him, he did pick up the check—and handed it to me. My brother won't even laugh unless it's at somebody else's expense.

I have a friend who's a two-fisted spender—both tightly closed.

One of my uncle's employees came in an hour early each day for a month—and my uncle charged him rent.

My neighbor is so cheap he even has a burglar alarm on his garbage can.

I know a guy so cheap, if he was a ghost, he wouldn't give you a fright.

My nephew recently bought some secondhand shirts cheap and changed his name to fit the monogram.

My cousin, before he was married, promised his fiancée the world, the moon, and the stars—so on their honeymoon he took her to the planetarium. How's that for cheap?

My butcher is very unhappy. He's had Blue Cross insurance four years—and hasn't been sick once.

My cousin doesn't always insist that his wife pay the dinner check—he sometimes offers to flip her for it.

I have a friend who is so cheap he tried to get a postage stamp wholesale. This guy took his girl for a taxi ride and she was so beautiful, he could hardly keep his eyes on the meter.

I know a guy who has a coin slot on his bathroom door for visitors.

How's this for a cheap bum: When his wife's kidnappers demanded ransom last December, he requested a 25 percent year-end discount.

I know a big spender who hands out IOUs to the drunken beggars on Delancey Street.

My country cousin is tighter than a train window: He got married in his own backyard so his chicken could have the rice.

My brother married a skinny girl so he could buy a small wedding ring.

The stingy salesman, while on an out-of-town sales trip, sent his wife a check for a million kisses as an anniversary present. The wife, annoyed at her cheap husband, sent back a postcard: "Dear Charlie: Thanks for the anniversary check. The milkman cashed it for me just this morning."

The cheapest? The guy with a pay phone in his car.

It is said that I have financial arthritis: Every time I reach for a check, I wince—but who listens to my mother-in-law? She says that when I break a dollar bill I sing "Auld Lang Syne."

I resent the fact that some people say I am still waiting for the Bible to come out in paperback.

The stingiest man I ever heard of was the guy who

brought his bride a ten-cent sack of candy and took her on a bus ride for their honeymoon. When she was halfway through the candy he nudged her and remarked, "Honey, suppose we save the rest of the candy for the children."

I don't know what my brother-in-law does with his money, but I can tell you this: He doesn't carry it with him when we go out for a drink.

I don't want to say my neighbor throws cheap parties, but I don't know anybody else, other than the grocery, who charges a deposit on a beer bottle.

A miser might be pretty tough to live with—but he's a nice ancestor.

I have a friend who is really cheap: He found a box of corn plasters, so he went out and bought a pair of tight shoes. . . . He told his kids Santa Claus stopped making house calls.

The old farmer had survived the Great Depression and never gave up his frugal habits even when he came into some money. A TV salesman visited and told him, "You must be lonely—a TV set would be a great source of companionship." The guy wasn't interested. "But you might as well spend your money," the salesman argued. "You can't take it with you!" The farmer snapped, "Can't take a TV set, neither."

I'm looking for the cheapest man in town. A man of rare gifts. A man who lives poor so he can die rich. One who gives nothing away but himself.

There's an old legend that if you break a mirror you get seven years hard luck. My brother feels the same way about breaking a dollar. He told me he got his wife pregnant—so they could fly family plan.

The skinflint was coming out of the restaurant one after-noon, when a lady stepped into his path, shook a coin box under his nose, and reminded him, "This is tag day for the poor. Give till it hurts." "Lady," the skinflint said with a slight quiver in his voice. "The very idea hurts."

Says my friend: "To me, there is no such thing as petty cash."

An undertaker advertised a few coffins at half-price. The next day there were six suicides. . . . Even cheaper: The girl said to her date when he took her home: "I'd ask you in but I know you must be anxious to get home to your money!"

Cheap? He's the type who gets mad because the gum machine won't take credit cards. Cheap? His idea of a honeymoon is booking the Bridal Suite at a welfare hotel.

A man entered his doctor's office the moment it was opened one morning. When asked the trouble, he stuck out his tongue. It was matted with small splinters of wood. "What happened?" the doc asked. "Last night I had an accident." "What kind? The rest of your body seems okay." The patient said, "Man, I spilled a glass of whiskey on the floor!"

I once said of my boss, "I happen to know he can be generous at times." My co-worker said, "Come off it. You know as well as I do that the only thing he ever gave to charity was a couple of poor relations." I said, "Do you know when he was in Paris it cost him ten dollars in tips?" My friend asked, "How many years was he there?"

I know a guy so cheap, his favorite pastime is sitting in the park on Sunday afternoon and stealing crumbs from the pigeons. To save money on his laundry bill, he puts soap flakes in all his pockets and walks through a car wash once a week. Cheap? He would have asked for separate checks at the Last Supper.

The cheapskate told trick-or-treaters, "Your candy is in the mail."

My neighbor hasn't changed—in thirty years he must have saved a bundle in laundry bills.

My brother was dining with me. He picked up the check, handed it to me, and said, "I wouldn't pay it if I were you."

My friend has worn an outfit so long it's been in style five times.

My broker is the only guy I know who tries to take the subway standby. He even went alone on his honeymoon.

My tough spender cousin fell heir to a million dollars, and all his pals in the saloon he frequented heard about it. Worried that his sudden wealth would change him, his buddy was discussing it when my cousin strolled in. The buddy waved all the guys to the bar: "When he drinks, everybody drinks," he shouted. "When he smokes— everybody pays."

He's so tight—the only thing he's ever withdrawn from his bank is free ink from the inkwell.

This bum came up against the cheapest lady of them all. She counts her money in front of the mirror so she won't cheat herself. The only thing she ever gave away was a secret. A bum was cold and he had no place to sleep. In desperation he climbed up four floors of the tenement, knocked on the door, and asked Madam Cheapskate if she could spare a dollar or two for a bed. "Well," she answered, considering for a moment. "Bring it up and we'll see what it's like."

Cheap? After making a three-minute phone call to California, a New York tightwad's stutter was completely cured.

My neighbor asked me for a cigarette. I said, "I thought you'd stopped smoking." He said, "Well, I've managed the first stage—I've stopped buying 'em."

The cheapest of them all? This guy named himself chief beneficiary of his own will. He lived poor so he could die rich.

A modern-day miser is a man who can live within his income.

I know a man who likes his wife in clinging dresses—the ones that have been clinging to her for years. This guy is so stingy—he won't even pay attention.

A cheapskate I know went into a shopping center with his wife, leaving their child and carriage with the other carriages in front. Afterward, as the family started for home and had gone a few blocks, the wife screamed, "That's not our child!" The skinflint answered, "Shut your big mouth—this is a much better carriage."

Talk is cheap—I'm sure it's nothing personal when they say I'm a big talker: A big spender gave me a check for my favorite charity. I was about to put it away when I said, "You forgot to sign this." He said, "I know—I was hoping to keep my contribution anonymous." This guy is so cheap, he takes off his glasses when he's not looking at anything.

A woman was complaining to her friend about her stingy husband: "Every time I need money I have to put on a big song and dance to pry it out of him. How come you don't have any trouble with that tightwad husband of yours?" Her friend smiled. "It's easy," she said. "I just tell him I'm going home to mother—and he gives me the fare."

Cheap? He remarried his wife so he wouldn't have to pay any more alimony.

This Wall Street big shot was showing his secretary a diamond ring he was giving his wife for her birthday. "Isn't it beautiful?" he asked. "Yes," said the secretary, "but I think your wife wanted a Rolls Royce." "That's true," the big shot agreed, "but you can't get a fake of those!"

The first clerk said, "I don't know what that guy does with his money. He's broke again." "Was he trying to borrow from you?" asked the second clerk. "No, I wanted to borrow from him."

I asked a friend, "Will you tell me, please, how you manage that you are never pressed for money, but always have plenty of it?" He said, "That's very simple—I never pay old debts." I asked, "How about new ones?" "I let them grow old!" he said. Would you believe this bum goes to a drugstore and buys one Kleenex?

The big star wasn't sure he wanted to accept a Vegas hotel's offer of half a million dollars a week, but they clinched the deal when they threw in the continental breakfast.

If you lend my brother-in-law some money, he'll be indebted to you forever. He even bought his daughter a dollhouse with a mortgage on it.

A man called up his girl and asked which night she would be free.

This bum got on a bus and read the sign PAY AS YOU LEAVE. He's still riding!

And the winner in the cheapskate sweepstakes . . . the guy who married a girl born February 29, so he only had to buy her a birthday present every four years.

When a man took his date home, she did not invite him inside. "Since we've been going dutch all night," she groaned, "you kiss yourself and I'll kiss myself."

Had dinner with my brother. I don't want to say he's cheap—but before he picked up the check, the restaurant changed hands three times.

I know a fellow who made a generous contribution to a home for the aged, but he's still a cheapskate: He donated his mother and father.

Another guy I know is determined not to go without taking it with him: He's bought himself a fireproof money belt.

My brother was complaining to his pal, "I don't know what to do with my wife—always asking for tens and twenties." His friend asked, "What the hell does she do with all the money?" My brother said, "I couldn't tell you—I never give her any."

Cheating

Guns don't kill people—husbands who come home early kill people.

The doctor told my brother: "You won't live a week if you don't stop running around with women." My brother said, "Why? There's nothing wrong with me. I'm in great physical shape." The doc said, "Yes, I know, but one of the women is my wife."

There's one hotel in town that's strictly for cheaters. In fact, when a couple registers, they sign in as Mr. and Mrs. To-Whom-It-May-Concern. One guy followed his wife there and he broke into the room and found her making love to his best friend. "You'll pay for this!" he shouted. The friend said calmly, "I've got my American Express. I never leave home without it."

Two doctors were talking: "I know you've been having a romance with my wife," one said. "What do you think of her?" The second doctor said, "Don't you know?" The first said, "Yes, but I wanted a second opinion."

Show me a man who kisses with his eyes open and I'll show you one who wants to make sure his wife isn't around to catch him.

The poor soul went to see the psychiatrist and cried, "When I came home from the factory last night, I found my wife kissing another man! How can I prevent that happening again?" The shrink advised: "Work more over-time."

Charlie told his friend, "I feel horrible—I'm going to be a father." His pal said, "Congratulations—but what's so horrible about that?" "Nothing—except my wife doesn't know about it yet."

The boss arrived at his office with a terrible headache. "That's funny, Boss," commented an employee. "A few days ago I had a terrible headache too, but it didn't last long. My wife pulled me over to the sofa, gave me a big hug and kiss, one thing led to another, and presto! My headache went away." The boss put on his hat. "I've tried everything else," he muttered. "Is your wife home now?"

Two pals were drinking at the bar: "Why the sad look?" one asked. "It must be a girl." The other said, "Yeah—but I can't tell you about it." After a few more drinks, he loosened up: "Okay," he said. "I hate to tell you this . . . but it's your wife." His pal said, "My wife?" "Yeah." "What about her?" The depressed guy put his arm around him and said, "Well, buddy-boy, I'm afraid she's cheating on us."

A man told me, "I know my wife's incompatible, although I've never actually caught her at it."

My neighbor's wife cried to me, "It was driving me crazy—I didn't know where my husband spent his eve-nings. One night I went home and there he was!"

The pretty model told me, "I knew that man couldn't be trusted. He has gone back to his wife."

My niece cried to me: "I see so little of my husband, I feel like I took his name in vain!"

One thing about the first man, Adam: He may have had his troubles, but he never had to listen to Eve talk about the other men she could have married.

"Just look at her," the headwaiter said about the girl at the bar. "She's had five husbands, including two of her own."

The captain was telling us, "My sex life has improved tremendously since my wife and I got twin beds." I asked, "How could that be?" He explained, "Hers is in Connecticut and mine is in Manhattan."

The obstetrician had just arrived at the hospital to help a woman who was about to give birth. "Will my husband be allowed to stay with me during the delivery?" she asked. The doc said, "Of course—the father of the child should always be present at its birth." The woman said, "Oh God—he and my husband have never liked each other."

My brother told me, "Now that I'm a free man, sex isn't as much fun as when I used to cheat."

My neighbor lectures, "They say one picture is worth ten thousand words. I found that out in divorce court. My lawyer had ten thousand words and my wife had one picture—of me and another woman."

I know I sound old-fashioned, but I just don't believe in trial marriages. I think they're very dangerous: If you're not careful, they could lead to the real thing.

My cousin told me, "When I met my wife she didn't have a social life. In fact, she didn't start dating until after we were married."

You know there really is such as thing as a happily married couple. It's any husband who's going out with another man's wife.

My neighbor and his wife make love all the time. That's why it's so difficult to catch both of them at home.

My sister overheard her neighbor talking about a married man with whom she was having an affair: "He's lazy, sloppy, not too bright, and very cheap, but I love him." That evening, at home, my sister confronted her husband and said, "Are you having an affair with our neighbor?"

The Indian was telling me that the squaws have been

practicing a variation of the wife-swapping bit—it's called "Passing the Buck."

The husband is leaving for work in the morning and he says to his wife, "You know, you're the worst wife, the worst cook, the worst lover a man could have." He comes back that night and finds her making love to another man. "What are you doing?" he screams. She says, "I'm getting a second opinion!"

My friend came home unexpectedly and discovered his wife in her lover's arms. Drawing a gun, he walked toward the guilty couple. "Don't shoot," his wife screamed. "Do you want to kill the father of your children?"

This short, fat, millionaire approached the beauty at the party. "Excuse me," he said, "I wonder if I could interest you in breaking up my marriage?"

The two salesmen approached the boss: "We weren't betting on whether your wife would have a boy or a girl—we were betting on which one of us it would look like!"

My neighbor told her friend, "I'm not a suspicious woman, but I don't think my husband has been entirely faithful to me." "What makes you think that?" "Well, my last child doesn't resemble him in the least."

"Of course I haven't been going out with another woman," said Adam. "You know perfectly well you're the only woman here." Eve was still suspicious. That night she sneaked over to where Adam was sleeping and quietly started counting his ribs.

Accused of having been seen with another man, the woman protested, "Darling—it was only my husband. You know there's no one but you!"

The woman's happily married—her latest boyfriend likes her husband. And even after ten years of marriage, her husband finds her entertaining—when he comes home unexpectedly.

A man said, "You're the best little wife a guy ever had—even if your husband doesn't think so!"

It's not only the TV evangelists and judges and politicians who cheat—it could happen to anybody. The Wall Street executive told the lawyer, "Hell, give me the bad news first." Said the lawyer, "The bad news is that your wife found a picture worth a hundred thousand dollars." "That's the bad news? In that case, I can't wait to hear the terrible news." "The terrible news is that it's of you and your secretary."

The lawyer and his wife were taking a stroll on Fifth Avenue, when the lawyer was greeted gaily by a sexy blonde. "And how did you meet her?" the wife asked. "Professionally." "Yours," asked the wife, "or hers?"

I have a married girlfriend who loved to entertain, but had to give it up—her husband started coming home.

The politician was late as usual. His opening line to his wife was, "I've just been talking to the senator and he agreed to do everything I want him to do." The wife sneered, "Well, first wipe the senator's lipstick off your lips."

The movie producer came home unexpectedly and found his wife in bed with the onetime B-movie hero. "Hey," he screamed. "What are you doing?" The actor said, "To tell you the truth, not much of anything these days."

The loving couple was startled by a noise in the corridor. The woman got up and cautiously opened the door just far enough to peek out. She returned to the bedroom looking greatly relieved. "Relax, darling," she said. "Nothing to worry about—it was just my husband sneaking into your apartment."

You know your wife is being unfaithful when you notice your dog taking your pipe and slippers to a house down the street.

Florence and Emily, two pretty young housewives, arranged to have cocktails and lunch together. When they met, Emily could see that something serious was bothering her friend. "Come on, out with it. What's depressing you?" Florence sighed, "I'm ashamed to admit it, but I caught my husband making love." Emily said, "Why let that bother you? I got mine the same way."

The young, attractive housewife was a bit surprised when her husband's best friend dropped by one afternoon and offered $500 to make love to her. Thinking that the extra money would come in handy, she led him into the bedroom and fulfilled her part of the bargain. Later that afternoon, her husband returned from work. "Did my friend stop by today?" he asked casually. "Yes, he d-did," she stammered. "Why do you ask?" "Well," her spouse replied, "he was supposed to return the $500 I lent him last week."

The reporters asked this beauty who was making it with the senator, "How come you never married?" She said, "I got nothing against marriage—some of my best friends are husbands."

The wife screamed at the learned judge: "You bum! You miserable cheat! I know everything now!" The judge said calmly, "If you know so much, when was the Battle of Gettysburg?"

My neighbor told me, "Three nights a week out with the boys . . . man, did the wife and I have an argument about that last night!" I asked, "How did it come out?" He said, "She agreed to cut it down to two."

A man came home and found his wife in bed with his partner. "What are you doing?" he shouted. She said, "See? Didn't I tell you he was stupid?"

I overheard a gal say to her girlfriend, "Helen, listen to this: That stinking husband of mine has been cheating on me. On Tuesday nights, when he's supposed to be playing poker with the boys, he's out with a young blonde. What do you think of that skunk?" Helen asked,

"How do you know this?" The gal replied, "My boyfriend Harry told me."

My brother just had a nose job. He really didn't need it, but his neighbor's husband came home unexpectedly.

His friend told him that his gorgeous wife had four lovers. He said, "Look, I know. But I'd rather have 20 percent of a good deal than 100 percent of a bad one."

A man was complaining to a friend about his marital troubles: "My wife has started rationing sex. It's now down to once a week." "Oh, I wouldn't worry about that," his friend consoled. "I know some fellas she's cut off completely."

The judge said to the lady: "Your husband charges you deceived him." The wife answered, "On the contrary, Your Honor, he deceived me: He said he was leaving town and he didn't."

When a man heard that his dearest friend was to marry a certain girl in West Centerville, he tried to halt the union. He went to his friend and cried: "This marriage must not take place! Why, she's had an affair with every man in West Centerville." "Listen, West Centerville isn't such a big town," replied the dope.

Computers

The computer has taken the place of labor, thinking, sex, productivity, and dating.

The machine can do more work faster than a human, because it doesn't have to answer the phone.

"This little computer," said the sales clerk, "will do half your job for you." The senior vice president decided, "I'll take two."

If you make a mistake, you're a bumbling idiot. If your computer makes a mistake, it's a malfunction.

The young man fed into the computer dating service a request for a girl who didn't drink, smoke, swear, or have any other bad habits. The computer screen blinked two or three times and then asked, "What for?"

My friend told me, "I had a tough time at the office today: My computer broke down and I had to think all day."

I know a computer and an IBM processor that got married and had a baby. The first word it said was "Data."

My uncle tells me about a fully automated bank in Miami. Seems somebody sent it a card saying, "This is a holdup," and the computer mailed the fellow $100 in unmarked bills.

One Wall Street executive tells me he has a solution to the twin problems of unemployment and low productivity: "I have invented a machine that will do the work of five men—it takes ten men to operate it."

I've got news for you: Computers do create jobs: Now it takes more people to correct each mistake.

It is good news when you are told the check is in the mail. It is bad news when you find out it was a recorded announcement.

Credit Cards

Money isn't everything—except when you've mislaid your credit cards.

These days, if somebody pays you in cash you get suspicious. You think maybe his credit is no good.

Credit cards have made buying easier, but paying harder.

Using a credit card is a convenient way to spend money you wish you had.

The main problem with paying by credit card is that Visa and Master Card don't accept American Express.

My wife is doing her best to stimulate the economy: She's the only one who has racing stripes on her credit cards.

My credit cards are in real bad shape—the only thing that will help right now is a cash transplant.

This year I'm determined to stay out of debt—even if I have to borrow money to do it.

I'm so used to buying with credit cards that when I bought something for cash, I signed all the dollar bills.

My neighbor is in big trouble: His credit is lousy. He even has to have a co-signer when he pays cash.

People who are too scared to steal, too proud to beg, and too poor to pay cash think credit cards are the answer.

I love the credit card commercials: "Tonight, steak in San Francisco—tomorrow, teriaki in Toyko"—Thursday, bankruptcy in New York.

The young wife said to her husband after looking over her budget: "If we miss two payments on the mortgage and one on the car, we'll have enough for a down payment on a color TV set."

I tried to use my credit card in a health food store, and the clerk told me they only accept natural cash.

With my credit cards, my wife has the world at her feet—while I have the creditors at my throat.

I admire the way my wife spends—she's a credit to her card.

Credit is a system of buying time with money you don't have.

Most people don't care how much they pay for something—as long as it isn't all at once.

The salesman tried to sell a refrigerator to the housewife: "Lady, you can save enough on your food bill to pay for it." She answered, "We are paying for a car on the carfare we save. We are paying for a washing machine on the laundry bills we save. We are paying for a TV set on the cost of the movies we don't see anymore. It looks like we just can't afford to save any more at this time."

No man's credit is as good as his money.

I know someone who pays cash every now and then just to throw the store management into a panic.

Two men were leaving a pub and one said, "You can't live with 'em and you can't live without 'em." The other agreed, "That's the way women are, pal." "Who said anything about women?" the first groaned. "I'm talking about credit cards."

I met my friend at a party and said, "You're looking a bit off color, pal. Anything wrong?" He said, "I'm afraid there is—I've had to give up drinking, smoking, and gambling." I said, "Hey, that's all to your credit." He cried, "It sure ain't. It's due to my lack of credit!"

My cousin told me, "My wife has the same attitude as the federal government: She never lets being in debt keep her from spending more."

With all the credit cards and mortgages available these days, anyone who isn't hopelessly in debt just isn't trying.

The owner of Joe's Pier 52 was asked if her restaurant honored any of the credit cards. She smiled. "We not only honor them, but we also love and obey them."

My neighbor says, "My wife must be a direct descendant of Teddy Roosevelt, the way she runs into stores yelling 'charge.' "

Muggers are complaining that credit cards are hurting their business: They claim too few people carry cash these days.

I asked a bankrupt debtor why he went bankrupt. He answered, "I hate to owe money."

Crime

Figures released today by the FBI show that for the first time there is now as much crime on the streets as there is on TV.

Organized crime in America takes in over $40 billion a year and spends very little on office supplies.

There's one neighborhood in the city so tough that the stop sign says, "STOP if you dare."

There's one area in my brother's city where you can walk twelve blocks and not leave the scene of the crime. Even the candy stores have bouncers.

The judge said to the bum, "You've committed six burglaries in a week." The bum said, "That's right. If everyone worked as hard as I do, we'd be on the road to prosperity."

The victim said to the mugger, "But my watch isn't a good one—its value is only sentimental." The crook said, "That doesn't matter—I'm sentimental."

The gangster handed his gal a beautiful mink coat. After admiring herself in it, she asked her fellow, "What is it worth?" He said, "Oh, five-to-ten, honey."

"When you leave here," the host advised his pal, "start running and don't stop until you get home." Later that night the host got a call from the hospital, where his pal was lying beaten up and without his money. "I did what you said," the patient reported. "I ran and ran—and I caught up with a crook."

The judge said to the character standing before him, "You can let me try your case or you can be tried by a jury of your peers." The bum asked, "What are peers?" The judge explained, "People of your own kind—your equals." The man said, "'Well, I don't want to be tried by no car thieves."

If crime doesn't pay, how come so many people want to be lawyers?

One thief told me, "My lawyer just got me off for robbery. Now I have to rob somebody to pay his bill."

The burglar said, "Don't be scared, lady. All I want is your money." She said, "Go away—you're just like all the other men."

One resident of the city told me, "Security is pretty lax in my building. I lost the key to my apartment and a burglar loaned me his."

One parking lot violator told the official he'd never forget him if he got him out of trouble with the police. And he didn't. The next time he was in trouble with the police, he called him again.

This character told me he got a $100 parking ticket. I said, "That's pretty expensive even for this city. Why so high?

I know a $20 ticket is for parking on a curb and a $40 ticket is for parking near a fire hydrant. What's a $100 ticket for?" He said, "For parking on top of a police car!"

I don't want to say he was crooked—but he bribed the traffic cop with counterfeit money.

New York is a friendly town: If you want to shake hands, you must reach in your wallet pocket.

In the city these days, when you make your budget, you get to put a certain amount aside for holdup money.

The judge asked the police officer, "Why did you bring this man in? You say he's a camera fiend, but you shouldn't arrest him just because he has a mania for taking pictures." The cop said, "It isn't that—he takes cameras."

What we need is a slogan to encourage politicians to stay honest: "Make laws—not license plates."

I live in a very quiet neighborhood—*very* quiet. Where else can you hear people whispering for help?

I asked my nephew, who recently moved into a new neighborhood, "How much of a walk is it from your house to the nearest subway?" He said, "I don't know, I don't walk—I run."

The girl was screaming at her boyfriend: "You bum," she cried. "You even forgot what day it is!" He said, "Geez no, I didn't fuhget ya boitday. I even went to the jewelry shop to get you something—but he was still open."

I'm tired of hearing people talking about my city's crime rate. We have 4 million people in New York and over a million of them have never even been mugged once.

One bank bandit was crying from his jail cell: "Twelve people out of 240 million find me guilty—and they call that justice?"

A street person was charged with stealing a pair of shoes. The judge said, "Stealing a pair of shoes, eh? Weren't you up here a year or so ago on the same charge?" The defendant confessed, "Yes, Your Honor. How long do you expect a pair of shoes to last?"

The magistrate said to the criminal before him, "The last time you were here, I told you I didn't want to see you again." The prisoner said, "I know, Your Honor. I told that to the policeman, but he wouldn't believe me!"

The accused strode forward: "Your Honor," she said, "I wish to plead guilty." The judge demanded, "Why didn't you do so at the beginning of the trial?" "Because," the lady replied, "I thought I was innocent, but at the time I hadn't heard the evidence against me."

The next case had the judge furious: "I note that in addition to stealing money, you took watches, jewelry, rings, and pearls." The prisoner said, "Yes, Your Honor. I was taught that money alone does not bring happiness."

Crime is so bad in my neighborhood, the bank keeps its money in another bank. My neighborhood is so rough that when I called the police, there was a three-year waiting list.

The woman was charged with shoplifting. The magistrate asked if she had anything to say on her own behalf. She replied hopefully, "Yes, sir, I have—I take only American goods."

All this talk about crime finally got to me: I equipped my front door with a dead bolt, a multipoint lock, a double chain, and a device that electrifies the doorknob. Now I never have to worry about a burglar ripping me off when I'm away from home—because I can't get out of the house.

"I can't understand," said the defendant, "why I should be charged with forgery. I can't even sign my own name." The judge said, "You are not charged with signing your own name."

The young man was arrested for robbery. The case against

him had been closed, and there was no testimony from the defendant. The judge turned to him impatiently and asked, "Where are your witnesses?" The crook said, "Witnesses? Not me—I never bring along any witnesses when I commit a robbery!"

If the number of crooks in this country keeps increasing, I don't know where we'll put them all—Our prisons and city halls are full.

I suppose it had to happen. . . . In the United States it is now as easy to buy a gun as it is to buy a politician.

A visitor told me, "This is a tough city. There's lots of stress. The other day I had a pain in my chest and I was fortunate—it was only a small-caliber pistol. Stress can kill you—a bullet you can get away from."

One prisoner said to his cellmate: "I am going to study and improve myself, and while *you're* still a common thief—*I'll* be an embezzler."

When Benny the Burglar climbed out the window of the house, his waiting pal, Charlie, asked, "What did you get?" Benny said, "It's a lawyer's house." Charlie asked, "What did you lose?"

I'll tell you about my neighborhood. . . . The most popular bumper stickers say, "Have you hugged your bail bondsman today?"

My cousin tells me he comes from a pretty rough neighborhood: The post office delivers arrest warrants in the mail marked "Occupant." That neighborhood is so tough, when you order in the restaurant they serve you broken leg of lamb. In school the kids were being taught, "An apple a day keeps the doctor away." One of the kids hollered up, "That's all well and good, but what have you got for the cops?"

My mayor has announced that crime is down in the city: They've run out of victims.

One rich lady was arrested for shoplifting. She explained to the police: "I did it because I was depressed. I found out the body work on my Mercedes is going to cost $3,500."

With all the juvenile delinquency, muggings, killings, strikes, bombings, and uprisings going on, I think maybe the Indians should have had some stricter immigration laws.

As a kid, I lived in a neighborhood that was so tough the school newspaper had an obituary column.

My apartment was robbed so many times I finally put up a sign that said, WE GAVE ALREADY!

"You still say you're innocent," repeated the judge, "in spite of the proof that seven people saw you steal the necklace." "Your Honor," replied the prisoner, "I can produce seven hundred people who didn't see me steal it."

I'm always courteous. Just this morning I gave my place on a checkout line to a guy with only two items—a note and a gun.

The DA intoned, "Your Honor, look at the prisoner. In the past year he has committed many outrages—purse snatching, forgery, grand larceny, embezzlement, arson, kidnapping, and murder." "What do you have to say for yourself?" asked the judge. "Well," replied the young man, "nobody's perfect."

The thief put a gun in the ribs of the man walking on Fifth Avenue: "You're wasting your time," the victim said. "I'm a married man."

The crook with the greatest chutzpa of the year is the one who held up a bank with a nylon stocking over his head: He made the first cashier fork over $50,000, then proceeded to the next cashier and tried to open an account with the money.

When it came time for the prisoner's release, the warden

said, "I'm sorry, we seem to have kept you a week longer than we should have." The ex-con said, "That's okay— just credit it to my account."

Daughters

She was only a boxer's daughter—but she knew what to do in the clinches.

She was only an upholsterer's daughter—but she knew what to do on a couch.

She was only a railroad man's daughter—but her caboose was the talk of the town.

She was only a cannibal's daughter—but she liked her man stewed.

She's only a senator's daughter—but she sure can advise and consent.

She's only a doctor's daughter—but she's ready to make house calls.

She's only a lawyer's daughter—but she knows how to break a guy's will.

She's only a hairdresser's daughter—but she knows how to tease a guy.

She's only a travel agent's daughter—but she cruises from bar to bar.

She's only a cab driver's daughter—but she can sure take you for a ride.

She's only an actor's daughter—but she'll make a play for anybody.

She's only a principal's daughter—but, boy does she have the faculties!

She's only a mechanic's daughter—but she can sure fix your wagon.

She's only a tattoo artist's daughter—but she's got designs on every guy.

She was only a suburbanite's daughter—but she could sure go to town.

She was only a globe trotter's daughter—but she certainly got around.

She was only a telephone operator's daughter—but she was never too busy.

She was only a waiter's daughter—but she sure could dish it out.

She was only a coin collector's daughter—but she showed all the guys her quarters.

She was only a plumber's daughter—but, oh, such fixtures!

She was only an artist's daughter—but she didn't know where to draw the line.

She was only a stockbroker's daughter—and all the boys got their share.

She was only a horseman's daughter—but she never could say nay.

She was only a rancher's daughter—but she horsed around with all the cowhands.

She was only a censor's daughter—but she never knew when to cut it out.

She was only a postmaster's daughter—but she liked to play with the males.

She was only an undertaker's daughter—but there wasn't anything she wouldn't undertake.

She was only a credit man's daughter—but she allowed anyone advances.

She was only a florist's daughter—but she was potted all the time.

She was only a surgeon's daughter—but she knew how to operate even better than Dad.

She was only a salesman's daughter—but she gave out plenty of samples.

She's only an astronaut's daughter—but she sure knows how to take it off.

She was only an electrician's daughter—but you're in for quite a shock.

She was only an architect's daughter—but, boy, was she built!

She was only a schoolteacher's daughter—but she had no principals.

She was only a real-estate agent's daughter—but she was easy to land.

She was only an optician's daughter—but, boy, did she make a spectacle of herself!

She was only a real-estate salesman's daughter—but she gave lots away.

She was only the dentist's daughter—but she went around with the worst set in town.

She's only a violinist's daughter—but she knows how to fiddle.

She was only a pilot's daughter—but she never put on the breaks.

She was only a sergeant's daughter—but she never knew when to call a halt.

She was only an explorer's daughter—but she always went too far.

Dentists

I hate going to the dentist: the suffering, the excrutiating agony—and that's just from filling out the insurance forms.

When a dentist is down in the mouth—the other fellow feels even worse.

The doctor complimented the lady: "You have very even teeth—it's the odd ones that are missing."

The dentist examined one of his patients and discovered his teeth were full of cavities. He asked, "Do you want me to fill them with gold or silver?" The patient screamed: "Gold or silver? I can't even afford to fill them with meat!"

Two cannibals are talking: "Have you seen the dentist?" asks one. "Yes," says the other. "He filled my teeth at dinnertime."

The man went to see the country dentist at midnight in a panic—he had dropped his front bridge down the kitchen drain. The country doc walked into the man's house with a pipe wrench, removed the bridge from the gooseneck, and cemented the bridge back in place. Four days later the man was pleasantly surprised that his dental bill was only $3—but was shocked that his "plumbing bill" was $485.

Orthodonture is the dental technique that keeps children braced and parents strapped. My neighbor told me, "I never even knew what an orthodontist was until I sent my kid to one. In only three years he straightened out his teeth and flattened out my savings."

The first thing you learn from orthodontists is that buck teeth is the condition—not the price.

All my dentist does is make appointments for me to see another dentist. I really don't know if he's a dentist or a booking agent.

The modern dentist lives up to his claim: "It won't hurt a bit"—until the bill arrives.

I go to a dentist who charges only ten dollars a cavity: I gave him ten dollars and he gave me a cavity.

My niece told me, "Every time I go to the doctor's, he makes me take off my blouse. I think I'm going to find a new dentist."

My grandfather called his doctor and said, "Doc, I don't mean to be critical, but every time I eat I have to use tenderizer." He said, "Lots of people use tenderizer." My grandfather said, "In soup?"

My grandfather told me, "I'm at the age where biting into a jelly apple brings me three things—memories, nostalgia, and a $100 bill from my dentist. My dentist really charges. Last week he put in a crown—I think it belonged to Queen Elizabeth."

Gold is now worth about $400 an ounce. I'll tell you how I found out—I was mugged by a dentist.

My dentist told me, "You've got nothing to worry about— I won't have to extract a single tooth. Of course, I'll have to take out the gums."

Do you ever get the feeling that your teeth are twenty years older than the rest of you?

I don't want to complain about my dentist, but last night I went to a dinner and swallowed 1,500 calories— and that was just in fillings.

My dentist is a wise guy. I said to him, "Tell me, doc, how are the X-rays?" He said, "The X-rays are fine—it's your teeth that are no good."

I asked my dentist, "Doc, I need some advice. What should I do about all this gold and silver in my mouth?" He said, "Don't smile in bad neighborhoods."

You know you're a dental coward if you let your mustache grow long enough so no one can see your teeth need work.

You know it's time to go to the dentist if no one tells you jokes because they're afraid you'll smile.

You know you're in trouble with your dentist when he keeps you seated till your check clears. How to get even? Bite down on his finger and tell him you thought it was a piece of cotton.

I just got my dentist's bill—I think he's pulling my leg, too.

"I've got good news and bad news," my dentist told me

one day. "Which do you want to hear first?" I said, "The bad news." The doc said, "You have six teeth that have to come out." "And what's the good news?" "I broke eighty on the golf course yesterday."

My dentist relieved the swelling in my gums—and he also relieved the swelling in my wallet.

I just paid my bill—now there's a cavity in my bank account.

My aunt told me she owed her doctor $500. "I couldn't pay," she explained, "so I went to him and he took out all my gold fillings. Now he owes me $100."

My doctor's practice is so good he can't see another patient this year without getting into a higher tax bracket.

The pretty patient said to her dentist, "My, what graceful hands you have—they belong on a girl." The doc moved forward, smiling, and said, "All right, if you insist."

Today's dentists don't fool around. I won't say what happens if you don't pay a bill, but did you ever have a wisdom tooth put back in?

I went to see my dentist, Dr. H. H. Cooper, and found out my wisdom tooth was retarded. I asked how much this was going to cost me. He said, "To put it simply—just put your money where your mouth is."

I complained to my doctor that my teeth were turning yellow and asked him what to do. The doc said, "Wear a yellow tie."

I think my dentist is in big trouble: Last week he took out all my gold fillings and put in IOUs.

According to the latest survey, nothing gets an old dental bill paid like a new toothache.

And here's another bit of advice: Never go to a dentist who has his office soundproofed. I was sitting in the chair when my dentist stuffed cotton in his ears. I asked if the sound of drilling was that hard to take. He said, "No—but the sound of screaming is."

When the dentist says "open wide" you aren't always sure what he means: your mouth or your wallet.

No matter what you say about dentists you've got to admit they keep up with all the new discoveries and progress going on in their profession. You go to a dentist's office and a receptionist gives you a form to fill out: Who are you insured with? Who insures them? Where do you bank? Do you have a safety deposit box? Do you pay your bills promptly? Are you an heir in anybody's will? They explain, "We've got the equipment here." They mean the billing computer.

The dentist said to his patient: "The bad news is you've got three cavities. The good news is your gold crowns have tripled in value."

Ted Berkelmann reveals: "I know a dentist who has his new office almost completely equipped. All he's waiting for is a shipment of old magazines."

Dieting, Health, and Exercise

Sophia Loren says, "Everything you see I owe to spaghetti." She is the greatest ad against dieting. Sophia also says, "Show me a girl with a beautiful body—and I'll show you a very hungry girl." My secretary says, "Why should I go on a diet to lose weight? More people look like me than Sophia Loren. Right now I'm on a low-salary diet."

You know you're ready for the diet bit when:
You wear two girdles—an upper and a lower . . .

It's hard to lose you in a crowd. You *are* a crowd . . .

You're so fat they had to let out your garment bag . . .

Every time you sit on a bar stool—you have a hangover . . .

Blue Cross charges you group rates . . .

The phone booth fits you like a girdle . . .

Jumbo the circus elephant makes a pass at you . . .

A guy has to make two trips to put his arms around you . . .

They want you to model for duffle bags.

Mrs. Plump was at a Weight Watchers meeting. She was sitting next to Mrs. Fatso, who was crying, "I think calories are very unfair! They keep hitting below the belt." Mrs. Plump said, "My husband insists I come here because he'd rather make love to a trim-figured woman." Mrs. Fatso said, "Well, what's wrong with that?" Mrs. Plump said, "It's just that he does it while I'm at these damn meetings."

The biggest thing to remember when you are dieting is—what you see on the table must wind up on the chair.

The first week of a diet is rough: I know, for I've undergone it. The second week is not nearly as rough, though, for by then I'm no longer on it.

America is the land where half our salary goes to buy food and the other half to lose weight.

Diet books can help you lose lots of weight. Just buy every one on the market and you won't have any money left to buy food.

More diets start in dress shops than in doctors' offices.

The "all you can eat" diet is for people who want to stay fat.

My aunt knew she was in trouble when she walked into Bloomingdale's and said to the clerk, "I'd like to see a bathing suit in my size," and the clerk said, "So would I."

Doctors will tell you that if you eat slowly you will eat less. It is particularly true if you're a member of a large family.

Somebody told me that it's always the people who are disappointed in love who are such compulsive eaters. So how come there are so many fat sultans?

Fat? I know a woman who used a hammock instead of a bra.

The Surgeon General and the entire medical profession tell us America is overweight. They're right. Now I know why we have so many fatheads in Washington.

A great diet is one in which you can eat anything you want with somebody else picking up the tab.

My niece goes to a great diet doctor who lets her eat anything she wants, as long as she pays his bills.

My sister lectures, '"Even if you'll never pose for *Playboy*, it's not a bad idea to diet and try to get rid of your centerfold."

My sister-in-law wanted to buy a book on dieting. She goes to a bookstore, picks out a book, and asks the clerk, "How much can I expect to lose with this diet book?" The clerk looks at the book and says, "Fourteen ninety-five plus tax."

My fat uncle's doctor told him only an operation could get him thin. My uncle asked, "Is this operation really necessary?" The doc said, "You bet it is—I have three kids in college."

My neighbor's wife is so fat she has to wear stretch jewelry. She put on so much weight she had to take out her appendix scar.

A woman tearfully phoned a reducing salon to cry that her husband had given her a lovely present but she just couldn't get into it. The secretary gave her an appointment and then added, "Don't worry, madam, we'll have you wearing that dress in no time." She sobbed, "Who said anything about a dress? It's a Mercedes!"

Everybody has a diet they call their own. My brother-in-law's: You eat anything you want, but you must also drink two quarts of Scotch a day. You don't lose weight but you forget you're fat.

I went on a simple diet: There are only three things you can't put in your mouth—a knife, a spoon, and a fork. . . . And if you use chopsticks—only *one*.

I went to one of those fat farms, and they really work. The first day alone I was $500 lighter. I always feel a little silly going to a fat farm. There's something about spending $500 to take off what cost you $5,000 to put on.

My wife has a new diet that allows her to drink anything that comes from a blender. Last night, she drank two chickens and a pot roast.

The nice lady went to see the distinguished lawyer: "My husband is terrible," she cried. "It's been a nightmare these last two years. He neglects me something awful. Insults me all the time. Cheap? I don't even get pocket money. Why he even skimps on money for food. I've already lost fifteen pounds!" The lawyer said, "Why don't you leave him?" She moaned, "First, I want to lose ten more pounds."

My wife said she plans to lose 180 pounds—ME!

I don't want to say my friend is fat, but he told me he is planning on opening a chain of fine restaurants across the country. He still hasn't decided if he'll serve the public.

My brother-in-law's got some body. His next job will be to model for beer kegs.

You know you're ready for Sweet 'N' Low when you get a high electric bill just from the light that goes on when you open the refrigerator. Or when the mayor asks you to donate your pants as a shelter for the homeless.

You'd better start that diet: When you fall down and you rock yourself to sleep trying to get up. . . . When you have no trouble watching your waistline—it's right there in front where you can see it . . . .

My sister, who's dieting, boasts she lost two pounds last week. "But I cheated a little: Before I got on the scale I shaved my head."

Even marriages change. Ten years ago I put my wife on a pedestal; yesterday I put her on a diet. Either she loses weight or we let out the couch.

There is a new invention now for women on diets—an ice cream bar with lettuce on the inside.

Of course, if you really want to lose weight, keep your mouth and the refrigerator closed.

My aunt told me she must go on a diet: During her vacation in Florida, she was ejected from a local beach for creating too much shade.

More signs when you know you're ready to go on a diet:
   If you're asked to be a model for slip covers . . .
   If you need a bicycle built for two and you're only one . . .
   If you look like the odd couple—by yourself . . .
   If you're two inches taller than your husband when you're lying down . . .
   If you're the front row in your graduation picture.

My neighbor's wife is so fat—when she got married they needed three relatives to give her away. On her honeymoon, she wore a six-piece bikini.

My son-in-law started counting calories when he was told the only way he's allowed on the street is with a parade permit.

It took a lot of willpower—but I finally gave up trying to diet.

The new fashions keep our gals in shape: They have pants

to make them look like boys and see-through blouses to prove they're not.

Almost every diet chart recommends yogurt as the best way to lose weight. They claim it's a magic food made from unwanted milk. I know a couple who went on this diet: They ate nothing but yogurt for six months. When they started he weighed 264 pounds and she weighed 130. After eating yogurt for only six months, the husband lost 140 pounds and his wife disappeared completely.

My doctor explained, "Jogging is better than romance for losing weight: You burn up the same amount of energy making love as you do jogging around the reservoir, except after two laps around the reservoir you don't want a cigarette." My doctor told me that every time you make love you lose about 200 calories. So far this year I've lost about 40 calories.

A recent report indicates that 34 million Americans are overweight. Those figures, of course, are round.

My brother is very unhappy about losing 120 pounds. You can't blame him—she was a very beautiful blonde.

Fat? She and the Statue of Liberty wear the same size dress. . . . She has to put on a girdle to get into her kimono. . . . Her charm bracelet has only old license plates. . . .

My friend tells me there's a new course in losing weight by yoga: They teach you how to tie a knot in your neck so nothing can go down your throat.

Exercise is good for you—for you, not me.

The physical fitness people say there's nothing like getting up at 5 A.M., jogging five miles, and ending it off with an ice-cold shower. There's nothing like it, so I don't do it. The truth is I don't need all that exercise—I can fall down by myself. In fact, the only exercise I get is bending to my wife's will.

One doctor told me I ought to do some swimming to stay in shape. He said it's good for the figure. I said, "Doc, you ever see a whale?" Me? I get winded reading the newspaper.

Running is when you use every muscle in your body. Incidentally, there are no muscles in the brain.

Running isn't as simple as it looks. Your feet have to control your stride; your feet have to control your balance. You might say, if you run ten miles a day, you've gotta have your brains in your feet.

The sheik hired a track star to run from the palace to his harem, about three miles away, to fetch one of his wives whenever he was in the mood. This happened three or four times a day. The sheik would nod and the track star would take off. This arrangement went on until the runner died at age thirty-six. The sheik lived to be ninety-six. The moral of the story is, sex doesn't kill you, it's the running after it that does.

The average executive will jog ten minutes for exercise and then take the elevator up to the second floor.

Joggers aren't very friendly. They pant rather than speak. My secretary says, "Jogging suits are really necessary for running. Otherwise you just look like you're late."

The elite have found a special way to fall down—it's called skiing. Skiing has to be the only sport in the world that requires you to spend an arm and a leg to break an arm and a leg.

When I was a kid, my only outdoor activity was chasing the Good Humor truck down the street. When I grew up I got my exercise hailing taxis. Now I take a cab to the Good Humor man.

Stay healthy and have a good brisk sit.

I have a modern diet that's taken twenty pounds off: I only eat when my wife cooks.

A man I know takes dozens of vitamin pills daily. "This blue one," he explained, "is for before dinner. The red one is for after dinner. And the yellow one—that *is* dinner."

My sister-in-law claims she isn't fat at all: "I'm just too short for my height—I should be nine feet seven."

Bob Orben preaches: "I'm all for yogurt, tofu, wheat germ, fish oil, and all those other good, healthy, and nutritious things. But, please, not while I'm eating!"

Carmine heard these two gals talking: "Gee, your husband is obese." "I don't know what that means, but to me, he's a big fat slob."

The two biggest sellers in any bookstore are the cookbooks and the diet books: The cookbooks tell you how to prepare the food and the diet books tell you how not to eat any of it.

Studies show that having a pet is good for your health. A dog keeps the doctor away—especially if it's big enough.

A fat man will never look old—there's no room for wrinkles.

I don't want to criticize my brother's weight—but his favorite food is seconds.

My neighbor's wife is a fitness fanatic who insists on teaching him some special exercises for every part of his body: To exercise his fingers, for example, she keeps making him take out his credit cards.

A new medical theory is that exercise kills germs. The tough thing is to get the germs to exercise.

Steven Kessler reminds us: "The toughest part of a diet isn't watching what you eat—it's watching what others eat."

Eat, drink, and be merry, for tomorrow they may not be deductible.

Eat, drink, and be merry—for tomorrow ye diet.

My sister claims: "Show me a girl with a beautiful body—and I'll show you a very hungry girl."

The fat man told me, "I don't think dieting is meant for everybody, so I took up weight lifting instead. I just use the wrong equipment, that's all—a knife and fork."

My wife told me, "I bought all those exercise videos—Richard Simmons, Jane Fonda. I love to sit and eat cookies and watch them."

The wife was hollering at her husband: "You want to know where all the grocery money goes? Stand sideways and look in the mirror!"

Quit worrying about your health—eventually it will go away.

The best way to keep healthy is to eat what you don't want, drink what you don't like, and do what you'd rather not.

The doctor gave the lady a bottle with three hundred pills in it. "How many do I take a day?" she asked. The medic said, "You don't take any—you spread them on the floor and pick them up three times a day."

Divorce

Divorce often turns a short matrimony into a long alimony. And when it comes to alimony, my brother is dean of the club. "Paying alimony," says the dean, "is like paying for a subscription to a magazine that is no longer published."

Marriage always begins with a small payment to a minister and often ends with a large payment to a lawyer.

Marry for love and you divorce for money. Marry for money and you divorce for love. The girl who marries a man for his money—sometimes has to divorce him to get it.

Another reason for so many divorces is that too many girls are getting married before they are able to support a husband.

To some women, marriage is always a gamble—because they never know in advance how much their alimony will be.

Alimony payments often give a husband a splitting headache.

Marriage is the price men pay for sex. Sex is the price women pay for marriage.

Divorce is a legal recourse for a couple that is determined to prove that love can find a way—out.

Overheard: "What's the name of your ex-wife?" "Plaintiff."

Man was this guy henpecked: When he got a divorce—*she* paid the alimony.

The sexy wife of the busy tycoon just won a divorce, charging her husband with lack of attentiveness. "If anything happened to me," the stacked missus claimed, "my husband wouldn't be able to identify the body."

They all have different reasons for divorce: A woman cried to her lawyer, "I want to lose this guy. Last month he asked me for my finger size. Today he gave me a bowling ball!"

A woman wanted a divorce because she said her husband never took her anyplace. He explained to the judge: "I never go out with married women."

One friend couldn't get a divorce. He said to his milkman: "Don't you guys run off with wives anymore?"

A woman said, "I want a divorce." The lawyer said,

"Sure—for a nominal sum I will start proceedings." She asked, "How much is a nominal sum?" He said, "Five hundred dollars." She screamed, "Forget it—I can get him shot for less than half of that."

Divorce has reached new heights this year: Even couples who aren't married are going to divorce lawyers.

Actually my wife and I would have been divorced years ago if it weren't for the kids: She wouldn't take them and I wouldn't take them.

People living together without getting married is particularly disturbing to the guy who just got arrested for fishing without a license.

On the road to divorce, the wife mumbles to the husband as his alarm goes off: "The coffee's ready—it's in the can in the cupboard."

A man's wife complained she had nothing to do, so he signed her up for a bridge club. She jumps next Friday.

I said to my niece: "It's been rumored around town that you and your husband aren't getting along too well." She said, "Nonsense. We did have some words and I shot him—but that's as far as it went."

Last night a man heard his wife saying sexy things. When he looked around she was on the phone.

"Honey," the new bride said, "I know that something is bothering you. I can tell. I want you to confide in me. Remember—we promised to share everything, for better or for worse." Her husband said, "But, dear, this time it's different." She said, "Nonsense—together we can face anything. Now tell me what our problem is." He sighed, "Okay, if you insist—we have just become the father of an illegitimate child."

A man packed his suitcase and told his wife he was leaving her. "I'm sorry," he said, "but it just has not worked out. In the last six weeks I've been back with you we haven't been able to agree on anything." Wife: "You've been back seven weeks."

Two women were talking about a couple they knew. One said, "Ten months after they got a divorce, they're living together again." "What a shame," said the other. "Nowadays, even divorce fails!"

It may be true that marriage originates when a man meets the only woman who really understands him—but then so does divorce.

A door-to-door salesman rang Mrs. Smith's bell and said, "If you have a rodent problem, I can solve it once and for all." She replied, "You're a little late—I divorced him last week."

This man is arrested for running away from his wife of twenty-five years. They're not sure what to charge him with. She claims it's desertion. He says it should be leaving the scene of an accident.

The lady said to the judge: "That's my side of the story—now let me tell you *his*."

My neighbor was telling her husband: "It seems to me that common sense would prevent many divorces." He answered, "It seems to me it would also prevent just as many marriages."

When you're divorced, everything you have is divided fifty-fifty: Your wife gets half and her lawyer gets the other half.

My uncle tells me: "After six years of marriage, my wife and I pondered whether to take a vacation or get a divorce. We decided that a trip to Bermuda is over in two weeks—but a divorce is something you always have."

Doctors

Everybody is concerned about crime today. I'll never forget the time when a guy wearing a mask took all my money—it was the time I was in surgery.

Always check the parking lot at your doctor's office. If there's a Rolls Royce in his parking space, you *know* who's going to pay for it.

I asked my uncle if his doctor was expensive. He said, "Well, he only charged me fifty dollars for my X-rays—but then he talked me into a dozen wallet-size glossies for twenty bucks a piece."

The young intern asked the professor what he should charge when he goes into his own practice. The doctor said, "I charge $200 for a house call after 8 p.m. It's $100 for an office consultation, and $50 if my advice is sought over the phone." The young medic asked, "How much do you charge for passing a patient on the street?" The prof explained to another young doctor, "After an examination, the doctors have a consultation: That's a medical term meaning 'share the wealth.' "

The patient said to the doctor, "How can I ever repay you for your kindness to me?" He said, "By check, postal order, or cash."

Money, in medicine, still talks. It's what doctors hear when they listen through their stethoscopes.

I asked my doctor if he could admit to any mistakes. He said, "Yes, I once cured a millionaire in only three visits."

The surgeon told the patient, "We'll need you unconscious for the operation—would you prefer sodium pentathol or a peek at your bill?"

An old doctor in a small town finally took a vacation. He left his son, who was about to graduate from medical school, in charge of his practice. When the father returned, he asked his son if anything unusual had happened while he was gone. "I cured Mrs. Stephenson of that indigestion she has been suffering from for the past thirty years," the son remarked proudly. "Oh, no!" the father exclaimed. "That indigestion has put you through high school, college, and medical school!"

The doctor said, "My dear sir, it's a good thing you came to see me when you did!" The patient said, "Why, Doc? Are you broke?" After undergoing extensive medical tests, he called on the doctor to see if the results were available. "Not yet," said the medic. "Why not?" the patient demanded. "Because," the doctor snapped, "I haven't figured out what kind of an operation you can afford."

Dr. Rosee said to the beautiful young girl, "Okay—just take your clothes off." She said, "But it's my grandmother here who's ill." The doc said, "Oh all right, madam, stick your tongue out."

The doc said to the pretty gal, "I suggest you curtail your running around, stop drinking, cut out smoking, begin eating properly, and get to bed early." She said, "Really?" He said, "Yes, why not have dinner with me tonight? I'll see to it that you have the proper food and that you're in bed by 9:00!"

Well, my doctor finally found out what I had—and he got every penny of it.

I just got out of the hospital. I'm okay—but my savings died.

My neighbor told me he went to the hospital to have his tonsils removed, but he swore he wouldn't go back again. I asked why not. He explained, "They also removed my wallet, my credit cards, my keys, and my car."

I asked my doctor: "What's the difference between a

specialist and a regular M.D.?'' He explained, ''The specialist has a bigger boat.''

Listen, anyone can find a doctor these days—the caddies all have walkie-talkies. In fact, recent surveys show that on any given day, during office hours, four out of five doctors would rather be on a golf course.

My doctor doesn't make house calls—but if you're sick more than five days he sends you a get well card.

I have confidence in my doctor. No matter what ailment I have, I'm confident he'll come up with a fee. A couple of weeks ago I complained to him that my nose was sore. He told me to stay off it for a few days. Finally, he said, ''I can't do anything for your problem—it's hereditary.'' I said, ''Then send the bill to my father, will you, Doc?'' After a while, the nurse called me: ''You haven't paid your bill in two months and the doctor is upset.'' I said, ''Tell him to take two aspirins and call me in a couple of weeks if he isn't feeling better.''

The sign in the doctor's office said: THE DOCTOR IS VERY BUSY. HAVE YOUR SYMPTOMS READY.

The patient said, ''I don't feel good all over.'' The doc asked, ''Do you smoke excessively?'' He said, ''No.'' ''Do you drink a lot?'' ''No.'' ''Keep late hours?'' ''Nope.'' The doctor shook his head and asked, ''How can I cure you if you have nothing to give up?''

The doctor was perplexed by his latest case. He had given his patient all kinds of tests, but his results were still inconclusive. ''I'm not sure what it is,'' he finally admitted. ''You either have a cold or you're pregnant.'' She said, ''I must be pregnant—I don't know anybody who could have given me a cold.''

Doctors have it made. In what other business could a man tell a woman to undress, examine her from head to foot—and then send the bill to her husband?

The doctor said, ''You have a severe, infectious, viral-type, influenza-ish sinus condition." The patient said, "Gee, Doc, sounds expensive—I only got ten dollars." The doc said, "You have a cold."

My doctor told me I shouldn't drink, smoke, overeat, or dissipate. What it all boils down to is this: Don't do anything that could interfere with paying his bill.

Medical costs are really rising nowadays. One doctor recently told me he's doing so well financially that now he can occasionally tell a patient there's nothing wrong with him.

The credo of the men of medicine: Always write your prescriptions illegibly and your bills plainly.

The doctor felt the patient's purse and admitted there was nothing he could do.

We all think we are born free—until the doctor's bill arrives. I know one who has an exclusive practice: He only treats people with fat wallets. He just made a major breakthrough in medicine: He raised his fee to $150.

My doctor has come up with an easy payment plan for me. Now I automatically deposit my paycheck in his account.

I'm always a little nervous about going to see a doctor when I realize that doctors are usually described as practicing. I wouldn't mind, but they do most of it on the golf course.

Forget about house calls—no doctor will come to your house today unless it's to foreclose on the mortgage.

My family doctor is very meticulous—he always washes his hands before he touches my wallet.

A doctor is a person who acts like a humanitarian and charges like a plumber.

Most doctors are so prosperous they don't have time for long diagnoses. Doctors now have a quick, healthy dose for this age of high-speed medicine: "Doc, what do I do if my temperature goes up another point?" "Sell—*next*."

"Doc, should I file my nails?" "No, throw them away like everybody else—*next*."

"Doc, I get this terrible pain in my back every time I bend over." "Don't bend over—*next!*"

"Doc, nobody ever pays attention to me." "*Next*."

The medic asked the lady, "What is the matter with your husband?" She admitted, "I think he is worrying about money." The doc said, "Ah—I think I can relieve him of that."

The doctor noted, "There goes the only woman I ever loved." The nurse said, "Why don't you marry her?" He said, "I can't afford to—she's my best patient!"

The young doctor asked, "Why do you always ask your patients what they have for dinner?" The old doc said, "It's a most important question, for according to their menus, I make out my bills."

My neighbor just came back from the doctor, and I asked, "Did he find out what you have?" He said, "No—he only charged me $50 and I have $100."

I went to one young doctor fresh out of medical school. I don't think he's making too much money yet: His stethoscope is on a party line.

Listen, it's not always the doctor's fault: "Congratulations," said the nurse to the man who was pacing outside the maternity ward. "You're a bouncing father—we just tried to cash your check."

After being informed there was nothing wrong with his car, the doctor was handed a bill for fifty dollars. "If there's no damage, how come you're charging me fifty dollars?" he screamed. The mechanic said, "It's like this, Doc, you charged me fifty dollars for a visit last week and I didn't have anything wrong either."

The doctor explained to the heart patient that he would be able to resume his romantic life as soon as he could climb two flights of stairs without becoming winded. The patient listened attentively and said, "What if I look for women who live on the ground floor?"

The doc asked my sister why she gave up taking tranquilizers. She said, "I had to—I found myself being pleasant to people I don't even speak to."

A new patient appeared in a doctor's office to explain, "Doctor, I'm disturbed. A week ago I came home to find my wife in the arms of another man, who talked me into going out for a cup of coffee. The next four nights, exactly the same thing happened." "My good fellow," said the doctor. "It isn't a doctor you need; it's a lawyer." "No, no," insisted the patient, "it's a doctor's advice I want. I've got to know if I'm drinking too much coffee."

It's easy to spot a hypochondriac: He puts cough syrup on his pancakes.

Two doctors were having a drink together. One noticed that the other was really getting loaded. The first doctor asked if anything was wrong? His friend said, "Well, yes—last night I got the ultimate rejection. I was in church praying for divine help—and a deep majestic voice answered, 'Take two aspirins and call me in the morning.' "

I had a peculiar thing happen to me: My doctor gave me a physical examination, then he put on rubber gloves to shake hands.

Surgeons appear to be getting younger all the time. I saw one this past weekend in a hospital with his rubber gloves pinned to his shirt.

Medicine is so specialized these days, one patient had to switch doctors when his athlete's foot moved from his right foot to his left.

If you have to go to the hospital, it may help you to remember, there is no such thing as a dangerous operation for less than $1,000.

My doctor told me there was nothing strange about my condition—except that it was so seldom encountered in a person who was still living.

I called my doctor to make an appointment and his beeper answered: "At the beep, leave your name, address, and credit reference."

The doctor told me, "Only an operation can save you." I asked how much it would cost. "Five thousand dollars." I said, "I don't possess that much money." The doc said, "Then we will see what pills will do."

The two young doctors were talking about their diagnoses: The first said, "You've cured your patient—what is there to worry about?" The second said, "I don't know which of the medicines cured him."

After the examination, the physician handed his patient a prescription and said, "Take this medicine after each meal." The poor soul said, "But, Doc, I haven't eaten in four days." The doc said, "Fine—the medicine will last longer."

"I'm getting a little worried about myself, Doc," I explained. "I need something to stir me up, something to take me out of my state of lethargy and put me in fighting trim. Have you included anything like that in this prescription?" He said, "No, not in the prescription—you'll find that in the bill."

My uncle, who is eighty-five, sat before the doctor: "My wife just gave birth to a baby," he said. "Do you think I can do it again?" The doc said, "Tell me—do you think you did it the first time?"

Medical science has made a lot of progress. No matter what illness you have, doctors can keep you alive long enough to pay your bill.

Malpractice insurance is so expensive doctors may go on strike to get public support for their cause. But it won't work: Nobody will be able to read their picket signs.

My brother-in-law tells me he is going to associate himself with some of the most famous and skilled medical practitioners in the country: He's going to be a caddy.

The Park Avenue doctor told the intern, "Doctor, I want you to look after my office while I'm on my vacation." The intern said, "But I've just graduated—I have no experience." Said the specialist, "That's all right, my boy, my practice is strictly fashionable. Tell the men patients to play golf and ship the lady patients off to Europe."

I think I first began to lose confidence in my doctor when I noticed the six-inch dollar sign tattooed on his chest.

My uncle was in the hospital recovering from surgery. After several days in a room on the fifth floor, he was being moved to the hospital's sixth floor. When I asked him why he was being moved, he told me, "Because I've just finished paying for the fifth."

Nowadays, the first thing a little boy learns to make with a toy doctor's kit is a bill.

A librarian was admitted to Doctor's Hospital for surgery. She got a get well card from her associates that read: "If they take anything out—make sure they sign for it."

I know a surgeon who will take your appendix out for $500—even if you don't have one.

I heard one doctor tell a hospital patient: "You're fine now. Why, you'll be up and complaining about my bill in no time."

The best thing about Medicare is that it lets you have diseases that would ordinarily be beyond your means.

The young actor told his pretty nurse, "I think I'm in love with you. To tell the truth, I don't want to get well!" The nurse smiled and said, "Don't worry—I don't think you will. The doctor is in love with me and he saw you trying to grab me this morning."

The doctor said to the young lady, "I'd like to give you a

thorough examination—take off your nightgown." The patient said, "But Dr. Schwartz found me perfect this afternoon." The doc said, "So he told me!"

"I'm going to operate on Mrs. Green," the doc told her nephew. "The fee will be ten thousand dollars." The nephew asked, "What does she have?" The doc said, "Ten thousand dollars."

When I was in high school I wanted to be a doctor—but that dream ended when I didn't make the golf team.

These days what four out of five doctors recommend is another doctor.

I went to my doctor for a physical. Now I know what M.D. stands for—mucho dollars.

The best way to tell real doctors from impostors is the way they hold medical instruments: A fake doctor doesn't know the proper way to grip a putter.

On Long Island, yesterday, a man who charged that doctors are more interested in playing golf than treating patients was attacked by a mob of angry doctors who beat him with their golf clubs.

I understand that green fees will soon be paid by Medicare.

The wife was screaming at her husband: "I pinch and scrape and save pennies for a whole year—and then you go and blow it on your gallstones." He said, "You should be happy. The surgeon did a marvelous job. He operated just in time—one more day and I would have recovered without it."

A busy businessman suffering from insomnia was told by his doctor, "Instead of counting sheep, try telling each part of your body to go to sleep." That night, as he lay with his eyes open, he remembered and began trying it. "Toes go to sleep . . . feet go to sleep . . . ," he ordered. "Legs go to sleep . . . thighs go to sleep . . . ." He was up to his arms when his wife walked in wearing a sheer nightie. The husband sat up and hollered, "Wake up, everybody!"

I don't think we should pick on doctors anymore—they have their own problems: There are so many malpractice suits brought against them these days that now if you want a doctor's opinion on something, you have to talk to his lawyer.

These days there are three kinds of doctors: expensive, exorbitant, and "you gotta be kidding."

My doctor doesn't believe in acupuncture. The only thing he sticks me with is the bill.

The doctor said to my neighbor's wife in the hospital: "I don't care how good you feel. I'll release you when I think you're ready to be released and not a dollar sooner."

I heard a lady say, "My operation was so serious that when the surgeon finished operating I was immediately put in the expensive care unit."

In America we spend billions of dollars a year just for health. No wonder we have so many healthy doctors.

The patient said to the pharmacist: "The doctor never mentioned that one of the side effects of this medicine would be poverty."

I have a friend who drowned while taking acupuncture treatments on a waterbed. Acupuncture is not new. As far back as thirty years ago it was big in my neighborhood in Brooklyn: Instead of a needle, they used an ice pick.

The last thing my eye doctor asked me to read on the chart was the figure 195 in very large type. He asked, "Is that clear?" I replied, "Very clear." He said, "That's good; that's the price of your new glasses."

A really smart doctor is one who can diagnose the ailment of a patient who doesn't smoke or drink and isn't overweight.

My doctor has a great stress test. It's called "the bill."

Doc gave his patient a new "wonder drug" pill. The poor soul asked, "Will this relax me?" The doc said, "No. You'll just dig being tense."

A mother of five told a friend, "I've been going to a psychiatrist since I last saw you." "What's bothering you?" the friend asked. "Nothing's bothering me," the mother said. "But that's the only place I can lie down without being disturbed."

I was practically cured of back pains by acupuncture. When I phoned the doc that the pains had returned, the acupuncturist yawned, "Just take two thumb tacks and call me in the morning."

If a man still has his appendix and his tonsils—the chances are that he is a doctor.

"I wouldn't worry about your son playing with dolls," the doc told the middle-aged matron. She said, "I'm not worried—but his wife is very upset."

The thing that bothers me about doctors is they give you an appointment six weeks ahead, then they examine you, then they ask you: "Why did you wait so long to see me?"

The doctor said to Fatso, "You need more exercise—but you'll get that trying to earn the money to pay my bill."

I don't believe people who say doctors won't treat poor people. My father is poor and his doctor treats him—even though his fees are what made my father poor.

I told my doctor I lost my job. The doc said, "That's a coincidence—I was just going to tell you, your condition is all cleared up."

There is one advantage to being poor—a doctor will cure you faster.

The patient said to the surgeon: "Look, I'm broke. Just cut out about fifty bucks worth."

Drinking

My uncle adopted an eleven-day-old baby: Now his wife will have to get two bottles ready every night.

My brother-in-law is an occasional drinker—any occasion will do.

My cousin wrote, "I don't smoke, touch intoxicants, or gamble. I am faithful to my wife and never look at another woman. I am hardworking, quiet, and obedient. I never go to bars or places of ill-repute and I go to bed early every night and rise with the dawn. I attend chapel every Sunday without fail. I've been like this for the past three years—but just wait until next spring, when they let me out of here!"

My neighbor really tried to go on the wagon last year—and three bars sued him for nonsupport.

My brother joined a weight-lifting class. Right now he's up to eight-ounce glasses.

One great thing about old Uncle Charlie: He never has a hangover—he stays drunk.

I asked the expert: "Tell me, what do you take for a headache?" He said, "Liquor the night before."

When you talk about heavy drinkers, my uncle has to win first prize: My poor old uncle drank a fifth of whiskey with each of his three meals, then took a nightcap at bedtime. When he finally died, the family tried to honor his last wish by having him cremated. It took them three days to put out the fire.

Nobody knew my boss drank—until one day he came in sober.

My father-in-law says he owes his success in life to a

streetcorner orator he listened to one noon hour many years ago. He was a prohibitionist and he lectured on the evils of drink, pointing out how people ruined their health, spent all their time in saloons and their very last cent for liquor. My father-in-law was so impressed that the very next week he bought his first saloon.

My cousin the drunk thinks Beethoven's Fifth is a bottle of Scotch.

Now they've got an organization called Teetotalers Anonymous. If you feel like going on the wagon, you call this number and two drunks come over to talk to you.

At a party I heard the host ask, "Will you have a drink? We have Scotch, rye, bourbon, and brandy." My uncle said, "Yes, please—that'll be fine."

Our mayor is on a kick against smoking, sex, gridlock, and bribing—I hope he never gets to drinking.

There are really no problem drinkers—except those who never buy.

Drinking removes warts and pimples—not from me, but those that I have to talk to.

My uncle's the nicest chap on two feet, if he could only stay there. His favorite drink is the next one.

"I don't remember too much about last night," the drunk told me, "but we did get a ticket for riding three in the front seat." I asked, "What's wrong with three in the front seat?" He said, "It was on a motorcycle."

The drunk went tearing around town honking his horn and running red lights. It's a good thing he wasn't in his car at the time.

My neighbor lamented: "A woman drove me to drink—and I never even had the courtesy to thank her."

The drunk noted, "I always keep a supply of stimulant handy in case I see a snake—which I also keep handy."

The lady said to the drunk, "Every time I see you, you have a bottle in your hand." He said, "You don't expect me to keep it in my mouth all the time, do you?"

"Pour me a cold one," the teenager said, walking into the bar. The barmaid looked him over and said, "Get lost, kid. You want to get me in trouble?" The boy answered, "Maybe later—right now all I want's a beer."

A man ordered a martini "extra rare." The bartender said, "You mean extra dry." The man insisted, "I mean extra rare—I'm having it for my dinner."

These two loaded gentlemen stood at the bar near closing time: "I got an idea," one lush said. "Les have one more drink and go find sum broads." The other said, "Naah—I got more than I can handle at home." The first guy said, "Great—then let's have one more drink and go up to your place."

I don't want to say that guy drinks a lot—but he's two thousand swallows ahead of Capistrano.

A guy was boasting of his grandfather: "He lived for ninety-four years and never once used glasses." "He had the right of it," nodded his brother. "I always said it was healthier to drink from the bottle."

"Stay out of that place, Mike," warned his friend. "If you go in, the devil goes in with you." "If he does," said Mike, "he pays for his own drinks."

The judge looked sternly at the defendant: "You've been brought here for drinking." The defendant answered, "Well, what are we waiting for—let's get started."

Today there's a diet for everybody. The most popular is the drinking man's diet. It's hard to tell how many people follow it, because most of them don't know they're on it.

My alcoholic uncle is a baby at heart: He still gets his two o'clock bottle—and his three o'clock—and his four o'clock.

My uncle suggests a great recipe for a Christmas turkey:

"Take a fifteen-pound turkey, add one quart of Scotch, heat it, then pour a quart of gin over it, then a quart of Burgundy, then put it back in the oven for one hour. Then you take the turkey out of the oven and throw it out the window—but, oh, what a gravy!"

One way to cut down on drunk driving would be for the saloons to offer free home delivery.

A restauranteur I know has a new cocktail in his bar made with vodka and carrot juice. You get drunk just as fast—but it's great for your eyesight.

Two insomniacs were discussing their problem. "I've lost ten pounds in the last two weeks for lack of sleep," one victim said. "I don't know what to do." "I do," the other said. "I just take a martini every hour after dinner." "Terrific. And it works?" "No, but it keeps me happy while I'm awake."

My alcoholic uncle told me he's considering filling his swimming pool with martinis. He claims that'll make it impossible to drown, since the deeper you sink, the higher you get.

My alcoholic cousin tells me the staff at his favorite hotel are very considerate: "The morning after, they always serve my breakfast on the floor."

A recent survey shows that whiskey drinkers get more cavities than milk drinkers, but they go to the dentist in a better frame of mind.

My alcoholic uncle told me: "I haven't quit drinking—never. Everybody hates a quitter."

I will not think of my brother-in-law as an ordinary drunk—not after I heard he donated his body to science, so he's preserving it in alcohol till they use it.

Dumb-Dumbs

America has now opened its borders to the independent kingdom of Slobbovia—as if we didn't have enough dumb-dumbs in Washington. The average Slobbovian pol never knows which foot he has in his mouth. If there's an idea in his head, it's in solitary confinement.

Did you hear about the Slobbovian grandmother who went on the pill? She didn't want to have any more grandchildren.

How does a Slobb make love? He hires a stand-in.

Do you know what they call anybody with an IQ of 80 in Slobbovia? Mr. President.

Slobey the Slobb went into the farm supply store and asked for six sticks of dynamite. The owner asked, "You want 'em to clear up your land?" Slobey said, "No—it's just that I'm going into town today and every time I go there, that wiseguy Dummy always comes up and yells, 'How are you?' and slaps me on the chest just to break the cigars he knows I carry there. Well, today when he does it, he's going to blow his damn hand off." This is the same guy who went to a doctor for an ulcer transplant.

Dumbrella, the Mayor of Slobbville, proposed that a gondola be put in the Dopey Park Lake. One councilman supported the idea with great enthusiasm: "Let's get two gondolas—male and female."

Slobbovians are loving people. Dan Dummy lived in a remote mountain village. One morning he was awakened by a postman delivering a letter. "You shouldn't have come all that way just to bring me one letter," he said lovingly. "You should have mailed it."

Did you hear about the Slobbovian skier with the frostbitten backside? He couldn't figure out how to get his pants on over his skis.

The newlywed asked his wife why she was cutting a block of ice into little cubes. The new wife said, "So they'll fit into the ice tray."

Dummy Stoopido passed a police station and noticed the sign that said, MAN WANTED FOR BANK ROBBERY. So he went inside and applied for the job. This is the same guy who spent hours looking for phone numbers in the dictionary.

Why don't Slobbovians throw dinner parties? They can't spell RSVP.

How does a Slobb increase his vocabulary? Easy—with a can of alphabet soup.

What can most Slobbovian kids do by the age of twelve? Wave bye-bye. Most Slobbovians are as smart as they can be—unfortunately.

What do you call a Slobbovian with half a brain? Gifted.

A Slobbovian's going to the hospital for a minor operation: They're putting a brain in. His wife's going abroad. When she went to her doctor for shots, she slapped him when he asked to see her itinerary.

Why did the Slobb buy a hundred bottles of aspirin? He needed the cotton.

The Kingdom of Slobbovia could have the biggest zoo in the world. All they have to do is build a fence around their country. The mayor is such a lamebrain—he wears orthopedic hats.

Dummy gave his wife a washing machine for her birthday, but he had to return it: Every time she got into it, she came out black and blue.

A woman I know doesn't buy brooms—because they don't come with instructions.

Dummy bought $3,000 worth of tires for his house because he wanted white walls.

This guy was going fishing and was buying bait. The store manager said, "I'll give you all you want for a dollar." Dummy said, "Good—I'll take three dollars' worth."

It's easy to spot a Slobb visiting this country: He asks what wine goes best with Alpo.

Slobbovian airlines are different: They show coming attractions of movies that will be shown on other airlines.

The doctor told Slobbina, "You're pregnant. You're going to have a baby." She said, "Sorry, Doc, but the baby isn't mine."

In upper Slobbovia, thieves escaped with over half a million dollars from the Slobbovia National Bank. The papers said, "Police are baffled trying to figure out the motive for the crime."

Did you know they installed TV sets in all Slobbovian stadiums—so the fans could see what was going on in their local bar?

Slobb drivers have never won the Indianapolis 500: They have to stop ten times to ask directions.

The two Slobb hunters were driving into the woods when they saw a sign that said BEAR LEFT—so they went home.

What happened to the Slobbovian Water Polo Team? The horses drowned.

The Mayor of Dumbville must be even smarter than Einstein was. Twelve people were said to have understood Einstein—*him* nobody understands.

What do you call a pregnant Slobbovian lady? A dope carrier.

The mayor had this sign put up on the door of the dance hall: ALL LADIES AND GENTLEMEN ARE WELCOME—REGARDLESS OF SEX.

What do they call an intelligent man in Slobbovia? A tourist.

Two Slobbs froze to death in upper Slobbovia: They went to a drive-in movie to see *Closed for the Season*.

Slobbina cried, "My boyfriend asked me to marry him and I'm so mad." "Why?" "Well, my mother married my father, my aunt married my uncle—so why should I marry a stranger?"

Did I tell you about Sam Slobb, who had a problem with spelling? He paid fifty dollars and spent the night in a warehouse. . . . Or how about Bob Slobb, who wouldn't go out with his wife because she was a married woman?

Slobey told his wife, "I'll never work for that man again!" She asked, "Why? What did he say to make you so mad?" He said, "He told me I was fired!"

There was a Frenchman, Englishman, and Slobbovian all sitting with their girlfriends and enjoying themselves. The Frenchman said to his girl, "Pass the sugar, Sugar!" The Englishman said to his girl, "Pass the honey, Honey!" The Slobb, in the spirit of things, said to his lady, "Pass the tea, Bag!"

The Slobb told me, "I just bought a suit with two pairs of pants, but I don't like it." "Why?" "It gets awfully hot wearing two pairs of pants." He was so dumb he thought Einstein was one beer.

A Slobb applied for a job as a prison guard. The warden said, "Now these are real tough guys in here—do you think you can handle it?" Dummy said, "No problem, sir. If they don't behave—out they go!"

I wouldn't say this guy was not a mental giant, but he thought a Band-Aid was a charitable organization for musicians.

Do you know they had to close down the library in Slobbovia? Somebody stole the book.

There was this guy in Lower Slobbovia giving evidence in a court case. He told the judge how he had seen a young girl beaten up by four muggers. The judge asked, "Why didn't you go to her aid?" Slobey said, "Your Honor, how was I to know who started the fight?"

The first dumb-dumb said: "I'm going to save my money and buy a Japanese radio." Answered the second dumb-dumb: "How are you going to understand what they're saying?"

The Slobbovian car dealer got caught turning back all the fuel gauges.

Eating (At Home and Out)

My wife never has to send out for junk food—she makes her own.

There's a simple rule to be followed when reading menus in fancy French restaurants: If you can't pronounce it—you can't afford it.

One restaurant customer said to another: "The service here is terrible, but you don't mind waiting, because the food is so poor."

I asked my wife, "Where am I when you serve those wonderful meals from which we always have the leftovers?"

A diner told his frantic waiter, "You know, I first came into this place in 1938." The waiter said, "I only got two hands—I'll get to your table in a minute."

Sam, my neighbor, said, "For the past two weeks I've

been eating like a king: three wonderful meals a day." I said, "Your wife must be a good cook." Sam snapped, "What good cook? She's away visiting her mother. I've been eating at Joe's Diner."

My wife is such a lousy cook, every time she leaves the kitchen, she runs the risk of being arrested for leaving the scene of a crime.

The diner to the waiter: "What's my offense? I've been on bread and water for almost an hour."

My sister admits she's a lousy cook: "In my house we have Alka-Seltzer on tap."

The hostess asked the man, "Do you have a reservation?" He said, "No." She said, "Fine—then I'll give you immediate seating."

While dining at a restaurant, my neighbor yelled to the waiter, "What's this fly doing in my vichyssoise?" The waiter replied, "He's probably cooling off. Sometimes it gets very hot in the kitchen."

My neighbor told his lady he would take her out to dine royally. Later she told her friends they went to Burger King and wound up at the Dairy Queen.

My wife is a lazy cook: She hires a hit man just to beat the eggs.

Egotists

I love people with big egos: To love oneself is the beginning of a lifelong romance. Take my friend: He's a self-made man—and he worships his creator. He who falls in love with himself will have no rivals.

The only exercise egotists get is throwing bouquets at themselves.

The youngster gazed at his father's visitor, a man of large proportions, who looked like a whale in heat. "My boy, why are you looking at me like that?" the man asked. "Well, Daddy told Mother you were a self-made man." The guest said. "Right—I *am* a self-made man." "But," said the boy, "why did you make yourself like that?"

My brother-in-law claims, "At school, everybody hated me because I was so popular."

"I'm afraid I'm unfaithful," my aunt told me. "I don't love myself as much as I should." I'll tell you one thing about my aunt: She likes you to come right out and say what you think—when you agree with her.

My cousin says modestly, "They didn't give me looks— but they gave me an absolute monopoly on brains and talent." He says, "I'm not conceited—although God knows I have every reason to be." He doesn't want you to make a fuss about him—just to treat him as you would any other great man. It is not true that his head is getting too big for his toupee.

In an age when the fashion is to be in love with yourself, confessing to be in love with somebody else is an admission of unfaithfulness to one's beloved.

I haven't seen so much respect and admiration for one man since my brother stood alone in front of his three-way mirror.

People who think they know everything are very irritating to those of us who do.

A conceited person never gets anywhere because he thinks he is already there.

When a civilian's house burns down, he calls his insurance man. The actor calls his press agent.

The reporter was passing along the river and heard

sounds of someone struggling in the water. He recognized the man who was hollering, "Help! I'm drowning!" as a famous actor. The reporter said, "Geez—you're just too late to make the late-night edition. But don't worry. You'll have a nice headline all by yourself in the morning edition!"

"How's your new publicity agent doing for you?" I asked the actress. She said, "He's great. I've had him less than a month and already my house has caught fire once, I've been robbed twice, been in an auto accident, had three suicide notes from admirers, and now I've been threatened with kidnappers."

The opera star screamed on opening night: "What's with the ten bouquets of flowers?" The manager said, "They're wonderful." She yelled, "What's wonderful? I paid for fifteen!"

You can't help admiring my boss: If you don't, you're fired.

His girl adores him and so does he. He's a very thoughtful kind of guy: Every time he has a birthday, he sends his mother a letter of congratulations. I saw him at dinner and asked how he was coming along with his psychiatrist. He explained, "I used to be the most conceited, arrogant, egotistical, prideful person you ever saw, until I saw my shrink. Now you just couldn't meet a nicer, more humble guy than I am anywhere."

The newspapers carried a story about the nation's most beautiful actresses and the insignificant men they sometimes choose as husbands. My neighbor sighed. "I'll never be able to understand why the biggest shnooks always get the prettiest women," he said to his wife. "Why, darling," she said, "what a very sweet compliment!"

My uncle never said an unkind word about anybody. That's because he never talks about anybody but himself.

England

England is a country surrounded by hot water. But they always pull out of it.

Two lords were talking: "I hear they buried your wife." "Had to—dead, you know."

The English poet once was asked if he would teach his daughter several languages. "No," he replied. "One tongue is enough for any woman."

The English like to laugh at themselves: "It does get foggy here in London; in fact, I've been in only one city that was more foggy, but it was so foggy at the time, I couldn't see what city it was."

A young barrister was a candidate from a Lancashire town. "I'm very pleased to address a working-class constituency," he started. "It may interest you to know that I am a working man myself. In fact, I often work when you are asleep." A voice in the rear hollered, "You must be a blooming burglar."

"Ah, yes, my late wife was a most remarkable woman," the mild old Englishman told one of his cronies on a park bench in London. "A very religious woman," he continued. "Never missed a day in church, and at home it was prayers and psalm singing from morning to night." "How did she come to die?" the friend inquired. "I strangled her."

The elderly English couple had won a small fortune on the pools and were paying their first visit to the south of France. "Isn't this a beautiful place, dear?" asked the wife. "Glorious," agreed her husband. "Do you know, dear," he went on, "if anything happened to either of us, I'd like to spend the rest of my days here."

After being injured in a cricket match, the English sports-
man went to see his doctor, who put three stitches in his
wound. "That will be five pounds," the doctor told him.
"Five pounds?" the injured one howled. "For three
stitches? I'm glad you're not my blooming tailor!"

Fashions

I think the fashion world is taking this designer label
business a little too far: Would you believe Calvin Klein
nasal spray?
Gloria Vanderbilt designer aspirin tablets?
Yves St. Laurent arch supports?
A truss with an alligator on it?
Milk of Magnesia in a Halston designer Lalique bottle?
Givenchy underarm spray?
How about Ex-Lax by Gucci?

The fashion world is going way out this year. One clever
Seventh Avenue dress designer is doing big business with
a line of teenage maternity fashions in school colors. Just
last week a big department store ran a full-page ad with
the headline: "Maternity Dresses for the Modern Miss."

Everybody is dying their hair: One woman dyed it so
many times, she has plaid dandruff.

A modern young lady had a little accident in Hollywood:
She fell off her seven-inch platform shoes. She would have
been injured—but her eyelashes broke the fall.

We've had slit skirts: Now, how about something more
practical—split jeans?

Slits in women's skirts now come in three different
lengths: high, higher, and "not guilty, Your Honor."

With the dresses today, if a girl has to have her appendix taken out and she doesn't want it to show—they'll have to remove it through her nose.

If women dressed to please their husbands, they'd wear last year's clothes.

My aunt explained why she finally decided to wear the mini: "If you're going to look ugly, you might as well look this year's ugly."

My niece told me, "I wore a see-through dress, but nobody wanted to."

My neighbor says, "I hope jodhpurs come back—they're the only pants that go out the same place I do."

This year the newest thing in women's hairdos are men.

My neighbor went into a clothing store and the salesman showed him one suit for $1,200. He said it was made from virgin wool. My friend said, "That's nice—but I'd rather see something for about $200 from a sheep who fooled around a little!"

My wife says I've got to start dressing better: "It's embarrassing to have people drop coins in your coffee cup."

The annual best dressed list is upon us again. My friends are all excited: They want to know what to wear on the unemployment line.

Fashion is so important in this country the president's wife just ordered a submarine to the coast of France to spy on the new spring line.

These days you can't judge a girl by the clothes she wears. There's not enough evidence.

I sat at a dinner table with a girl last night whose dress was cut so low that I had to look under the table to see what she was wearing.

This season, gowns that are in leave most of the wearer out!

The most attractive thing about the latest fashions for women is that they won't last.

Fashion is a personal thing. My sister is the only girl I know who wears prescription underwear.

Designer jeans are great if you don't care about blood pressure below the waist.

You can always tell a widow in Beverly Hills: She wears a black tennis outfit.

I can't understand why women want to show their knees? Who ever said wrinkles were sexy?

The credo of today's fashion is: If it's comfortable—forget it. A lady was having trouble with her new shoes at a fashionable salon. "They're not comfortable," she said. "I just can't walk in these shoes." "Madam," said the manager, "people who have to walk don't buy their shoes here."

One fashion-conscious lady tried on a dress at a posh boutique and cooed, "It's very nice—but it's a lot less than I wanted to spend."

No wonder they call it high fashion: Take a look at the price tags.

Designer jeans prices are ridiculous. If I spend $150 for a pair of jeans, I expect a woman to be in them.

Girls' jeans come in three sizes: small, medium, and don't bend over.

The good news is, we're living in a time when millions of Americans are finally beginning to turn the other cheek. The bad news is, it's to show the designer label on their jeans.

One model told the clerk, "I don't care about the style or color of shoes, but I want low heels." He asked, "To wear with what?" She said, "A short, plump, elderly millionaire."

The fashion maven was explaining why women's boxing never caught on: "Did you ever hear of a woman putting on gloves without shoes and purse to match?"

A designer tells me women's clothes are getting more masculine and men's clothes are getting more feminine. Pretty soon you'll be able to save a fortune by marrying someone your own size.

My neighbor's wife always wants to buy a new outfit every time she's invited out. My neighbor thought he'd play a gag and accepted an invite to a nudist wedding. The gag was on him: She spent $3,000 on a body lift.

It's bikini time on the beaches. "I saw some of those new fashions," my sister notes. "I have earrings that cover more than that." Those bathing suits are really getting brief: I've seen more cotton in the top of an aspirin bottle. In fact, this year's bikini gives about as much coverage as a lapsed insurance policy.

My tailor made up six suits for the rock star for $18,000. That's not much considering that the price includes batteries.

Fathers

Father's Day is the day when father goes broke giving his family money so they can surprise him with gifts he doesn't need.

Father's Day and Mother's Day are alike—except that on Father's Day you buy a much cheaper gift.

I don't know why, but Father's Day never seems to grow up—it's like Mother's Day after taxes.

A father is a banker provided by nature.

My neighbor told me, "Every year my wife gives me the same present on Father's Day: A list of presents she wants for her birthday. This year my son gave me something I always wanted—the keys to my car."

I have good news and bad news. The good news is the kids all got together and sent me a check for $100 made out to cash. The bad news is—they asked me to sign it and send it back.

My father told me about the birds and bees—he didn't know anything about girls.

My uncle is always unhappy on Father's Day because he never had any children to celebrate it with him. "Weren't you happy at home?" I asked him. He said, "Oh, sure. My wife laughs at everything I do—that's why we have no children."

My uncle is a little naive: He thinks a paternity suit is something you wear when your wife is pregnant.

The man who says he runs things around the house is probably referring to the lawnmower, the vacuum cleaner, and the washing machine.

That father of five children had won a toy at a raffle. When he got home, he called the kids together and asked, "Who should have this present? Who is most obedient? Who never talks back to your mother? Who does everything she says?" Five small voices answered in unison, "You can have it, Daddy."

Father admits he would never be what he is today without his family—BUSTED.

Father: The person who can't get into the bathroom, on the phone, or out of the house.

"Dad is a great guy," my nephew told me. "Just about the

time he gets his daughter off his hands, he has to start putting his son-in-law on his feet."

Every year my mom gave my dad the perfect Father's Day gift: She sent us kids to summer camp for two weeks.

My friend said, "I knew Father's Day was coming up when my daughter asked me what size cologne I wear."

Every father thinks he is the master of his home—but mostly he is the paymaster.

On Father's Day give Dad money—it's the one thing you can be sure he doesn't have.

Hollywood kids always have a problem on Father's Day. It's not so much a question of what to buy—it's who to give it to.

My brother-in-law the drunk told me the most embarrassing thing happened to him one Father's Day: "My wife had a Scotch on the rocks as a nightcap, then went up to kiss Junior good-night. The kid opened his eyes and said, 'Mommy, you're wearing Daddy's perfume!' "

Last Father's Day was really something. I got up early and called my dad long distance. I wished him a happy Father's Day, and then we stayed on the phone for about an hour, reminiscing about my childhood and the great times we had together. Then, when we were ready to hang up, my father said six words that I'll never forget for as long as I live. He said, "By the way, who is this?"

Gambling

They say that every election is a gamble, which is ridiculous. When you gamble, at least you have a chance to win.

I love to gamble but I just can't throw my money around on gambling and drinking and women—I've got a government to support.

I just heard a touching story: There's a bookie down the street who changed his name to Red Cross—just so his customers' losses would be tax deductible.

Atlantic City is now mad for gambling. My brother pulled into a parking space at one hotel and dropped a quarter in the meter; three little wheels spun around—and he lost his Chrysler.

I was lucky in Atlantic City—I got a ride home. I just hope they have more luck with my money than I did.

Las Vegas: Now there's a town for my money. They've got some pretty classy hotels there—you have to wear a tie to lose your shirt. I just love the town. You can't beat the climate, the people, the food—or the slot machines. I had the best system for beating them at the craps tables—but then the casino opened.

I go to Atlantic City once a month to visit my money—and leave a little interest. Money isn't everything—but if you stay there long enough, it's nothing.

Horseplayers are a breed of their own.

My neighbor put four kids through college. Unfortunately, they were his bookmaker's kids.

I'd probably do more gambling if I had a better bookie. The one I've got now had me bet on Harold Stassen in five elections.

When I do gamble I like to play the horses, but before I bet I always talk to people who know horse flesh—trainers, jockeys, my butcher . . . .

At the track, I met my very dejected uncle, who was tearing up his stubs. "Why so sad?" I asked. "I've got reason to be sad," he lamented. "I came here today with enough money to choke a horse, but I made a terrible mistake." I asked, "What was that?" He said, "I didn't choke him—I bet on him."

When you enter Nevada, they have big signs that say: KEEP NEVADA GREEN—LOSE!

Gambling is a sure way to get nothing for something! I learned how to make a small fortune in Atlantic City: Go there with a big one.

They now have five-dollar slot machines. They're for the man who has everything—but not for long.

Most hotels have signs in the rooms that say: HAVE YOU LEFT ANYTHING? At Atlantic City the signs say, HAVE YOU ANYTHING LEFT?

Gambling has done wonders for Atlantic City: It's the first time I saw slot machines that take welfare checks.

A lot of people are planning to spend their vacations in Atlantic City. Which is appropriate. A vacation is where you get away from it all—all your money, your savings, your stocks.

Atlantic City is jumping. I walked away from an Atlantic City laundry machine for five minutes—and somebody won my wash.

The trouble with hitting the jackpot on a slot machine is that it takes so long to put the money back in.

I'm going back to Atlantic City this weekend. I hope I break even—I need the money.

My neighbor told me, "Gambling brought my family

closer together: I lost all my money and we had to move into one room."

The only way to win at blackjack is to use a real blackjack.

They even have slot machines in the men's room in Las Vegas—if you don't win, you don't go.

I went into a drugstore and asked for some aspirin. The clerk said, "I'll toss you double or nothing." I ended up with two headaches.

Everybody in Las Vegas has a system to beat the system. I asked one maven, "What do I do? One day I lose, one day I win." He said, "Jerk, play every other day."

In Vegas, even the houses of worship are a game of chance. At one church on the strip the priest calls the Bingo numbers in Latin—so the atheists can't win.

Gamblers are nice people. I have a friend who always observes Be Kind to Animals week: All the money he earns he gives to the horses.

Drinking and gambling are a powerful parlay in Nevada: "But we have it under control," one friend told me. "Monday night, at my Gambler's Anonymous meeting, we all get drunk. Then Tuesday night, at Alcoholics Anonymous, we have an all-night poker game."

One seventy-year-old gambler said to his wife, "Enough already, let's go upstairs and make love." She said, "I don't like the odds."

One loser approached me, "I know, I know, I owe you $300." I said, "It's only $200." He said, "It's gonna be $300."

It is estimated that Americans spend over $7 billion a year on games of chance alone—and that doesn't include weddings.

Gambling in Las Vegas or Atlantic City is a little ridiculous. You take your money out of the bank and pay your own transportation to bring it to them.

In Reno, you can get rid of your wife and your money at the same time.

My uncle is a loser. He pumped $150 into the first machine he saw and never won a nickel. He *did* win 100 packs of cigarettes.

It was their first time in Vegas, and the elderly couple couldn't wait to try it all. They pulled slot machines and played bingo, craps, roulette, blackjack with all kinds of exuberance. After each thrilling excursion, they returned to their rooms to recuperate and count their losses. The fourth night, the husband said, "Honey, I'm too tired to go again—let's just send them a check."

Las Vegas has had a steady increase in population since the 1960s. This is because half of the people who visit there can't afford to leave.

Vegas is the type of town where celebrating a blessed event is getting three sevens on the slot machines.

My brother had a rough weekend in Atlantic City: "I went for $600 at the tables—and that was just the dinner tables." Remember when people went to Atlantic City to get tanned—instead of faded?

My neighbor groans he hasn't been having much luck playing the horses: "Yesterday the nag I bet a bundle on ended up in a photo finish with the truck that waters the track."

Gambling is basically a foolish vice. It's kind of like diving into an empty swimming pool! The chances that you'll hit bottom are about the same.

A man once saw a priest blessing a horse at Aqueduct, which convinced him to bet a bundle on the nag. When the horse ran out of the money, he remarked to the priest, "Father, it looks like a blessing doesn't work at the track." The priest replied: "My son, I wasn't blessing that horse, I was giving him last rites."

Las Vegas has the only hotels in the world where if you call down for room service, they send up three slot machines and a change-maker.

My sister suggests: "The best way to prevent your husband from gambling is for you to spend it first."

You can't win . . . I know a guy who only made mental bets. He lost his mind.

Getting Old

Age is a matter of mind—if you don't mind, it really doesn't matter.

Believe it or not, sex with a younger man is not all a bed of roses. There are some drawbacks. For example, he may expect you to respond.

You know you're getting old when you pay for sex and get a refund.

Age creeps up on a woman—especially when she's married to an older man.

These two octogenarians on their honeymoon check into the Plaza Hotel. As soon as they get into bed he reaches out and holds her hand. In a little while they fall asleep. The next night, again he reaches for her hand, and again they fall asleep. The third night, as he reaches for her hand, she hollers, "What are you, a sex maniac? Three nights in a row?"

My neighbor claims he's gotten to the point in life where he loses his place during romance.

My cousin claims: "Your whole life turns around when you hit middle age. You start to eat and you feel sexy; you go to bed and you feel hungry. By the time a man is able to read a woman like a book—his eyes go bad."

This Social Security dude got on a very crowded bus. This pretty young thing got up and offered him her seat. He was pleased but embarrassed. "How about getting on my lap?" he suggested. She took him up on his offer. After five minutes, he said, "Miss, I'm sorry, but you'll have to get off my lap—I'm not as old as I thought I was!"

You know you're old when:
   Your wife wakes up feeling amorous, and *you* have a headache . . .
   Your sex drive is in park . . .
   You bend down to tie your shoe and you try to think of other things to do while you're down there . . .
   Heartburn is more frequent than heartache . . .
   Your friends who accuse you of robbing the cradle are more jealous than shocked . . .
   Whether you're desired for your money or your looks becomes less of an issue . . .
   There's less of a mad scramble to arrange your face when you wake up next to someone.

I know a guy who married an old gal for her money, and he earned it. "Drink makes you look young and gorgeous," he told her. "But I haven't been drinking," she said. "No," he agreed. "But *I* have."

I'm at the age now where I look at *Playboy* through an interpreter. . . . Even my hairpiece is turning gray.

The old guy was boasting at the party: "I'm as good now as I ever was. I can do everything now I could do at thirty." He turned to his wife and said, "Isn't that right, Mildred?" She said, "That's right—which gives you an idea of how pitiful you were at thirty."

The big trouble with us is that when we're old enough to know better—we don't want to.

Nine out of ten doctors will tell you that sexual activity can lengthen your life. It can also shorten your life: I know one twenty-five-year-old fellow who was very active physically with this older lady—until her husband shot him.

Having sex at eighty-eight isn't the problem. The problem is getting the girl.

I'm fortunate to be around at ninety. Somebody up there must like me—or somebody up there does *not* want me. Many of my contemporaries who have retired say, without something to do their lives became boring. They say the only time they actually *have* to do anything—is when they get up during the night.

I won't say he's old, but the picture on his driver's license is by Van Gogh. He looks the same as he did twenty years ago—but so does a dollar bill. But he's found the secret of eternal youth: He won't go with girls over twenty—even if the price is much higher. He brought his young bride to his Park Avenue home. "Isn't she gorgeous?" he asked his valet. "Could be," the valet answered. "But I do hate to see a man begin a full day's work so very late in the afternoon."

I nicknamed my waterbed Lake Placid.

"Our song" was Taps.

An eighty-year-old man was reading in his hotel room when he heard a knock on the door. He opened the door and a gorgeous girl looked in and said, "Did you send for room service?" He said, "I don't think so." She said, "I must have the wrong room." The old guy said, "You got the right room—but you're twenty years too late."

Middle age—that's the period of life when one look at a man's checkbook and his waistline reveals the same thing: He's overextended again.

You know you're getting old when you go to a drive-in movie and keep the seat belt fastened.

Grandpa told me, "I'm at the age where sex is a four-letter word—H-E-L-P!"

"I must be growing old," a man grumbled to his friend. "I can tell by the way people talk to me." "You don't look old," the friend told him. "What do people say?" "They used to ask me, 'Why don't you marry?' Now they ask, 'Why didn't you marry?' "

For a man, the most disturbing part of being a grandfather is that he's now sleeping with a grandmother.

I don't mind being a senior citizen—I just don't look forward to graduation.

The one good thing about old age is that you only go through it once.

The thing that worries me about temptation at my age is that if I resist it—it may never come again.

I'm at that age where I'm beginning to wonder if my sex drive was taken over by the post office. . . . Sometimes it takes me five days to deliver.

You know you're old when you have to use tenderizer in Cream of Wheat.

You know you're old when you sit in a rocking chair and you can't get it started.

People ask, "What is the dividing line between middle age and senior citizenship?" You know you've reached the "golden years" when:
   What you want for your birthday is a hot water bottle . . .
   You use the stairs to get in and out of a swimming pool . . .
   You believe it is okay for other women to wear a bikini but not your wife or daughter . . .
   You take a little nap before going to bed at night . . .
   You're with a girl for a romantic evening and you hope for only two things: that the stars come out and your teeth don't . . .
   You celebrate your fortieth anniversary by sending out for hors d'oeuvres, champagne, and oxygen.

I'm in favor of senior citizen sex—I'm in favor of anything that's a spectator sport.

I asked my grandmother, "Is there as much sex among senior citizens today?" She said, "Probably—because it takes twice as long."

I'm at the age now where I find Farina spicy.

My big nighttime cocktail is Serutan on the rocks.

This widow and her elderly boyfriend were alone in her apartment but were having no success in making love. She said, "You can't think of anyone either?"

A widow in her late seventies was sitting on a park bench sobbing her heart out. Her friend asked, "What's wrong?" She said, "I have a beautiful house, I just married a young man who loves me and can't do enough for me, I get love day and night." "Then why are you crying?" her friend asked. "I forgot where I live."

My aunt tells about the widow who moved to Florida and was sitting on the beach, when she saw this handsome young man sunning himself. She rushed over to introduce herself: "You're new here? You look so pale." He said, "Yes, I've been in prison." She said, "My dear, really? What for?" He explained, "I bludgeoned my wife to death!" "Oh," she cried, with joy in her face. "You're single!"

Widows don't object to men who kiss and tell—they need all the publicity they can get.

It's not your age that matters—it's how your matter ages.

An old maid is a yes-girl who didn't have a chance to talk.

A spinster is a woman who knows all the answers—but nobody asks her the questions.

The sweet old lady went to the post office to mail a package. She was afraid she didn't put enough stamps on it, so she asked the clerk to weigh it. He told her she used too many stamps. She said, "Oh dear—I hope it won't go too far."

One resident at a senior citizens center: "A lady asked me if I play bridge. I replied, no, but I play post office." She said, "Good—now, you go and become a letter that just got lost."

The Social Security agent told the applicant: "Feeling sixty-five isn't good enough. You have to *be* sixty-five."

An elderly man was driving way below the minimum speed limit, when a policeman pulled him over to the side of the road. "Do you know why I stopped you?" the cop asked. "Sure do, sonny. I'm the only one you could catch."

A little old lady crossed the street against the light and was promptly stopped by a policeman. "Didn't you see that sign up there? It says DON'T WALK!" "Oh, *that* sign," she said. "I thought the bus company had put those up."

Old age is in: An archaeologist is the best husband any woman can have: The older she gets, the more interested he is in her.

What is age? My first girlfriend was Cleopatra—and I'm still interested in romance, although now it's a memory course. I remember when a union man meant a supporter of Abraham Lincoln. I'm at the age now where every time I see a girl I used to know—it's her daughter.

My brother complained about his loss of physical desire. I explained, "It's not to worry—it's natural at your age." My brother said, "But my neighbor is past ninety and he says he makes love every night." "So," I advised, "why don't you say the same thing?"

There are two ways to keep from getting old: Lie about your age and drink while you're driving.

A friend was telling me: "It's no fun getting old—nearly all my friends are gone now. Of course, Andy Marshall is the one I miss most." I asked, "Why is that?" He said, "Because I married his widow."

The ten best years of a woman's life come between twenty-eight and thirty.

My old sister says she doesn't have wrinkles, she has laugh lines. She must do a lot more laughing at her age.

My old sister tells me she has discovered a wonderful way to eliminate wrinkles: "When you look in the mirror take off your glasses."

I always tell people I'm much older than I actually am— just to hear them tell me how good I look for my age.

You know you're growing old when a pregnant woman offers you her seat on a bus.

Advice on dating much younger women: Don't try too hard or her kisses may turn into mouth-to-mouth resuscitation.

My brother was at a party, where he was staring at an attractive young lady. She asked, "Why are you undressing me with your eyes?" He answered, "Because I have arthritis in my hands."

You know you're old when:
    You don't mind when someone else drives . . .
    You produce a heretofore unheard sound when kneeling or bending . . .
    Your biological urge dwindles into an occasional nudge . . .
    You have an insurance policy actually signed by John Hancock . . .
    Your favorite night spot is a seat in front of the television.

How to have a young mind and a healthy body at age ninety: Have a young mind and take a healthy body out to a disco tonight.

I once asked Betsy Ross to go dancing with me, but she couldn't: She was busy sewing something at the time.

Getting old is terrific—I mean, considering the alternative.

I knew I was getting old when I took my dog out for a walk

and I couldn't keep up with him—so I swapped him for a turtle.

My friend's doctor told him to slow down—so he took a job with the post office.

You've got to enjoy old age. . . . Take my friend: He has no respect for age—unless it's bottled.

The definition of a dirty old man: A guy who has three daughters and only one bathroom.

A man who correctly guesses a woman's age may be smart—but he's not very bright.

A woman starts lying about her age when her face begins telling the truth about it.

If you can't afford to touch up your face, touch up the date of birth on your driver's license.

You can usually tell when you hit middle age: It starts hitting back.

My brother was telling me about his two friends, Irving and Irene, who finally got married after all these years. "Why, how old are they?" I asked. "Well, he's at the age when the only thing he can sink his teeth into is water. She doesn't show her age, but if you look under her makeup it's there." "So, what's the problem?" "Well, I'm not sure—but if they waited this long, you'd think they would have held out for a couple of more months—they could have charged the wedding to Medicare."

Have you noticed that you have to get old before anybody will say you look young?

Growing old has its compensations: All the things you couldn't have when you were young you no longer want.

The first hint I got that I was getting older was when I played the slot machine and it came out three prunes.

Old age is when a man wakes up tired and lustless.

I love it when people say, "You're not getting older—you're getting better," but I have one problem with that: The only thing I seem to be getting better at—is getting older.

Whatever Mother Nature gave me—Father Time is taking away.

My aunt never reveals her age. I told her, "That hat makes you look ten years younger—How old are you?" She said, "Thirty-nine." I said, "I mean without your hat." She admitted she was touching forty. "Touching it?" I squealed. "You're beating the hell out of it."

Auntie wouldn't even tell the judge her real age. She told him she was thirty. He said, "You may have trouble proving that." She explained, "You will find it difficult to prove the contrary. The church that had the record of my birth burned down in 1920."

My aunt even lies about her dog's age.

The ninety-one-year-old tycoon married the eighteen-year-old doll. She told him he looked like a million and she meant every penny of it. Everybody laughed but the groom. He went to see his doctor and said, "I'm in trouble." The doc said, "Sure, you're ninety-one and she's eighteen." He said, "No, it's not that. My romance is great—but after I make love to her, I can't remember her name."

What a lovely couple. They married late in life but they keep trying. She takes vitamins and he takes iron. The trouble is, when she's ready—he's rusty.

If you want to live to be a hundred, first you've got to make it to ninety-nine, and then the last year—take it easy.

My neighbor admits, "I'm at the time of life when a woman buys herself a see-through nightgown and then can't find anybody who can still see through one."

I see nothing wrong in an older woman marrying a young doctor—lots of ladies put their guys through medical school—but a teething ring instead of a stethoscope? And operating with surgical mittens?

Woman, forty-six, married designer, twenty. She wore formal clothes and he wore pampers. The wedding was held in the afternoon—because his mother wouldn't let him stay up late. Young? This fellow signed his marriage certificate in crayon.

As people become older they tend to become quiet. They have more to keep quiet about.

My uncle was seventy-two but he still liked to chase girls. A neighbor brought this to my aunt's attention and asked what she was doing about it: "Who cares?" she said. "Let him chase girls. Dogs chase cars, but when they catch them, they can't drive."

Childhood is the time when you make funny faces in the mirror. Middle age is the time when the mirror gets even.

The eighty-five-year-old man was crying to his friend: "My secretary is suing me for breach of promise." His friend said: "At eighty-five what could you promise her?"

You're getting old when:
   You're more interested in hearing "yes" from a banker than a girl . . .
   You proposition a girl and hope she says "no" . . .
   You know your way around—but you don't feel like going.

Most of the things I liked to do as a kid are now being done by batteries.

The way to live longer is to fall in love with what you're doing. Then you can't wait to get out of bed in the morning and get to work—unless you got someone in bed with you.

I was driving through one little town when I saw this little old man sitting in a rocking chair on the stoop of his house. I said, "You look as if you don't have a care in the world. What's your formula for a long and happy life?" He said, "Well, I smoke six packs of cigarettes a day, I drink a quart of bourbon every four hours and six cases of beer a week, and I go out with girls every night." I said, "That's great—how old are you?" He said, "Twenty-five."

Growing old means never having to walk into a maternity ward and say you're sorry.

He's at the age now when a girl flirts with him in the movies. She's after his popcorn.

There is one thing about getting older: All the people you could have married now look like the one you did.

There's a bright side to getting older: You get fewer calls from insurance salesmen.

The octogenarian said: "I don't have an enemy in the world—I've outlived them all."

My mother-in-law reports, "Cosmetics are nice, but old Mother Nature still always has the last laugh. Careful grooming may make you look twenty years younger, but it still won't fool a flight of stairs."

Being nearsighted has its advantages and disadvantages. An advantage is that there seem to be more pretty girls on the street. A disadvantage is that they are usually on the other side of the street.

You know you've reached middle age when weight lifting consists of just standing up.

Middle age is when women stop worrying about getting pregnant and men start worrying about looking like they are.

Retirement is that part of life when you have twice as much husband and half as much money.

Golf

The teacher said: "Johnny! Remember what happens to little boys who use bad language playing marbles!" The kid said, "Yeah, Teach, they grow up and play golf."

The club grouch was unhappy about everything—the food, the assessments, the parking, the other members. The first time he hit a hole in one, he complained, "Dammit, just when I needed the putting practice!"

The wife came into the bedroom and found her husband hugging his golf bag. "What's going on?" she asked. "You told me I had to choose," he answered, "and this is my choice." She followed her husband to the country club and watched as he had a terrible day with the clubs. "How can you prefer this to making love to me?" she cried. "Ah, come on honey," he said. "This is for money."

Sam married a beautiful twenty-two-year-old redhead, and before they left on their honeymoon he thought he would be completely honest. "Look, I have a confession to make. Golf is the most important thing in my life. I sleep golf, I dream golf; golf is all I think about twenty-four hours a day. Just golf. I just wanted to set things straight." She said, "Good. I also have a confession. I'm a hooker." "Oh," he said, grabbing her wrists. "I can fix that. Just hold your left hand over your right hand, like this."

My neighbor was crying because her husband left her for the sixth time. I said, "Don't be unhappy—he'll be back again." She said, "Not this time—he's taken his golf clubs."

I was playing golf with my dear friend, the priest. I watched as he bowed before each shot and mumbled a few words. After a very poor performance on the front nine, I stared over the course, turned to the priest, and asked, "Father, would it help me to pray a little, too?" He said, "I'm afraid not, my boy." I said, "Why not?" He said, "Because you're such a lousy putter."

Charley was lining up his putt on the sixth green, when suddenly a woman dressed in a bridal gown came running toward him. "This is our *wedding day*," she shouted. "How could you do this to me?" "Listen, Sarah," the golf nut said. "I told you only if it's raining—*only* if it's raining."

They're saying golf is so popular that it has replaced sex. Of course, it's the guys over sixty who are saying it. Take my neighbor, who is over seventy; he told me, "My sex drive has turned into a putt." This is the same husband who will walk through thirty-six holes of golf—but won't get up to get his own glass of water.

Sunday is the day we all bow our heads: Some are praying and some are putting.

My neighbor's wife wanted a new Caddy—so he sent her a sixteen-year-old boy.

My doctor told me, "Golf is healthy. It matters not whether you win or lose. What matters is whether *I* win or lose."

The doctor told Al: "You look pretty run down. . . . I suggest you lay off golf for a while and get in a good day's work at the office."

Some golfers are just natural cheaters. My brother-in-law cheats so much that the other day he had a hole in one and he marked a zero on his scorecard.

There was one golfer who told the truth: He called another golfer a liar.

Nothing counts in golf like your opponent.

"I'm sick and tired of being left alone every weekend!" the wife cried. "If you think you're going to play today . . . ." "Nonsense, darling," the husband said, as he reached

for the toast. "Golf is the furthest thing from my mind—
Please pass the putter."

Gossip

A gossip is a person who will never tell a lie—if the truth
will cause more damage.

Most people can keep a secret—it's the person they tell it
to who can't.

Raquel told Gloria at the manicurist's: "Ellen told me that
you told her the secret I told you not to tell her." Gloria
said, "Gee, and I told her not to tell you that I told her."
Raquel said, "Well, I told her I wouldn't tell you she told
me—so don't tell her I told you."

Make someone happy today—mind your own business.

At any party, don't talk about yourself—it will be done
when you leave.

Four women met every week in each other's houses to play
bridge. One day, one of the women said, "Instead of playing, let's talk. You don't know this: I'm a kleptomaniac—
but I swear I never took anything from any of your homes."
The second lady said, "I'm a nymphomaniac—but I never
made a play for any of your husbands." The third said, "I'm
a dipsomaniac—but I never stole any of your booze." The
fourth said, "I'm a gossip—and I can't wait to get to the
beauty parlor."

A good gossip can't believe everything she hears—but she
can repeat it: Two ladies entered a restaurant. One noticed
a familiar face at the other end of the room. "Do you see

who I see sitting over there?" she said to her friend. "Tell me, do you believe that terrible story about her?" Her friend replied eagerly, "Yes—what is it?"

I never repeat gossip—so please listen carefully the first time.

Plastic surgery is a science that can do anything with a nose except keep it out of other people's business.

Hear no evil, see no evil, speak no evil—and you'll never be a success at a cocktail party.

Happiness

True happiness is when you marry a girl for love and then find out later she also has money.

Happiness is fitting into your jeans and then realizing they're your daughter's.

Maybe money won't buy you happiness—but at least it will keep you company while you're looking for it.

The guy stormed out of the house after an argument with his wife: "You'll be back," she yelled after him. "How long do you think you'll be able to stand happiness?"

Two lady shoppers were having high tea. Packages were piled all around them—they had obviously been taking full advantage of the post-holiday sales. One of the ladies lifted her wine glass in salute to her companion and said, "Whoever said that money can't buy happiness just didn't know where to shop."

One star I know has three swimming pools: one with salt water, one with fresh water, and one with Perrier.

Perhaps it's just as well that money can't buy happiness. Considering today's prices, most of us couldn't afford it anyway.

Happiness is seeing your favorite girl in a two-piece outfit—slippers.

The only really happy people are married women and single men.

Happiness is when your girl sees you out with your wife—and forgives you.

Happiness is your secretary becoming pregnant and her boyfriend marrying her.

Happiness is signing your marriage license with disappearing ink.

Happiness is an income tax collector allowing you to list your wife's hairdresser as a dependent.

Happiness is the income tax man accepting your mistress as a deduction.

Happiness is when your wife gets in the wrong line at the bank and makes a deposit.

Happiness is when an old man marries a frigid woman.

Happiness is a martini before and a nap after.

Money can't buy happiness, but it will get you a better class of memories.

It's true that money can't buy happiness, but it sure goes a long way toward the down payment.

My neighbor told me, "There's only one thing that keeps me from being happily married—my wife."

A woman gets married to make two people happy—herself and her mother.

I asked my girl to marry me and she said no—and we lived happily ever after.

My first wife and I were happily married for five years—then she lost her job.

For twenty years my wife and I were very happy—then we met.

"What happened?" I asked my down-in-the-mouth neighbor. He said, "I had a rough battle with my old lady: She promised she wouldn't talk to me for thirty days!" I said, "Well then, you should be happy!" He cried, "What happy? This is the last day!"

A solicitous wife is one who is so interested in her husband's happiness that she hires a detective to find out who is responsible for it.

A guy is never happy until a girl comes along and makes him miserable.

Happiness is a No Tipping sign.

Holidays

April Fools' Day

Today is April Fools' Day. Did you ever get the idea that political elections should be held today? The biggest April Fools are the politicians. According to FBI estimates, only a small number of career criminals will be caught this year: The rest will be reelected.

It's April Fools' Day, so don't take any wooden nickels—even though they're worth more than the real ones.

My neighbor warned me, "Be careful about the practical jokes you play today. My mother played a practical joke on my dad and he reminds me of it every time my birthday rolls around."

The landlord told my neighbor, "It's April Fools' Day and I've decided to raise your rent." My neighbor beamed, "Now that's swell of you. I was wondering how I could raise it myself."

The groom was enjoying his honeymoon. He was at the bar in his hotel, having his wedding drinks, when a friend asked, "Where's your bride?" The groom said, "She's upstairs with my best friend making love." He said, "What are you going to do about it?" "Nothing—April Fool—he's so drunk he thinks he's me!"

The man complained to the slumlord in his building, "There's no ceiling in my bedroom." The slumlord answered, "That's okay, the man upstairs doesn't walk around much!"

How did I know it was April 1? My neighbor took his car for a walk and left his girl to be washed and polished.

April Fools' Day is when your brother sleeps on his waterbed wearing a life jacket.

It's April Fools' Day, the day the dumb-dumbs sound smart—like the dope who picked a guy's pocket in an airplane and made a run for it. . . . Or the garage mechanic who told the women's libber, "You have a short circuit." She answered, "Well, just don't stand there like a dummy—lengthen it."

Christmas

Do your shopping now—before the prices go down.

My cousin told me, "I have no idea what gifts I'll receive for Christmas—but I sure know what I'm going to exchange this for."

My aunt lost her charge cards, so her husband put an ad in the paper offering a $100 reward for each card, no questions asked. The only catch is, the offer is not good until after the Christmas shopping season.

With this inflation, I can't believe the prices they are getting for Christmas trees. It's true that only God can make a tree—but I wish he would investigate his salesmen.

Our kids are so sophisticated today. My neighbor asked his six-year-old, "What are you gonna ask Santa Claus to give you this year?" The kid said, "Nothing—I'll use my charge plate."

Christmas worries me—that's when my wife always gives me presents I can't afford. I told my wife that the start of the Christmas shopping season makes my heart pound, my knees shake, and my pulse race. She said, "Thinking of all the money you're going to spend?" I said, "No, thinking of all the money *you're* going to spend."

It's too bad Election Day isn't held on Christmas: When we see some of the guys we elected, we could exchange them for something else.

Have you noticed that many people who laugh at kids for believing in Santa Claus are the same people who believe in campaign promises?

Can you imagine if the Christmas story happened today? The Three Wise Men would be fellas who got out of the stock market in time.

Ever wonder why Santa Claus goes Ho Ho Ho? Listen, if you had to work only one day a year—you'd laugh too.

Just remember that the Christmas presents of today are the garage sales of tomorrow.

Last year my beautiful wife gave me a smoking jacket for Christmas. It took me an hour and a half to put it out.

I asked my dentist what he wanted for the holidays. He said, "All I want for Christmas are your two front teeth."

What do you give a man who has everything? Shots!

It was a slow Christmas: Santa Claus lost a bundle in the stock market.

We all hope for the same thing at Christmas: that Santa will visit us and our relatives won't.

Christmas shopping gives everyone who didn't go broke in the stock market crash a second chance.

My favorite Christmas story is about my friend who took his little grandson shopping. They went to one department store and the lad dutifully climbed on Santa's lap. "Ho Ho," Santa said. "What do you want for Christmas?" The kid said, "You better get a pencil and paper and write it down." "No, it's okay," Santa said. "I'll remember." The little boy recited his list and left. Grandpa and the boy went to another department store and another Santa asked, "Ho Ho, what do you want for Christmas?" The kid screamed, "You dumb-dumb—I told you to write it down!"

What my wife is giving me for Christmas is priceless: She's not giving me anything.

Christmas is a time I'll long remember—I charged everything.

I'm giving money for Christmas presents; it's the cheapest thing I could find.

If you think it's the thought that counts, just try sending somebody a Christmas gift COD.

It's always better to give than to receive. Then you don't have to bother exchanging it.

This is the season when you buy this year's presents with next year's money.

I have a friend who didn't know what to give his wife, who has everything—so he decided to give her a husband who could afford it.

I just figured out why we're having so much trouble in the

world: All the wise men are under Christmas trees instead of in Washington.

Happiness at this time of the year is a craps table in Atlantic City that will take gift certificates.

One kid looked up at Santa Claus and said: "Are you a politician?" Santa said, "Of course not. Why would you think I'm a politician?" " 'Cause you always promise more than you deliver."

Santa Claus has the right idea—visit people only once a year and you'll always be welcome.

In Russia they have Santa Claus in department stores, too, but it's a little different: You sit on Santa's lap and *he* tells *you* what you're getting.

Columbus Day

Columbus and his men came over on the *Nina*, the *Pinta*, and the *Santa Maria*. Today, all Americans are in the same boat.

I'm very proud and thrilled to celebrate Columbus Day with every Italian in the world, but between you and me, what's so great about Columbus discovering America? It's so big how could he miss it? In fact, discovering America is like discovering Orson Welles in a telephone booth.

Columbus discovered America for one reason: He wanted to give the rest of the world a place to borrow money from.

When Columbus came to America in 1492, everybody thought the world was flat . . . and the way prices are going, it soon may be.

Don't get me wrong. America is still the land of opportunity. The only foreigner who didn't make any money here was Columbus.

Times sure change. Before Columbus found us, America

was controlled by the Indians, who hunted and fished so much that they didn't have time to work and worry. Columbus changed all that. Now that the white man controls the nation, he works and worries so much that he doesn't have time to hunt or fish.

You can't blame the Indians for not getting too excited about Columbus Day. Five hundred years ago, when the Indians were running this country, there were no taxes, no national debt, no foreign entanglements, and the women did all the work. What they can't understand is how white men thought they could improve on a system like that.

July 4th

Thanks to our founding fathers, every child born in the U.S.A. today is endowed with life, liberty, and a share of the government debt.

Every American still has a chance to become president of the United States—that's one of the risks he has to take.

When John Hancock signed the Declaration of Independence, it was the first insurance policy he wrote that guaranteed that all men are created equal. I wonder if he intends to pay off on Mickey Rooney.

Nathan Hale said, "I regret that I have but one life to give for my country." His wife said, "Before you give your life—let's talk to John Hancock about insurance."

Patrick Henry said, "Give me liberty or give me death." His wife said, "You'll drop dead before you get a divorce from me."

Abe Lincoln is known for his Gettysburg address, which is very surprising—it didn't have a zip code.

How about Honest Abe's living in a log cabin? No lights, no heat, no running water—I think I have the same landlord!

New Year's

Millions of people will start the New Year by drinking to somebody's health—while they ruin their own.

My brother-in-law welcomes in the New Year: "Everyone has to believe in something: I believe I will have another drink."

Me, I don't go out on New Year's Eve. Why should I spend all that money on things I won't even remember?

A toast to the New Year! May all your troubles last as long as your New Year's resolutions.

I'm not making New Year's resolutions this year—I've got a few left over from last year I never used.

A New Year's resolution: Starting next month I resolve not to procrastinate.

My friend made a resolution: "From now on I'm just going to have a little Scotch in the afternoon—and in the evening a sexy Italian will do."

My uncle reminds you to watch the drinks if you're driving: "Because they have a tendency to spill if you make a turn."

At the stroke of midnight, I want you to give a long, smoldering, passionate kiss to the one you love the most—and if your husband is handy, give him a kiss too.

I think I know why we celebrate New Year's Eve. It gives us time to recall the past year and then drink enough to forget it.

The drunk told me: "I never drink on New Year's Eve: That's amateur night."

Thanksgiving

Have a happy Thanksgiving—you sure have a lot to be thankful for. If nothing else, be glad you're not a turkey.

In my house we're not having a new turkey this year—we've still got some left over from last year.

I try to be grateful for little things—like my lifetime pension lasting out the week.

My neighbor was complaining: "Grateful? What have I to be grateful for? I can't pay my bills." I told him, "Well, be grateful that you aren't one of the creditors."

And most of all, let us all be grateful that we live in the United States of America—where a man can still do as his wife pleases.

Thanksgiving is a day for happiness: Money can't buy happiness—but it helps you look for it in many more places. And even if happiness could be bought there would still be those who would try to chisel on the price.

Thanksgiving is when turkeys that have fattened up all year go to the chopping block. With humans, it's April 15.

Oh, I'm grateful and all, but as long as the pilgrims were making the effort to come over here and make a big meal, why did it have to be turkey? Why not lamb chops? Or a corned beef sandwich?

Valentine's Day

Tomorrow is Valentine's Day. You still have time to send a note to the one you love best—and don't forget to send a card to your wife or husband as well.

My neighbor got this Valentine: "Roses are red/violets are blue/my alimony check/is six weeks overdue."

Valentine's Day is named after St. Valentine, the patron saint of lovers, florists, candy companies, and divorce lawyers.

My uncle told me: "My wife is on a diet, so I got her what I consider a very thoughtful Valentine gift: I sent her a lettucegram."

"Dear Joe," she wrote. "Be my Valentine—words cannot express how much I regret having broken off our engagement. Will you please come back to me? Your absence leaves a space no one can fill. Please forgive me and let us start all over again, I need you so much. Yours forever, Sylvia. P.S.: By the way, congratulations on winning the lottery."

Washington's Birthday

George Washington was first in war, first in peace, and the first to have his birthday juggled to make a long weekend.

Father's Day is dedicated to George Washington. There are hundreds of hotels, motels, and boardinghouses all over the country that have signs that say, GEORGE WASHINGTON SLEPT HERE. No wonder he was called the father of our country.

Hollywood and Beverly Hills

Two Hollywood ladies were bragging: "Charles and I made our money the old-fashioned way," said one. "We were born rich." "You gotta be kidding," said the other. "My Irving is so rich, he bought his son a kiddie car with a built-in telephone." "Yeah? Well Charlie built me a house with seven dining rooms—one for each course!" "Is that so? Well Irving bought his son a set of trains—the Pennsylvania and the Central." "Really? At parties, my husband serves only money. . . ."

Beverly Hills is Hollywood's show-off place. Even their motorcycle gang is different: It's not every gang whose members ride chauffeur-driven motorcycles.

Somebody asked the star how many bathrooms were in

his Holmby Hills mansion. He said proudly, "I can seat sixteen."

Beverly Hills matrons never look you straight in the eye—they're too busy searching your face for signs of a face lift.

A panhandler on Rodeo Drive: "If you don't have cash, sir, how about lending me your American Express Gold card for the day?"

This film star is really upset. Her secretary didn't keep the records straight, and now she finds she has had two more divorces than she had weddings. One handsome actor told her, "I'd love to be married to you some day." She said, "Okay—I'll put you on my wedding list." One impatient wolf insisted on a date. She put him off with, "You know I'm going to be married tomorrow—call me in about three weeks."

Then there was the Beverly Hills society girl who only partially returned affection: She returned all the love letters—but kept all the rings.

Even grandmas are different in Beverly Hills: "My daughter married a big producer," one was bragging. "They even have four cars." The second grandma said, "That's wonderful—do they have any children?" She said, "Yes, they have a little boy—a beauty. He's fifteen months old." Her friend asked, "Does he walk yet?" She said, "You joking? With four cars, why should he walk?" The other said, "My grandson, only three years old, God Bless him, has already five fathers."

You know you're down and out in Beverly Hills when:
    Your wife starts asking for the household expense money in traveler's checks . . .
    You start carrying cash again . . .
    You're invited to a screening and it turns out to be a police lineup.

Hollywood. Land of the stars, the has-beens, the would-like-to-bes; playground of the rich, the famous, and the phonies—I finally figured out what the Hollywood Hills are made of: bull.

Things aren't always what they appear: A $1 million house in Beverly Hills could be a $600,000 house with a $400,000 burglar alarm system.

I saw this sign in a Beverly Hills shop on Rodeo Drive: JAPANESE AND ARABIC SPOKEN HERE—CASH UNDERSTOOD.

Hollywood is where the poverty level is a two-car garage.

Two old stars met at their club in Beverly Hills: "I say, Tony old boy," said one looking morosely into his drink, "as your best friend I hate to tell you this—but your wife is fickle." His pal said, "Oh? So she's thrown you over too?"

The producer came home and found his wife in the arms of his leading man. "I beat the hell out of her," he told me. "Didn't you hit the guy?" I asked. He said, "Hell, no— he's the star of my picture."

They're talking about the woman shopper on Rodeo Drive who was arrested for vagrancy because she was carrying only three credit cards.

Some folks have said that Hollywood people are not real. That's not true. Some of them may be phonies—but they're real phonies.

Did you hear about the elephant who appeared in so many jungle pictures he went to Hollywood? He just had his tusks capped.

A Hollywood star never cheats. Who is he going to find that he loves as much as himself?

The Hollywood gals never cheat—they just have unlisted husbands.

A Hollywood couple I know has finally ironed out the divorce settlement. Now they can go ahead with the wedding.

Why did the famous drinking actress leave her dress on the floor all night? She was in it at the time.

How does an actor in Hollywood know when he's getting old? There are more lines in his face than there are in his script.

Two actresses who hadn't seen each other for years were catching up on things at the Beverly Wilshire Hotel: "I haven't seen much of Marvin lately," one said. "Oh!" said the other, "then you didn't marry him?" "Yes," said the first. "I did."

A woman walked into the lobby of the hotel with her cleavage down to her ankles and her hips moving on fast forward. "We should all pray for that woman," one actor said. The other looked up and replied, "Believe me, I have. But she prefers her husband."

Beverly Hills is a pretty expensive town: There was an old lady who lived in a shoe—it's all she could afford for $90,000.

One actress reported that the wire wheels were stolen from her Rolls Royce and the police didn't seem properly sympathetic. When she asked why, the cop shook his head and said, "Crime is relative. Who's the bigger thief—the kid who steals them? Or Rolls Royce, which gets $500 a wheel for them?"

The reason some Hollywood stars postpone their weddings is because they have trouble finding baby-sitters.

The Hollywood teacher told the actress's son, "Tell your mother to come to school next month." The kid said, "I can't tell my mother." The teacher asked, "Don't you know where she's going to be next month?" The boy said, "I don't even know *who* she's going to be next month."

I love Hollywood—it's the only place in the world where they take you at face-lifted value.

One actress wouldn't acknowledge her plastic surgeon at

a Beverly Hills party. He sniffed, "How do you like that? She's lifting my new nose at me."

Beverly Hills is a fabulous place. This town is so rich, every Christmas they distribute food baskets to people with only one swimming pool. And where else do traffic lights come in decorator colors? In fact, Beverly Hills is so chic the breadline has a complimentary caviar bar, and the unemployment line has a complimentary car wash.

In Hollywood psychiatrists advertise: "Two couches—no waiting."

One Beverly Hills mother was telling her friend, "My son has never gone to a psychiatrist." The friend said "Really? What's wrong with him?"

An underprivileged child in Hollywood these days is a child with only one set of parents.

In Hollywood schools are different. It's the only place where truancy officers work from a surfboard.

There's a shortage of water in Beverly Hills at the moment: Two Perrier trucks collided.

Recipe for making chicken soup in Beverly Hills: "Bring the Perrier to a slow boil. . . ."

You have no idea what class is until you've visited Beverly Hills. Where else can you find monogrammed garbage? Talk about class: One producer's wife told me, "We've got cats here that won't scratch because they might chip their nailpolish—and dogs are paper trained on fifty-dollar bills!" And if you think all of this is too much—they've got the only fire hydrants that you have to open with a corkscrew.

There's a new deodorant for sale in Hollywood that gives off the odor of chlorine. It's for people who want others to think they have a swimming pool.

The nightlife in Philadelphia starts at about 10 P.M. and runs to about 3 in the morning. The nightlife in New York starts at midnight and runs until about 7 in the morning. In Hollywood, the nightlife starts at 10 in the morning and ends at 3 in the afternoon.

You know you're down and out in Beverly Hills when:
    You see your 8-by-10 glossies in the post office . . .
    Thieves break in your house and leave something . . .
    The organist at your daughter's wedding has a monkey with a tin cup . . .
    The local thrift shop refuses your clothes . . .
    Your friends' answering machines won't take your calls . . .
    They want to use your house to shoot a remake of Tobacco Road . . .
    The authorities pick you up for wearing polyester . . .
    You see your accountant on "Lifestyles of the Rich and Famous."

You know you're still on top in Beverly Hills when:
    You've got two chauffeurs—one only makes left turns . . .
    Your kid's kiddie bank has a vice president . . .
    Your kid's nurse has a maid . . .
    You have a chauffeur-driven sled . . .
    Your kiddie car has whitewall tires . . .
    You have an air-conditioned baby carriage . . .
    You have an unlisted Social Security number, an unlisted wife, and an unlisted zip code.

Would you believe even AT&T in Beverly Hills has an unlisted phone?

The Beverly Hills police cars are Mercedes—the fire trucks are convertibles.

This Beverly Hills star can afford a dentist who makes house calls. The star's husband was on a diet—so he hired someone to swallow for him. This star has more money than she can spend—but a sleep-in TV repairman?

The Hollywood hills are alive with the sound of con artists.

Hollywood is where the people accept you for what you're not.

Hollywood is over a hundred years old—and that ain't easy in a town where even the senior citizens claim to be under thirty. In fact, the only time you're over thirty-six here is when you're listing your bust measurements. It's the only place in the world where they have live-in plastic surgeons.

I like the people in Hollywood—it's the Hollywood in people that I don't like.

Hollywood is a small town bordered on the north by producers, on the south by starlets, on the west by agents, and on the east by ulcers.

Many a starlet admits: "I owe everything to my first producer—who made me."

This producer hesitated at offering a once-famous movie actress a part in his newest picture: "Darling," he cooed to the star, "you may not want to play this role. It calls for a lovely but immoral prostitute who runs from the arms of one bum to another—a woman who lies and cheats—a real witch. Tell me, how do you feel about it?" She said, "Feel about it? It's the first decent part I've been offered in years."

Hollywood is where the wedding cake outlasts the wedding.

This bride walked into her new home and she turned to her new husband and said, "John, darling, this house looks familiar. Are you sure we haven't been married before?"

These Hollywood kiddies were playing house. One said, "We're going to have a big family—I want three fathers and three mothers."

This schoolboy asked his teacher for a larger report card, explaining, "I'd like to get *all* my parents to sign it."

In Hollywood they don't ask, "How's your wife?" They ask, "Who's your wife?"

Beverly Hills officials have passed a law banning sex in restaurants, because they're afraid it might lead to smoking afterwards.

Have you heard about the latest hit TV show in Hollywood? It's called "Bowling for Alimony."

There are four things that every genuine Beverly Hills star must have: A Japanese gardener, a Filipino houseboy, a French maid, and a Mexican divorce.

I love Hollywood: It's got everything under the stars—including the starlets.

Did I tell you about the expectant father who wanted to name the baby Oscar—because it was his best performance of the year?

Beverly Hills is one of the richest and swankiest areas in the country. It's a great place to live provided you never need a policeman or a fireman in a hurry: They come by appointment only.

Beverly Hills is a place where, if an actor's wife looks like a new woman—she probably is.

Hollywood is where the movies are running longer and the marriages are running shorter. In Beverly Hills they figure the marriage has a chance of succeeding if the couple leaves the church together.

Two Beverly Hills princesses were discussing their boyfriends. "My new boyfriend is a dream," said one. "He doesn't drink, gamble, or even so much as look at another girl." The other said, "Gee—how will you ever get a divorce?"

Beverly Hills, it's a helluva town: The kids' bunk beds don't have a ladder to get up to the top bunk—they have a little self-service elevator. One kid is now working on his fifth father by his fourth mother, and I'll say one thing for him: He never talks back to his dad. Why should he? He hardly knows the man. The kids there don't play good guys and bad guys—they play clients and agents.

I know one actress who never got an Oscar, Emmy, or Tony—but she's had every Tom, Dick, and Harry.

In Hollywood film circles everybody lies, but it doesn't really matter because nobody listens.

It was a bitter Hollywood divorce and a rough custody battle: She got the children and he got the scrapbooks.

Hollywood is a place that seems to forget that wives are like cars: If you take care of them, you don't have to get new ones all the time.

One actress said: "I have so many movies where I've played the role of a hooker the producers don't pay me in the regular way anymore: They just leave cash on my dresser."

I wouldn't say she's a fickle actress—but she does have a wash-and-wear wedding gown.

In Hollywood, it's usually the little things that break up a marriage: the little blondes, the little redheads, the little brunettes . . . .

The swinging actress was complaining to her director: "You're not photographing my best side." He answered: "I can't, you're sitting on it."

In Beverly Hills an amicable divorce is one in which the husband gets to keep anything that falls off the moving van as it leaves the driveway.

A Hollywood couple got married—and their lawyers lived happily ever after.

The accepted custom is to ask a girl's father for her hand in marriage, but in Hollywood, you ask her husband.

The pretty girl said, "I won first prize and a movie

contract." "What did you enter?" I asked. "A producer's apartment."

Hospitals

What ever happened to good old-fashioned medicine? I can remember when the first thing that happened when you were rushed to a hospital was they took your pulse. Now all they take is your Blue Cross number.

I know a doctor who is so independent he won't even make hospital calls.

It now costs more to go to the hospital than it once cost to go to medical school.

The patient was leaving the hospital and wanted to see his bill. The doctor told him, "Sorry, old man, you're not strong enough yet."

Private hospitals have other strange ways of making money—like selling tickets for the visitor's hour.

I don't think anyone should complain about the high cost of medical care—especially while they're still in the hospital.

My friend Myron told me, "When I was in the hospital, I had a day nurse and a night nurse. In the afternoon I rested."

I was operated on at a great hospital—Our Lady of Malpractice. Five years ago they spent $3 million on a recovery room—it hasn't been used yet. After the operation, the doc told me: "Your sex life will be terrific—especially the one in the winter."

My brother told me he just returned from minor surgery at Doctor's Hospital. "What kind of treatment did you get?" I asked. "The nurses always say, 'How's our leg today?' or 'How's our back today?' But when I touched our thigh, she slapped our face."

This guy came to the emergency ward at the hospital and cried: "Help me—my backside hurts terribly." The doc said, "What kind of work do you do?" The guy said, "In Coney Island, I put my head through a hole in the canvas and people throw baseballs at me—and Doc, I haven't been able to sit down for a week." The doc said, "What's throwing baseballs at your head got to do with your sitting down?" "My boss also rented out the back of me for a dart game!"

Today's hospitals don't kid around. I won't say what happens if you don't pay a bill—but did you ever have tonsils put back in?

Hospital costs are so high these days it's become impossible for a patient to be ill at ease.

A hospital's a place that keeps you three days if you have big troubles—and three months if you have big insurance.

I know hospital costs are out of hand—but I never thought I'd see a self-service operating table.

A hospital bed is a parked taxi with the meter running. Everything is so expensive; hospitals should really use cheaper equipment—like an X-ray machine that takes four poses for a buck. I really don't blame hospitals for trying to keep costs down, but I do think a coin-operated bedpan is going a little too far.

The patient was complaining about the hospital food: "I hope the doctors didn't go to the same school as the cooks."

After she visited her uncle in the hospital, a woman took the nurse aside and asked, "Confidentially, is he making any progress?" The nurse said, "Not at all—he's not my type."

After two weeks in a hospital I realized how bad my wife's cooking is. When I was discharged, I hated to leave, the meals were so good.

Last week I ate nothing but $100-a-plate dinners—I was in the hospital. I had my first bath in bed in the hospital. A nurse washed me down, then gave me a wet cloth and said, "You know what to do with this." I didn't really, but for three days my room had the cleanest windows on the floor.

Inflation

Inflation that used to be creeping is now jogging.

I saw a TV commercial the other night that said, "Please don't buy our product. It costs so much to make it, we can't afford to sell it."

Inflation is getting worse. The grand prize in this year's lottery is an all-expense-paid trip to your supermarket.

The guy who blew a fortune in the market may have just returned from a trip to the *supermarket*.

Statistics prove that the best time to buy anything is a year ago.

A sign in the gift shop read: FOR THE MAN WHO HAS EVERYTHING: A CALENDAR TO REMIND HIM WHEN THE PAYMENTS ARE DUE.

My neighbor told me: "I made two big mistakes last year. The first big mistake was starting a new business. The second was starting it in a fireproof building."

"I wouldn't mind the rat race," a friend told me, "if I could just have a little more cheese."

My banker always made it a practice to give credit where credit was due. Now he's bankrupt.

One merchant known to be neglectful in paying his bills was seen arguing with a manufacturer. "Why bother?" I asked him. "You won't pay the guy anyway—so why all the bargaining?" The storekeeper said, "I like him—and I want to help keep down his losses." The truth is, he pays his bills with a smile. Most creditors would prefer cash.

Inflation is the nation's number one pickpocket.

Inflation is when you pay cash for something and they ask to see your driver's license.

Listen, inflation may have been arrested, as the economists claim, but whenever we go shopping, it seems to be out on bail.

Prices are so high, we eat like politicians: Every dinner is fifty dollars a plate.

Nowadays, even apples are so expensive, you might as well have the doctor.

Maybe you can't take it with you, but where can you go without it?

At least you know Russia will never invade the United States—they couldn't afford to live here.

I know, I know, money can't buy happiness. Even if it could, think what a luxury tax there would be on it.

These days "passing the buck" is hardly worth it.

"Twelve dollars!" the woman exclaimed, as she checked out of the supermarket with two very small packages. "Why, that's highway robbery. The owner must be crazy to charge prices like that." The cashier replied, "No, ma'am, the boss ain't crazy—he's a philosopher." The lady demanded, "What kind of philosopher?" The cashier said, "Well, he figures that if you can't take it with you—you might as well leave it here!"

Many of us would be delighted to pay as we go—if we could only catch up with paying where we have been.

I lead a life of wine, women, and song—it's cheaper than gas, food, and rent.

Just remember: A two-dollar bill is not only unlucky—it won't buy anything either.

My neighbor's wife can never figure the prices in the supermarkups. It upsets her. She says one store tried to buy back at twice the price all the groceries she bought there the week before.

A bargain is anything these days that's only a little overpriced.

The dollar is worth nothing these days. The value of the buck is so low, police caught a man passing counterfeit bills and gave him a ticket for littering.

The husband embraced his wife: "Darling, I've got good news: We don't have to move to a more expensive apartment. The landlord just raised our rent."

I'm independently wealthy. Thank God I have enough money to last me the rest of my life—unless I have to buy something.

The high cost of gasoline may wind up saving us money. By the time you fill the tank you don't have any money to go anyplace else.

Sign in a midtown restaurant: OUR PRICES HAVE NOT GONE UP SINCE YESTERDAY.

Remember the good old days when you spent ninety dollars on a meal and a plane ride came with it?

A husband poring over the checkbook said, "Honey, we can make it through the rest of the year—providing we don't buy anything, eat anything, or turn anything on."

The most common cause of car sickness is still the sticker price on the window.

The cost of living is always the same—all you have.

Insults

He's got a photographic mind—too bad it never developed.

I don't mind him being born again—but did he have to come back as himself?

He's the kind of friend you can depend on: Always around when he needs you.

He never says an unkind word about anybody—because he never talks about anyone but himself.

If I gave you a going away present—would you?

Cleancut? He once asked a hooker if she'd like to have some fun. When she said yes—he took her bowling.

If you were a building—you'd be condemned.

I can read you like a book. . . . How I wish I could shut you up like one.

He was the kind of kid who made his parents wish that birth control was retroactive.

If I don't get in touch with you in a year or two—please show me the same consideration.

I'm responsible for bringing together all the people who love and respect you. They're waiting outside in the phone booth.

Some of you may not recognize him tonight—he came disguised as a human being.

I feel like making small talk—let's discuss your IQ!

You know, you'd make a perfect stranger.

You're really not such a bad person—until people get to know you.

He doesn't have an enemy in the world. He just has a lot of friends who don't like him.

You're okay in my book, but I only read dirty books.

You're a man who has no equals—only superiors.

It's been so long since you paid for anything, you still don't know prices have gone up.

At least you give your wife something to live for—a divorce.

Look at your face—was anyone else hurt in the accident?

You have a lot of talent—but it's in your wife's name.

I think the world of you, pal, and you know the shape the world is in right now!

I'm proud to be a friend of yours, pal, and it isn't easy being a man's only friend.

It's good to see you—it means you're not behind my back.

You're a good egg—and you know where eggs come from.

You're not yourself today, and I notice the improvement.

He knows a lot; he just can't think of it.

He looks the same as he did forty years ago—old.

He knows how to break up a party—he joins it.

I don't know what makes you tick—but I hope it's a time bomb.

I'll never forget the first time we met—but I'm trying.

I looked high and low for you—but I didn't look low enough.

If you have your life to live over again—do it overseas.

You are a humble and modest man—and with good reason.

You are a man of rare gifts. You haven't had one in years.

Your folks never told you the facts of life—because they never thought you would have to use them.

In her own eyes, she's the most popular girl in town—in the country. "You know," she told me with characteristic modesty, "a lot of people are going to be miserable when I marry." I said, "Really? How many men are you going to marry?"

The lady diner said to one waiter, "Why aren't you in the army?" He snarled, "For the same reason that you're not a Rockette."

Insurance

I'm a believer in insurance, but honesty is the best policy if you don't have general coverage.

What really hurt Humpty-Dumpty wasn't that he had a bad fall—it's that he had recently let his accident policy lapse.

My insurance company is pretty good but they're reluctant to pay off claims: My policy has a $100 debatable.

I'm paying so much insurance to take care of the future that I'm starving to death in the present.

A few weeks ago I tried to get some health and accident insurance. I had to go to three doctors and get three estimates on what it would cost to fix me up before I could get any insurance.

My neighbor told me: "After years of nagging, I finally bought one of those annuities but, of course, I didn't read the small print. Now I've discovered that to be eligible for compensation I have to be run down by a herd of wild animals on Fifth Avenue. Then I collect three dollars a week. If I lose my hair, the insurance company helps me look for it. And they take marvelous care of my wife: All maternity costs—after the age of eighty-seven."

My job provides me with a real good health insurance policy. For instance, should I ever come down with yellow fever, the insurance company will repaint my bedroom so that I don't clash with the walls.

They have a new kind of fire and theft insurance: They only pay you if your house is robbed while it's burning.

A woman asked her insurance agent, "Should my husband die overnight, what would I get?" He said, "That depends on how the evidence is presented to the jury."

My neighbor told me, "I had a policy on my first husband." I asked, "What did you get out of it?" She said, "My second husband."

Those were memorable days in the early history of our country. . . . Nathan Hale saying, "I regret that I have but one life to give for my country." Patrick Henry saying, "Give me liberty or give me death." John Hancock saying, "Have I got a policy for you!"

Taxes and life insurance are just about the same thing: You pay out the money, and someone else has the fun spending it.

In every insurance policy the big print giveth and the small print taketh away.

My house is thoroughly insured. For instance, if a burglar gets hurt robbing me—he can sue.

My friend Myron has so much life insurance that he can make his wife's day just by sneezing.

This man went to his insurance agent to report that his car had been stolen and he would like to get his money immediately. The president was polite, but firm: "Sorry we do not give you money. We replace your car with a new one." The indignant man screamed, "If that's the way you do business, you can cancel the policy on my wife!"

A broker lectures: "Honesty is the best policy—except when trying to collect on your insurance policy."

The broker received a phone call from an excited woman: "I want to insure my house," she said. "Can I do it by phone?" The broker said, "I'm sorry, but I'd have to see it first." The woman cried, "Then you'd better get over here right away—because the place is on fire."

This insurance adjuster was annoyed. "How come," he asked the man who sent for him, "you didn't call the police the minute you discovered your car had been stolen?" The man answered, "Well, for one thing, my wife was in it!"

A manufacturer was considering joining a lodge, but first he asked the president, "Does your lodge have any death benefits?" The prez said, "It sure does. When you die, you don't have to pay any more dues."

I asked my neighbor's wife, "When will your husband's leg be well, so he can return to work?" She said, "Not for a long time." I said, "Why? I thought it was almost well." She explained, "It was—but then compensation set in."

A woman awoke to see a burglar going through her jewel box. "Jules," she whispered to her husband, "stop that thief." He said, "Suppose he's armed?" She said, "*Please*. That jewelry isn't insured—*you* are."

Today the only guy who likes to see a girl fully covered is her insurance agent.

Sex is like life insurance: The older you get, the more it costs.

The newest policy is no-fault auto insurance: If you have an accident, you call the insurance company, and they tell you it isn't their fault.

Life insurance is a system that keeps you poor so you can die rich.

I have a very reliable insurance company. In all the fifteen years they have been insuring me, they never missed sending me the bill.

When I was sick my wife sat up all night reading to me—my insurance policy.

Kids

Youngsters today are more advanced than ever. Recently, I did a show for a bunch of Cub Scouts—and they all brought their wives.

One ambitious kid asked his father if he could do any work around the house to help make himself some extra money. The old man told him he couldn't think of anything. "In that case," the kid said, "how about putting me on welfare?"

The hardest part of telling young people about the facts of life is finding something they don't already know.

I'm not worried about what kids know today—I'm just worried about how they found out.

One Scout told me, "I don't know why parents get upset about sex education in schools—it's like chemistry except they don't let you experiment."

I think kids should learn about sex the same way I did—with a pair of high-powered binoculars.

Two kids were discussing their future: "Now that your old

man has given you the car, does he still give you a weekly allowance?" "No." "Then how do you pay for gas?" "Simple. When the tank is near empty I let the old man drive it."

The most important thing to learn about rearing children is how to protect yourself.

Pop got this letter from his son, who was camping upstate: "Dear Dad, I have come to the conclusion that it is time for me to stand on my own two feet. I shall call collect Sunday night to explain. Love, Stanley."

Kids have it made today—their mothers drive them everywhere. They drive them to school, to their friends' houses, to the movies, to dancing lessons. . . . I know one kid who wanted to run away from home and his mother said, "Wait, I'll drive you!"

What's the use of raising your kid to talk when in a few years you'll wish he'd shut up?

My accountant was telling me, "Not only is my son Donald the worst-behaved kid in the class, but the teachers complain he has a perfect attendance record."

Pop said, "It's all my fault. . . . All my life I worked and slaved to provide a safe and beautiful home for our kids to grow up in; a friendly, happy place to bring their friends; a secure refuge against the storms of the world. And now that they've grown up—they won't leave."

Charlie and Frankie were playing on the beach in Atlantic City. "I'm really worried," Charlie said. "Dad slaves away at his job so I'll never want for anything, and so I can go to college. Mom spends every day washing and ironing and taking care of me when I don't feel well. I'm worried!" Frankie asked, "What have you got to worry about?" "I'm afraid they might try to escape."

A kid walked into the living room and spoke to his father: "Pop," he said enthusiastically, "I've got great news for you." The old man smiled and asked, "I'm glad—what is it?" The kid said, "Remember you promised me $100 if I passed in school?" Pop nodded. "Well," the son said, "I'm sparing you the expense this year!"

Parents were stricter in the old days: One day I said, "Mom, my shoes are too tight." She said, "Why don't you fold your toes?"

A mother used to cry over her baby's first haircut. She still does, only now it's the price.

I've put two kids through college already—my doctor's son and my plumber's daughter.

Okay, so the kids are back in school. Back to the three R's—reading, writing, and rioting. In my day the kids had shoulder bags—now they have holsters. Instead of crayons they carry mace. I saw a gun shop having a "Back to School" sale.

In one school instead of a guidance counselor, they have a parole officer. Instead of overtime, the teacher's union is now asking for combat pay. Talk about tough high schools, at the front door, they search you for weapons. If you don't have any they hand one to you.

In some schools kids don't enroll anymore—they're fingerprinted. No more is it called art appreciation class: Today the kids major in graffiti. In one school, the students even kept the teacher in after school.

A lot of young high school kids are graduating pregnant cum laude. Even the nursery rhymes are coming into modernity: I heard a little fifteen-year-old say, "Mary had a little lamb." Her friend said, "Yes, but Gloria had a daughter."

Energy in youth is confusing. The same kids who are too tired to help with the dishes can wait up all night for the box office to open for a rock concert.

Warren, age eight, was asked by his grandfather, "What's the first thing you notice about a girl?" The boy replied,

"Well, that all depends on which direction she's facing."

First day back in school, my neighbor's kid was asked to write a paper entitled, "How I Spent My Summer Vacation." The kid told the teacher, "I'm not making *any* statement without my lawyer here!"

The old man was hollering, "You young kids with your wild ideas about sexual experience and free love! Let me tell you, it may be free, but it's not love. It's just plain free lust. What's this world coming to? These kids make me so mad I could bust." His wife said, "Calm down! You can't change things. Why are you so angry?" He said, "Because I'm not part of it!!!"

There's no such thing as "kids" any more. With sex education being taught in grammar school, a minor becomes a major before he can spell. One little girl I know carries an umbrella with mistletoe in it.

The class assignment was to write a short paper called "Things I'm Thankful For." One fourth grade boy said, "First my glasses: They keep the boys from punching me—and the girls from kissing me."

My neighbor and his wife told me, "We decided to have children because we felt there might be something missing in our lives. Now we're sure of it: We're missing our freedom, our privacy, and our sanity."

A father decided to teach the facts of life to Myron, his ten-year-old son. He sat down and nervously explained all about the bees and the flowers. When he finished, the old man suggested that the boy pass on this information to his eight-year-old brother. Myron went to his younger brother's room and said to him, "You know what married people do when they want to have kids? Dad says that bees and flowers do the same thing!"

A father knows his kids are growing up when his daughter starts applying lipstick and his son starts wiping it off.

Shortly after my neighbor had a new baby, her five-year-old daughter was sitting with her friend Myrtle. "Do you think you'll have a baby soon?" Myrtle asked. "Have a baby?" the little girl screamed. "I can't even tell time yet!"

When my kids became wild and unruly, I just used a nice, safe playpen. Then, when they finished—I climbed out.

A teacher knows he's in trouble when he tells his kids the facts of life—and the kids correct him.

Our schools don't need more money; they must learn to save money. They can start by teaching driver education and sex education in the same car.

Students are in favor of discipline in school: They want the teachers to do exactly what they tell them.

The principal said to her second grade teacher: You just can't send thank you notes to your pupils when they stay home because of illness.

Parents of a ten-year-old boy were concerned about the introduction of sex education in the school, and were worriedly discussing the possibility that their youngster might have to attend classes in the subject. The kid overheard their discussion and disposed of the problem neatly by saying, "I don't want it if there's any home-work."

"I'm trying something new," the young mother was saying. "Next summer I'm sending my dogs to camp—and my kids to obedience school."

My nephew came over to the house the other night. He asked me to help him with his arithmetic. After two hours, he said to me, "If it takes you so long to do fourth grade work—what am I gonna do next year?"

Parents have to learn to see the best in things. For instance, if your daughter comes home from college with a little bundle in her arms, be glad when it's laundry.

My neighbor said, "My nephew who took violin lessons is

now a conductor." I replied, "Great, does he conduct the Philharmonic?" He snapped, "What Philharmonic? He's a conductor on the A train."

A teenager asked a clerk in a Beverly Hills department store: "If my parents like this blouse, can I return it?"

The father yelled, "Always you ask me questions! What would have happened if I asked so many questions when I was a kid?" His son said, "Maybe you'd be able to answer some of mine."

My eight-year-old nephew wonders, "If teachers are so smart—how come they're still in school?"

Two kids talking: "We had a spelling bee at our school last week." "So what? Yesterday our school had a cockroach that did calculus."

The way our young kids are behaving these days—it's now the parents who are running away from home.

Poverty is hereditary: You can catch it from your children.

Parents spoil their kids these days. I bought my kid a space suit—cost me twenty-eight dollars—and you know something? He won't go!

The youngster hollered at his dad, "I didn't ask to be born." The old man answered, "If you had the answer would have been no."

My neighbor told me: "I'm so proud of my son the college graduate. He got his first job." I said, "Great—when did he graduate?" He said, "Twelve years ago."

"Maria," Mom said to her eight-year-old. "Have you given the goldfish fresh water?" The youngster replied, "No, Mom. They didn't finish what I gave them yesterday."

Pop said to his daughter, "You usually talk on the phone for two hours, but this time it was only forty-five minutes. Why?" She said logically, "Well, this time it was a wrong number."

Sending a kid to college is educational for the parents. It teaches them how to do without a lot of things.

If you have any good advice to give to your kids, do it while they're young enough to still believe you know what you're talking about.

A man used to sing his children to sleep until he heard one of them whisper to another, "If you pretend to be asleep—he stops."

Every time my daughter smiles at me it brings a tear to my eyes. I just can't forget how much those braces cost.

Teenagers today are people who express a burning drive to be different by dressing exactly alike.

A woman's neighbor consoled her: "I wouldn't worry about your son flunking second grade." The mother said, "Well, I do worry—and so does his wife."

College is an institution that really does prepare its students for the real world: Right off the bat it puts them in debt.

Mother said to her little boy, "Every time you are naughty, I get another gray hair." The kid said, "Gee, Mom, you must have really been a wild swinger when you were little—look at Grandma."

"Did you hear about Myron? He's supporting two wives." "Myron is a bigamist?" "No, his son got married last month!"

The kid said to the little girl in the next seat: "Let's play Adam and Eve: You tempt me to eat the apple—and I'll give in."

For most kids an unbreakable toy is something you use to smash those that aren't.

A wealthy stockbroker's son was overheard saying, "I haven't finished learning about the birds and the bees. Now my Dad wants me to learn about the bulls and the bears."

The boy who had just been graduated from college went

to work for his father. "Go out and sweep the sidewalk," the father commanded. "But, Dad," the lad protested, "I'm a college graduate!" "Oh, I forgot about that," the father said. "I'll come out and show you how."

The little boy told his mom when he came home from school one day that he was in love with a girl classmate. Mom asked, "Now how do you know you're in love?" The kid said, "She told me."

Labor

Today is the birthday of the American Federation of Labor. I'm strictly for labor unions—they protect their people. My furnace broke down and I can't get it fixed. The furnace repairman says that his union won't permit him to work in an unheated house.

Nobody wants to make house calls anymore. I called an exterminator and asked him if he could kill rats. He said, "Sure . . . when can you bring them in?"

I went into the deli for lunch and, after waiting twenty minutes for a waiter, called one over and told him that I had only one hour. He growled, "I don't have time to discuss your labor problems now."

The waiter told the boss, "We want a guaranteed annual wage, a guaranteed annual bonus, a guaranteed pension plan, and we would like a guarantee that you won't go broke."

A steam shovel was digging an excavation when a union official stomped in. He said, "A hundred men could be doing that job with shovels." The contractor agreed but added, "Why not a thousand men with teaspoons?"

There are still people who will do an honest day's work—but they want a week's salary and fringe benefits to do it.

Nothing helps a sick employee get well like running out of sick benefits.

"We've got the greatest union in the world," the husband told his wife after dinner. "Why what happened?" she asked. He explained, "Well, I've got good news and bad news. First the good news—I got $50,000 severance pay." "That's just great," said the wife. "Now, what's the bad news?" He said, "Wait till you find out what they severed!"

The unions protect their workers and their wives—in both cases, by putting more men on the job.

God only needed six days to create the world—but then, that was before labor unions.

My TV repairman took out his diamond-studded screwdriver and his platinum tweezers, twisted a few controls, and said, "That'll be $185." I said, "What could you possibly have done to warrant a $185 charge?" He explained: "Three things: I coagulated the circuit rectifier, I goldwatered the azalea bushing, and I let my wife go shopping in Saks."

In union there is strength—and in unions even more strength: The handsome young union house painter attracted the lady of the house. She asked him to drop his brush and come make love to her. The union man complied. An hour later the same thing happened. At noon, he took out his lunch box and started to eat, when the lady beckoned him again. He said, "Nope—not now, madam. I'm on my own time."

A New York sign painter who made a specialty of lettering signs for union strikers was picketed by men who wore signs saying: THESE SIGNS WERE NOT PAINTED BY THE FIRM WE'RE PICKETING.

My neighbor told his son, "Learn a trade—and then you'll be able to go out on strike."

One lady called up the owner of a restaurant: "Would you mind calling my husband, Andy, to the phone? He's the waiter." The boss said, "Andy the waiter? Does he work for me?" She said, "Yes, of course, but at present he's outside picketing the place."

The only work my neighbor's ever done full time is picket.

Myron was called to the office by the supervisor for talking back to his foreman: "Is it true that you called him a liar?" "Yes, I did." "Did you call him stupid?" "Yes." "Slave driver?" "Yes." "And did you call him an opinionated, bullheaded egomaniac?" "No, but would you write that down so I can remember it?" Myron's boss hated him so much, just before he fired him, he gave him a raise so he would be losing a better job.

The chief called his assistant into his office. "Frank," he started, "I want you to slow down. Take it a little easier. Stop pushing yourself. What I'm saying is—you're fired."

The electrician knocked on the back door and said to the lady who answered, "I came to install the TV cable." The woman said, "I didn't order any TV cable, mister." He said, "Are you Mrs. Davis?" She said, "No, I'm Mrs. Rosen. Mrs. Davis moved away last year." The electrician screamed, "How do you like the nerve of some people? They call us, say they want TV cable right away—and then they move!"

Latest statistics show that there are over 1 million people who are idle in New York. Fortunately, most of them work for the government.

One city employee mentioned, "Maybe it's true that hard work won't kill a person—but you never heard of anyone who rested to death either."

The waiter asked the owner, "If I take this job, will I get a raise every six months?" The owner said, "Well, yes, if you do a good job." The waiter said, "I knew there was a snag to it someplace."

The shop steward asked the porter what he was doing.

"Sharpening pencils," the porter said. "Ain't allowed," said the steward. "That's a job for a carpenter."

The old politician said to his son, "When I was your age I was working twelve hours a day, with half an hour for lunch, six days a week—and believe me, I loved it and worked hard every minute." The kid said, "Please, Father, be more discreet in voicing your antilabor, union-baiting sentiments. You'll never get reelected with radical statements like that."

Things are tough in the job market. I met a guy who said he just lost his job. "Where did you work?" I asked. He said, "The unemployment office."

You think you've got problems? We have a plumber who no longer makes house calls.

The new man on the road crew told the foreman he hadn't been given a shovel yet. "So what? You're getting paid aren't you?" "Sure, but all the other guys have something to lean on!"

Two Hollywood actors were talking. One said, "We have to picket tomorrow. Shall I pick you up in the Jag or the Rolls?" The other said, "We're striking against deplorable living conditions. You'd better make it the Jag—it's a small car."

Lawyers

A license to be a lawyer makes stealing legal. Today, when you get done paying the lawyer—you don't have anything left to pay the judge.

I consulted a lawyer to find out if I needed a lawyer. He

said no and sent me a bill for $300. Two days later, I was at a party and met another lawyer. I told him how all I did was ask the first guy if I needed a lawyer and he socked it to me for $300. Can he do that? I asked. Yes, the second lawyer said. The next morning *he* sent me a bill for $300 for legal advice.

Every lawyer has a meter going, and he doesn't even drive a taxi. He says "Hello," it costs $25. "How are you?" is at least $40. Even a call girl doesn't charge $175 an hour. I know one lawyer who charges you if he dreams about you. Thinking about you while going up in an elevator is double time. One attorney received a birthday gift from a client. He didn't like it. He sent her a bill: "For time spent while returning your gift—$150."

A friend told me, "Boy, do I have an expensive lawyer. He handled my medical malpractice suit and I wound up owing the doctor a liver and a kidney and my attorney an arm and a leg."

Ignorance of the law does not prevent the losing lawyer from collecting his bill. One of the defendants in Connecticut was saying he thought he'd had pretty good lawyers. Said a co-defendant, "I'd trade you both these lawyers for one good witness."

The client said to his attorney: "Say, man, your bill is ridiculous: You're taking four-fifths of my damages. This is extortion." The lawyer replied quietly, "I furnished the skill, the eloquence, and the necessary legal learning for your case." The client said, "Yeah, sure, but I furnished the case itself." The lawyer sneered, "Anybody could fall down a hole."

The guy told the judge: "My doctor says I can walk, but my lawyer says I can't."

The butcher pushed open the door marked PRIVATE and stood before Forster, the attorney: "If a dog steals a piece of meat from my shop, is the owner liable?" The lawyer said, "Of course." The butcher said, "Okay, your dog took a piece of

sirloin steak worth twenty dollars about five minutes ago."
The lawyer said, "Is that so? Then just give me another
twenty dollars and that will cover my fee."

A lawyer is a learned gentleman who rescues your estate
from your enemies—and keeps it himself.

You can't live without lawyers—and you sure can't die
without them.

A businessman was involved in a lawsuit that dragged on
for years. One afternoon he told his attorney, "Frankly, I'm
getting tired of all this litigation." The lawyer replied,
"Nonsense—I propose to fight this case down to your last
nickel."

The two attorneys were talking: "As soon as I realized it
was a crooked deal, I got out of it." "How much?"

What's the best way to save a marriage? Go out and price
a few divorce lawyers.

"I know the evidence is strongly against me," the crook
said, "but I have $75,000 to fight the case. Can we win?"
"As your attorney, I assure you that you'll never go to
prison with that kind of money."

I'll tell you how smart my lawyer is—he never graduated
from law school. He was so smart, he settled out of class.

The judge leaned over the bench and said to the prisoner,
"How come you can't get a lawyer to defend you?" The
defendant said, "As soon as they find out I didn't steal the
money, they won't have anything to do with me."

"Before I take this case," the counselor said, "you'll have
to give me a hundred-dollar retainer." Myron agreed: "All
right—here's your one hundred bucks." The lawyer said,
"Thank you—this entitles you to two questions." Myron
screamed, "What? One hundred dollars for just two
questions? Isn't that awfully high?" The attorney said,
"Yes, I suppose it is. Now what's your second question?"

A lawyer is a man who helps you get what's coming to him.

"I borrowed $2,000 from my father so I could study law," the young attorney said. "My first case was when my father sued me for $2,000." The kid now works for a law firm—making loopholes.

This same young counselor was advising his pretty new client, "When we go to court, I want you to wear a short skirt." She protested, "But they're not in good taste." He said, "Do you want to be acquitted—or do you want to be in good taste?"

The lawyer said to his client, "Now, madam, I will take your case, but do you think it's advisable for you, a mother of twelve children, to accuse your husband of neglect?"

If you want to make a short story long, tell it to a lawyer: "When you go into court, you are putting your fate into the hands of twelve people who weren't smart enough to get out of jury duty."

Lawyers are now allowed to advertise, just like the butcher, the baker, or the plumber who overcharges.

My friend is such a great lawyer, the government just named a loophole after him. He even could find a loophole in the Ten Commandments.

A lawyer and a doctor were arguing about the relative merits of their professions: "I don't say," said the doc, "that all lawyers are thieves, but you'll have to admit that your profession does not make angels of men." The lawyer answered, "You're right—we leave that to you doctors."

The two cellmates were talking. One said, "Me? I robbed from the rich and gave it to my lawyers."

Would you believe there is a "lawyers referral service" with the slogan, "Our lawyers can relate to your particular problem: Most of them have been in jail, too."

The attorney said: "Are you sure you're telling me all the truth? If I'm going to defend you, I've got to know everything." "Yeah, I told you everything." "Good, I think I can get you acquitted—your alibi is excellent. Now, are you sure you told me everything?" The defendant said, "Yeah—all except where I hid the money."

Talk is cheap—if lawyers don't do the talking.

The law is a system that protects everybody who can afford to hire a good lawyer.

Norman had just won his first case, and the client, a man acquitted of a burglary charge, came over to congratulate him. The crook said, "Thanks a lot. I'll drop in on you sometime!" The lawyer said, "Fine—all I ask is that you make it in the daytime."

I've known lawyers who sometimes tell the truth—they'll do anything to win a case.

The lawyer was walking down Fifth Avenue when he saw two cars collide. He rushed over and yelled, "I'm a lawyer. I saw the whole thing—and I'll take either side."

Harvard U. claims it produces most of the nation's lawyers and politicians: That's a good enough reason to close the place down.

The attorney said to the judge: "One hundred thousand dollars isn't nearly a big enough settlement, Your Honor. After all—my client deserves something too."

"If we win this case," said the client, "I'll pay you $3,000." The lawyer agreed, "Okay—get some witnesses." The man hunted up several witnesses and won the case. "Now that we've won," the lawyer said, "how about my $3,000?" The client agreed, "Okay—get some witnesses."

The pickpocket was crying: "I should have been a lawyer. Crime sure as hell pays them."

Where there's a will there's a lawsuit.

The divorce attorney was telling the couple, "Your husband gets custody of the car, you get custody of the house, and I get custody of the money."

This lawyer and his wife were walking in Central Park, when a robber stuck a gun at them. "Tell him you're a lawyer," the wife snapped. "There's supposed to be honor among thieves."

My neighbor told me: "I asked my son the lawyer for some advice. Yesterday I received a bill. I said to him, 'You'd charge your own father?' He replied, 'But Dad, didn't you notice the 50 percent discount?'"

He's such a great lawyer, once he got the jury so confused they sent the judge to jail.

Some men are heterosexual, some are bisexual, and some don't think about sex at all—they become lawyers.

My lawyer's great. I broke a mirror, which means seven years hard luck. He got me off with five.

Lazy People

For my brother, laziness is a career: He never puts off till tomorrow what he can put off forever.

My neighbor's wife was complaining about her man: "He's so lazy. He's been sitting there all day doing nothing." I asked, "How do you know?" She answered, "I've been watching him."

My uncle refuses to drink coffee in the morning—it keeps him awake all day. He has a watch that tells how many days till his retirement. Lazy? When he leaves the house, he finds out which way the wind is blowing and he goes in that direction. If his ship ever did come in, I doubt if he'd bother unloading it.

The lazy man cries, "Everything gets easier with practice except getting up in the morning."

I know a bank robber who was so lazy he made carbon copies of the hold-up note.

I have the laziest friend of all: He married a widow with five children. The first thing he does when he gets up in the morning is to take a sleeping pill. He finally fell off the couch and had to be taken to the hospital in an ambulance. The doctor examined him and reported, "I'm afraid I've got some bad news for you, sir. You will never be able to work again." The poor soul said, "Thank you, doctor, now what's the bad news?"

The laziest guy in town? He listens to the weather on the morning show and won't go to work if it's raining any place in the country. . . . The directions on his medicine say, "A teaspoon before going to bed"—and in one day he uses seven bottles. . . . He has the seven-year itch and is already nine months behind in his scratching. . . . His idea of cleaning house is to sit in a corner and collect dust.

People who throw kisses are hopelessly lazy.

I know a man who's so lazy, he always goes through a revolving door on somebody else's push. Automation could never replace him—they still haven't found a machine that does nothing. He bought a book on exercise and then lay down on the couch to read it.

Women have a tough life. They have to clean, cook, sew— and that's very hard to do without getting out of bed.

My neighbor told me, "I couldn't work if I wanted to. All my life I've had trouble with my back: I can't get it off the bed. Besides, I've found that the hardest thing in the world is doing nothing—you never know when you're finished." I went to see him and found him in bed, as usual. "Why are you lying down?" I asked. "Are you tired?" He said, "No, I'm lying down so I don't *get* tired."

How about the hillbilly who was reclining under a tree? I

said, "Hey there! Your house is on fire." He said, "Know it," without moving. "Well, why don't you do something about it?" He said, "Doin' it now. Bin a-prayin' for rain ever since she started."

My Uncle Charlie's very superstitious: He won't work any week that has a Friday in it. Some people would call him a failure. He isn't—he just started at the bottom and liked it there.

The laziest man I know is also the richest. He's an oil man from Texas who bought his wife a yacht for Christmas so he wouldn't have anything to wrap.

"Doc," a man said, "if there's anything wrong with me, don't give me a long scientific name. Say it so I can understand it." The doctor said, "Very well—you're lazy." The patient said, "Thanks, doc. Now give me a scientific name, so I can tell my boss."

Lazy? His wife has kept her promise to keep the kitchen spotless. They eat out.

Lazy? He counts calories not because he wants to lose weight but because he doesn't want to have any excess energy.

The boss told the young office clerk, "I think you're the laziest person I ever met. I don't believe you do an hour's work in a week. Tell me one single way in which this firm benefits from having you here?" The young man said, "Well, when I go on vacation, you don't have to hire somebody to take my place, and no extra work is thrown on the others."

The news that Steve had lost his job got around quickly, and Myron asked, "Why did the foreman fire you?" Steve shrugged, "You know what a foreman is—the one who stands around and watches the other man work." Myron asked, "What's that got to do with it?" Steve explained, "Well, he just got jealous of me—people thought I was the foreman."

Lazy? Coffee doesn't keep him awake—even when it's hot and being spilled on him.

The guy told his boss, "I'm late because the escalator got stuck." The boss said, "Why didn't you walk up?" He said, "I couldn't—it was going down!"

"My father pays our rent," complained the woman to her husband. "My mother buys our clothes and my aunt pays for our groceries. My brother helps with the children's school fees, and my sister arranges our holidays. I'm ashamed that we can't do better." "I know how you feel," soothed her husband. "You have at least two uncles who give us nothing."

Lies

Remember, the person who agrees with you . . . will lie about other things too.

With most men, a lie is a last resort. With a politician, it's first aid.

I asked my neighbor, "Have you seen one of those instruments that detect falsehoods?" He said, "Seen one? I married one!"

An honest politician is one who's never been caught.

What do you tell a guy who is wearing a new suit that looks like a Salvador Dali copy, when he asks you how you like it? Try: "That suit is really *you*." Or: "I don't care what anybody says—I like it. But what the hell do I know?" He'll take the lie as a compliment.

My friend's wife is a great gal, except she just can't be

trusted. Even if she *told* me she was lying, I still wouldn't believe she was telling the truth.

You've just concluded a passionate love scene with the temporary love of your life. She doesn't want you to go home to your wife, and cries, "You're only interested in me for one thing!" Be ready with the lie of your life: "That's the one thing my wife wishes I was interested in *her* for."

Sometimes the truth can be rougher than a lie. My neighbor confided to me: "I told my wife the truth. . . . I told her I was seeing a psychiatrist, two plumbers, and a bartender."

Cynthia cured her husband from coming home early in the morning. I asked her how she did it. "Easy," she explained. "Last night when I heard him fumbling downstairs, I yelled, 'Is that you, Myron?'" "How did that help?" I asked. She said, "My husband's name is John."

Lies can be used for good instead of evil: My boss received offers from four publishers for the fiction rights to his expense accounts.

My neighbor says, "The only time my husband tells the truth is when he admits he's lying."

It's always the best policy to tell the truth, unless, of course, you are an exceptionally good liar.

The way my brother-in-law handles the truth, he should work for the weather bureau.

My friend said, "I don't trust my wife. Last night she didn't come home at all, and this morning, when I asked where she had been, she told me she spent the night with her sister Carol." I asked, "What makes you think she didn't?" He said, "I *know*, because *I* spent the night with her sister Carol."

"I dabble in oil," said the gas station attendant.

"My husband is a liver, brain, and lung specialist," said the butcher's wife.

The actor bragged, "I have a big following." (Five finance companies, three department stores, four landlords, and seven collection agencies.)

Losers

Talk about losers, Marty Brill had this triska thing: He took this gal to the Tunnel of Love at an amusement park and she told him to wait outside.

My neighbor told me, "I was in Atlantic City for only three days and lost my car, my watch, and my money—I lost everything but my good-luck charm."

My friend always bets on number 8. At the races he put a bundle on the number 8 horse and always lost. In Atlantic City his chips were always on number 8—always lost. I asked, "Why always 8?" He said, "It's my lucky number."

A loser? When his bookie's place burned down, the only thing the firemen saved were his IOUs. . . . He's the only person who can buy artificial flowers and have them die on him. . . . He crossed in front of a black cat the other day and it's had bad luck ever since.

A friend told me, "As a kid I was very dull and really a loser. I used to belong to this teenage club which liked to hold wild parties at my house. I wouldn't have minded, but they would never invite me."

I suspected my marriage was in trouble from the first day: Her parents sent me a thank you note.

When I was a baby, my parents bought me a carriage with no brakes.

I know a girl who was so ugly she never made *Who's Who* but was featured in *What's That?*

I went to a computer dating service—and they sent me the number of Dial-a-Prayer.

I went to a psychoanalyst for years and it helped: Now I get rejected by a much better class of girls.

My parents didn't want me: They put live teddy bears in my crib.

I was kidnapped when I was a kid. Soon as my father got the ransom note, he sprang into action—he rented out my room.

When I was born, my father gave out cigar butts.

Even my bank doesn't have confidence in me. I have the only checks in town with three things printed on them: my name, address, and "insufficient funds."

No wonder I have no confidence in my looks: On Halloween my parents sent me out *as is*.

I remember the time I had an operation: While it was going on, I heard the doctor tell the nurse, "I'll take all calls."

My parents spent ten years trying to find a loophole in my birth certificate.

My brother was such a loser that in school during fire drills, his teacher told him to keep his seat.

Talk about losers: I went to a real wild party at a nudist camp. My luck, everybody got drunk and started putting their clothes on!

My neighbor is a real loser. He has a slight impediment in his speech—his wife.

My uncle claims he's so henpecked, his parakeet gets to talk more than he does.

I'll give you a loser: He's so henpecked, he still takes orders from his first wife.

I know another man so henpecked he never knows what he and his wife are arguing about—she won't tell him. He's such a loser, on his wedding night she told him they were seeing too much of each other.

You're a sure loser when your junk mail arrives "postage due."

It's not a matter of whether you win or lose—it's whether you can deduct your losses.

Sign at Las Vegas dice table: SHAKE WELL BEFORE LOSING.

A born loser is a guy whose ship comes in, but it's loaded with relatives.

I hung up my stocking last Christmas and all I found was a note from the health department.

I was an unwanted child from birth: I had to take a taxi home from the hospital.

Are you ready for the loser of the year? He got a letter from a magazine sweepstakes telling him he may owe them a million dollars.

My brother proposed to his girl, saying, "Marry me and I'll go to the ends of the earth for you." After the wedding she said, "Okay, now you keep your end of the bargain." Last week he called up for the right time. The recording hung up on him.

A loser is a guy who's been unlucky in two out of two marriages: His first wife left and the second one won't.

My brother's a born loser. When his ship finally came in, he was waiting at the train station.

I know a guy who's so thickheaded he'd make the perfect contestant for a game show called "Strike It Poor."

My wife wants her sex in the backseat of a car—and she wants me to drive.

This character I know has a twin sister and she forgot his birthday.

My bank demands my identification—even when I deposit money. . . . Even as a kid, my luck was bad: On my tenth birthday my father bought me a bat. The first day I played with it—it flew away. . . . My education was dismal—I went to a school for mentally disturbed teachers. . . . My parents did not love me—they bronzed my baby shoes with my feet still in them. . . . I have no luck with women. The other day I asked a girl to see her apartment—she drew me a sketch.

Marriage

The matchmaker said to the young man, "I have a girl for you with $50,000." The chap said, "Can I see her picture?" The matchmaker snapped, "With $50,000 we don't show pictures."

The marriage agent said, "I will be honest—she squints and has false teeth." The applicant said, "False teeth? Are they gold?"

A woman told the marriage broker she wanted a man with a nice business. The man he found insisted, "I'm a businessman. In my business I get samples. How do I know if she's any good? Find out if she'll give me a sample." "But she's a good girl," said the broker. "No samples, no deal." The broker told this to the girl, who screamed, "He's a businessman? Well, I'm a business-woman. Samples he wants? References I'll give him!"

A young woman brought her fiancé Rocky home to meet her parents. The old man asked his prospective son-in-law about their future. Rocky said he would keep his bride in the manner to which she had become accustomed.

"How?" asked her father. "I'll move in with you!" Rocky answered.

She said, "You look like my third husband." He asked, "How many husbands have you had?" She said, "Two."

She waited for him outside his office on February 29. "It's a leap year," she smiled. "Come on, my parents and my lawyer say we should get married." He tried to change the subject: "Tell me," he said with a rather painful smile, "how's that diet of yours going?" She said, "Just fine—last week I lost eight pounds." He said, "That's wonderful— how did you do it?" She said, "I had your baby."

"Are you proposing to Charlie this leap year?" Sylvia asked her friend Ruth. She said, "No—my feelings toward him have changed." Sylvia asked, "Then you will return his diamond ring?" Ruth said, "No—my feelings toward the diamond ring have not changed."

She said, "All I want in a husband is a man who is good looking, kind, and understanding—I don't think that's too much to expect from a millionaire."

The wealthy lawyer put all his stocks and bonds and money in his daughter's name, but of course she fell for a jerk. There was nothing he could do but look up his prospective son-in-law and tell him, "Sylvia is going to be a wealthy girl in her own name. If we let her bring you her extensive dowry, what can we expect from you in exchange?" The young lover said cheerfully, "I'll be glad to give you a receipt, sir."

A man in love is incomplete until he has married. Then he's finished.

"Darling, you have deceived me," the young bride said to her husband shortly after the marriage. "But I told you I was a millionaire, and I am," the groom answered. "Yes," the bride retorted. "But you also told me that you were seventy-four years of age and in poor health—and now I've discovered that you are only fifty-six and fit as a fiddle."

This report was printed in a local paper: "The couple were married on Saturday, thus ending a friendship that began in their school days."

"Did you hear they've got a new product that cuts down on a man's sexual urges?" I asked my neighbor. He said, "So what's new with that? I married one thirty years ago."

A fellow was testifying in court about the serious injuries he received in a loading platform accident. He said: "Ever since I fell off that loading platform, I have been unable to have marital relations more than five times a week." The judge leaned over and said: "Tell me, where is that loading platform?"

Some marriages are made in heaven—but so are thunder and lightning.

You know what it means to come home to a wife who will cook for you, love you, take care of you, adore you? It means you're in the wrong house.

Marriage is a lot like the army: Everyone complains but you'd be surprised at the large number that reenlist.

The only people who make love all the time are liars.

The difference between sex for money and sex for free is that sex for money usually costs a lot less.

When it comes to broken marriages most husbands will split the blame—half his wife's fault and half her mother's.

The wife said to her husband: "Sylvia next door tells me that her husband makes love to her three times a day. Why don't you do that?" He said, "I would, but when I run into her I usually have garbage in my hand."

It's not letting a wife have the last word that worries most husbands—it's getting around to it.

Attorney: "For many, divorce is a great relief. The only problem is you have to get married to enjoy it."

My brother told me, "I'll never forget my honeymoon. My

wife put on her sexiest negligee, snuggled up close, and in a very shy voice said, 'Dear, now that we're married, can I do anything I want?' I said, 'Anything you want.' 'Anything?' 'Sure, anything.' So she went to sleep!''

The only time my wife pays strict attention to what I say—is when I'm asleep.

Hard work is the soundest investment: It provides neat security for your wife's next husband.

The secret of a happy marriage is to find someone you could be happy arguing with.

My wife practices the rhythm method. That means she won't make love unless there's a drummer in the room.

My wife is allergic to money: As soon as it gets in her hands, she gets rid of it.

There are still more marriages today than divorces—which proves that preachers can still outtalk lawyers.

Marriage is like a lottery. The trouble is, you can't tear up your ticket if you lose.

My wife sure knows how to spend money—she's extravagant. I mean, who tips at toll booths? My wife is easy to please: She'll go anyplace for dinner except her own kitchen.

Everybody is always trying to find a cure for marriage: My neighbor bought a book, *How To Be a Boss in Your Own Home*—but his wife hasn't permitted him to read it.

I know one husband who doesn't permit his wife to have her own way. She has it without his permission.

Outside of maybe making love once in a while, the average housewife doesn't want to work anymore.

I believe the young people today are getting married much too young. Imagine having your father drive the car on your honeymoon.

Helping with the dishes and housework makes for a happier marriage—it's too bad more wives don't do it.

They say opposites attract. That's why I married a girl with money.

The judge asked one witness, "What did you do before you were married?" "Anything I wanted to," was the answer.

The old-fashioned couple used to *stay* married. Nowadays, the old-fashioned couple is the one that bothers to *get* married.

A wife lasts only as long as a marriage—but an ex-wife is forever.

My neighbor's daughter asked him, "Daddy, what does a woman do when she loses interest in sex?" He said, "She gets married."

Definition of a guy who's been married five times: spouse broken.

The only difference between in-laws and outlaws is that outlaws don't want to live with you.

A gentleman is one who holds the door open while his wife lugs in the bags of groceries.

A woman told the shopkeeper, "I want a small revolver for my husband." He asked, "Did your husband give you any indication of the make he prefers?" She said, "No—he doesn't know yet that I'm going to shoot him."

Marriage is the only war in which you sleep with the enemy.

I was married by a judge. . . . I should have asked for a jury.

My neighbor told his wife: "If you really loved me, you would have married somebody else."

Me and my wife go fifty-fifty on everything: I tell her what to do—and she tells me where to go.

The guys were playing golf at the Concord Hotel and

saying only good things about their wives: "I just love being with my wife," Schwartz said. "She has such a way about her; and our credit cards are in her name—so I never leave home without her."

One nurse swears to me she was on duty in the maternity ward, where, after showing a father his newborn baby, she asked him if he'd like to see his wife. "No," the man replied. "We haven't spoken in two years."

Marriage is a game you must know how to play: During the marriage vows, one groom said to the rabbi, "Hurry it up. We have an appointment with the marriage counselor in an hour."

You know you've made a bad marriage if you go in for wife swapping and you have to throw in the maid.

My cousins tried to save their marriage for the sake of the children—and *they* are the children they tried to save it for.

"I was a fool when I married you," he snarled. "I know," she answered, "but I was too infatuated to notice at the time."

"Darling," the young wife said hesitatingly, "I hardly know how to tell you, but soon there will be a third sharing our little home." The husband was ecstatic. "Sweetheart," he cried, "are you sure?" She said, "Positive—I had a letter from my mother this morning saying that she would be here next Saturday!"

The poor soul said to his wife, "Look, dear, we're low on money now—we're just going to have to cut down on luxuries. If you would learn to cook, we could fire the chef." She answered, "In that case, if *you* would learn to make love—we could fire the chauffeur."

My wife lets me run things in our house—errands.

My neighbor told me, "When I first met my wife, she was a schoolteacher. I used to write her passionate love letters —and she'd send them back corrected. I must be the only man in the whole world who returned from his honeymoon and received a report card. It said, 'Dick is neat and friendly and shows a keen interest in fun and games.' "

A diplomatic husband to his wife, "How do you expect me to remember your birthday when you never look any older?"

A woman asked the clerk at the fur shop, "Will a small deposit hold it until my husband does something unforgivable?"

My wife is exactly like life insurance: The older she gets, the more she costs.

Marriage is a romantic story in which the hero dies in the first chapter.

Let's face it, men, you really need a wife. . . . Think of all the things that happen that you can't blame on the government.

Wives are the opposite of fishermen: They brag about the ones that got away and complain about the one they caught.

My neighbor's wife told her husband, "You certainly made a fool of yourself at the party. I only hope no one realized you were sober."

My sister says, "My husband is a very versatile man. He can do anything wrong."

The angry wife confronted her husband and said: "That twenty-dollar bill that was in your pants pocket last night—did you steal it out of my purse this morning?"

The angry husband screamed, "Supper's not ready again? That's it—I'm going out to a restaurant!" The wife said, "Wait just five minutes." He asked, "Why? Will it be ready then?" She said, "No, but I'll go with you!"

They can never forget the time they first met—but they keep trying.

Marriage is coming back: Even couples who are living together are getting married.

Remember the old-fashioned wedding ceremonies and the little flower girls? The flower girls are now the couples' own kids.

You can usually tell early if a marriage is going to work. Like this last wedding I went to is a good example: About halfway down the aisle, the bride stopped and asked if anyone in the audience had an aspirin.

The nice lady said to the psychiatrist: "It first occurred to me that our marriage was in trouble when my husband won an all-expense-paid trip for two to Las Vegas—and he went twice."

You can always tell when a marriage is shaky: The partners don't talk to each other during the TV commercials.

"Irving," the new bride cried, "when you married me you promised to love, honor, and obey." He said, "Yeah—but I didn't want to start an argument in front of all those people."

The wife says, "Hoping our marriage will improve is like leaving the night light on for Jimmy Hoffa."

My neighbor told me, "We had a church wedding because my wife's parents didn't want to miss Bingo."

Here's what you need to have a very happy marriage: The first thing is to establish who's boss. In my house what I say goes. The trouble is when I raise my hand, my wife never calls on me.

"Do you and your wife ever have a difference of opinion?" my friend asked. I said, "Sure we do—but I don't tell her about it."

They have all kinds of books on marriage, like *How to Make Your Marriage Work*. Then there's the sequel: *How to Make Your Wife Work*.

"You know, dear," the beleaguered husband said, trying to appease his wife, "I've been thinking over our argument and—well—I've decided to agree with you after all." She said, "That won't help you a bit—I've changed my mind."

The definition of a bachelor: A rolling stone gathering no boss.

During a lifetime, a man goes through three economic stages: What he spends on his date is charity, what he spends on his wife is tribute, and what he spends on his ex-wife is ransom.

My wife was an immature woman: I'd be in the bathroom taking a bath, and she would walk right in and sink my boats.

The only time you see a blushing bride these days is when the groom doesn't show up.

Ours was a small wedding—just her parents, my parents, and the obstetrician.

Home is where the husband runs the show, but the wife writes the script.

A woman never knows what kind of husband she doesn't want until she marries him.

My neighbor brags that his wife deserves all the credit for stopping him from gambling away his salary: She spends it before he gets it.

A playboy enjoying his feast at the deli insisted that no matter what anyone else says, the most dangerous food of all time is the wedding cake.

The average man has probably thought twice about running away from home—once as a child and once as a husband.

All most men want from their wives is affection, admiration, encouragement, and the ability to live grandly on an inadequate income.

A wife is a woman who always says, "I'll admit I'm right—if you'll admit you're wrong."

Wife to husband as they leave a marriage counselor's office: "Now that we're back on speaking terms, shut up!"

The most trusting husband we know is the one who thinks his wife spent the night in church because she came home with a Gideon Bible in her hand.

"Say, that's a beautiful sable," I told my neighbor's wife. "Must have cost you a fortune." "No," she said, "it only cost a kiss!" I asked, "One that you gave your husband?" She said, "No, one that he gave the maid."

My wife cooks religiously: Everything she serves is either a burnt offering or a sacrifice.

The couple was having an argument: She hollered, "If it weren't for my money, this furniture wouldn't be here!" He answered, "If it weren't for your money, *I* wouldn't be here!"

The wife was complaining to her friend: "No wonder I'm sick of marriage—Tommy hasn't made love to me once since the honeymoon." "Why not divorce him?" "Because Tommy isn't my husband."

My neighbor told me, "I'm all upset. My wife hasn't spoken to me in a week—and I can't remember what I said to make her shut up."

Old saying: He married her to get rid of her.

A fellow asked his girl's father for her hand in marriage. Pop asked, "Well, the point is do you think you can make her happy?" The suitor said, "Heck, man, you ought to have seen her at the motel last night!"

Her husband demanded, "Is there another man, Shirley?" And she said, "No, course not. Only you and Pat and Oscar and Henry, as always."

Young wives are more practical nowadays. I know one who was so economical that she went without her honeymoon so that her husband could save up for alimony.

"I don't want to say my wife's cooking is bad," says my neighbor, "but every time somebody drops food on the floor—the dog runs and hides."

It's no wonder my wife feels so much at home at the racetrack. After all, she is a nag.

A bachelor has nobody to share his troubles. But then, why should a bachelor have troubles?

My sister tells all girls: "Look for an older man with a strong will—made out to you."

He's always taken his troubles like a man—he blames them on his wife.

Adam would never have taken a wife if God didn't put him to sleep first.

A bachelor's a man who believes that one can live as cheaply as two.

A wife can usually live within her husband's income, provided he has another one for himself.

Two guys downing Martinis: "Did you hear Joe's wife got another baby?" "Another baby? That's her eighth." "Yeah, he wants to get her a special gift—but he doesn't know what." "How about a *stop sign?*"

Slapping the groom on the shoulder, the bride's father said cheerfully: "My boy, you're the second happiest man in the world."

The guy wrote to the collection agency: "Sorry I have not been able to pay this bill but I recently got married and am short of funds. My honeymoon took more out of me than I expected. As soon as I am back on my feet I will bring this account up to date."

My sister-in-law says: "Husbands are like fires. They go out when unattended."

My wife has her own way of keeping our kitchen immaculate: She never goes in it.

My neighbor embraced his daughter lovingly and said, "Your young man told me today he wanted you as a bride and I gave him my consent." The daughter cried, "Oh, Dad, it's going to be so hard leaving Mother!" Dad said, "I understand perfectly—just take her with you."

When kids today go dancing, it's a little crazy. The kids don't look at each other, don't talk to each other, don't touch each other—it's like being married.

The only form of gambling allowed by the church is marriage.

My sister suggests: "The best way to hold on to a husband is to treat him as you would any other pet: Give him three meals a day, plenty of affection, and a loose leash."

The lady cried, "My husband accuses me of overdrawing our checking account. I haven't overdrawn—he has under-deposited."

My neighbor told me, "I can honestly say that since I married my wife, I haven't looked at another girl—I'm completely discouraged."

Two men were discussing their wives. One said he loved his wife very much, but every time they got into an argument, she became historical. "You must mean hyster-ical," his friend corrected. "No, historical. She keeps bringing up the past."

My neighbor was told that his wife ran away with his best friend. He said, "Anybody who would take her away *is* my best friend."

My neighbor told me he's marrying a girl with a $100,000-a-year income. I said, "And you told me it's a love match." He said, "It is—I love money!"

For a man, marriage boils down to two adjustments regard-ing give and take: When it comes to money, you give, she takes. When it comes to orders, she gives, you take.

Polygamy would never work in this country. Think of four wives in a kitchenette.

The cop stopped the couple driving seventy-five miles an hour. The signs on the windshield and the back of the car announced JUST MARRIED. The officer said, "I should give you a ticket for speeding—but I figure why add to your troubles?"

A couple were dining out on their wedding anniversary. The husband lifted his glass for a toast and said, "I can't think of anything good to say: We have rotten kids, we lost our house, we don't have a car." His wife interrupted, "But you have me." The husband replied, "You're not listening. I'm trying to think of something good to drink to."

A woman's hardest years are those before she finds a husband. A man's hardest years are those after he finds a wife.

My sister-in-law told me: "My idea of an unbalanced budget is one in which I find I'm spending less than my husband is earning."

If it weren't for marriage, people could go through life thinking they had no faults at all.

My wife says, "I admit my husband is more intelligent than I am. The proof is that he was smart enough to marry me—and I was dumb enough to marry him."

A man can say anything he pleases in his own home—nobody listens anyway.

A practical nurse is one who's married to a rich old patient.

A young minister was called upon to perform his first wedding ceremony. After the rites, the bashful couple just stood there. The nervous parson knew he had to get them started back up the aisle, so habit dictated his next words. "It's all over now," he told the couple. "Go—and sin no more."

I said to my neighbor: "The trouble with you is you don't relax. You take your troubles to bed with you." He said, "What can I do? My wife refuses to sleep alone."

Jones: "I wish my wife were a dentist." Bones: "Why?"

Jones: "I'd love to have her say to me, 'Open your mouth,' instead of her usual, 'Shut up.' "

I'm not having any trouble meeting expenses. My wife keeps introducing me to new ones.

I went to a mob wedding recently. It was the only time I ever saw a groom cut the wedding cake with a switchblade.

The fat lady at the circus married the Indian rubber man—and in three weeks he erased her altogether.

The paradox of marriage is that a man hitches up to one woman to escape many others, and then chases many others to forget the one he's married to.

My neighbor told me, "I'm really getting absentminded. Just the other day I kissed a woman by mistake." I said, "You thought it was your wife?" He said, "No, that's just it—it *was* my wife!"

A husband is a person who is under the impression he bosses the house when in reality he only houses the boss.

My neighbor notes: "I subscribe to the theory that people should never get married on Sunday—it's just not right to gamble on a holy day."

My neighbor describes a family man as one who has several mouths to feed, and one big mouth to listen to.

The man who holds the car door open for his wife either has a new wife or a new car.

The women's lib organization is advocating that wives be paid for housework. My neighbor says he's agreed to pay his wife—if she comes in only on Thursdays.

The newlyweds had just sneaked off to the honeymoon resort. After dinner, the groom went to bed, but the bride pulled up a chair and sat gazing out the window at the stars. "Aren't you coming to bed?" asked the husband. "No," she announced. "Mother told me this would be the most beautiful night of my life and I don't want to miss a minute of it."

Wife: "When are you going to get window shades for the bathroom? The neighbors will see me if I take a bath."
Husband: "Don't worry about it. Take your bath. If they see you, *they'll* buy shades."

My sister believes, "All men are alike—which is probably why the mother of the bride always cries at the wedding."

Second wives always work out better. Like the ads say, when you're number two—you try harder!

"Today is my birthday," Alice told her neighbor, "and Harry served me breakfast in bed." The neighbor said, "You're lucky—I had to go to the hospital and have a baby to get breakfast in bed."

I won't say she married for money—but the ceremony was performed by an accountant.

Miscellaneous

I definitely believe in reincarnation. Did you ever notice how many dead people come to life every day at five in the afternoon?

This guy won $1 million on his lottery ticket. I asked, "Are you deliriously happy?" He said: "Yes! Yes! Yes!" I asked, "What is the first thing you are going to do?" He answered, "Tell my friends it wasn't me!"

The guy said, "My apartment is being turned into a condominium, but I told the owner forget it. I'll rent his roaches—but I won't buy them!"

The obituary editor of a Boston newspaper was not one who would admit his mistakes easily. One day, he got a phone call from an irate subscriber who complained his name had been printed in the obituary column. "Really," was the calm reply. "Where are you calling from?"

One pile of garbage has been on our street so long it was declared a landmark.

"I can't understand it," madam cried to her maid. "How can you leave me after all these years? Haven't I always treated you like one of the family?" The maid said, "Oh, so now you admit it?"

Myron tells me, "I told the manager of my building the apartment had roaches. He raised my rent for keeping pets."

My neighbor told me: "My dog was my only friend. I told my wife that a man needs at least two friends—so she bought me another dog."

Someone once asked my mother if everybody in our family suffered from insanity. She said, "No. We all enjoyed it."

He crossed a turkey with a kangaroo—and now has the first turkey you can stuff on the outside.

The computer may save a lot of guesswork—but so does a bikini.

I love circus people—like the acrobat who married the tattooed woman because, "If I can't sleep in the middle of the night, I can sit up and look at the pictures."

The guy was crying at the bar: "I don't understand my wife. I don't understand my boss. I don't understand my girl. I don't understand my kids. And now I don't understand my personal computer."

Money

This handsome young actor married an elderly lady with millions: It was a marriage made in Chase Manhattan. . . . He loves her company: It does $6 million a year. . . . He explained to his pals in the show: "The great thing about money—it never clashes with anything you're wearing." He told them, "I keep a diary of all our good times together—it's called a bank book."

The very handsome young man amazed the very rich dowager with a proposal of marriage. "What?" she gasped. "You really want to marry me? Why you silly, sweet young man, you've only known me for three days." The young suitor said, "Oh, no—it's much longer than that. You see, I've worked for two years in the bank where you have your account."

The young man said, "The Boy Scouts have the right idea—I help little old ladies across the street to my place. You should see all the merit badges—made of gold."

I know a man whose wife was twice his age but two thousand times his bank account. But pretty soon she started to complain, "You're making it with other girls. This must stop." He said, "Calm down. Don't I let you pay the bills? Don't I let you buy all my clothes?" She said, "Yes, of course." He said, "Well, what are you grumbling about? I only use the others for lovemaking!"

Carmine Santulli tells me: "My wife has the personality and mannerisms of a flea: When she gets on my back, I can't shake her off. The only way I can get her off is to use a special lotion—it's called money."

A budget is a plan that enables you to pay as you go—if you don't go anywhere.

A budget is a complete record of how you manage to spend more than you earned.

The wife was crying to her mother, "We always have too much month left at the end of our money!"

Mothers and Mothers-In-Law

To Mom on Mother's Day
You surely are a winner.
One question do I ask:
What time is Sunday dinner?

I appreciate the chance to visit my mom on Mother's Day—it's like taking a refresher course in guilt.

My mama was an extravagant saver—she saved more than my father earned. My father was always strictly business: Every year he had her Mother's Day card notarized.

My neighbor told me it took his wife three hours to get her new mink coat for Mother's Day: one hour of shopping and two hours of tantrums.

The woman said to her husband, "Is it true that money talks?" He said, "That's what they say, dear. Why do you ask?" She said, "Well, I get so lonely during the day, I wish you'd leave a little here to talk to me!"

I don't think my dad was too happy when I was born—on Mother's Day he sent my mom a sympathy card.

My mom will always remember the Great Depression: It was the day I was born.

Let's hear it for Mom—the only woman with a Ph.D. in laundry.

I asked my friend, "What did your mom get for Mother's Day?" He said, "A new washer/dryer." I said, "What happened to her old washer/dryer?" He said, "She divorced him last year!"

I never could have achieved the position in society that I now hold without my mother—but honestly, I don't hold that against her.

The most remarkable thing about my beautiful mom is that for years and years and years she served the family nothing but leftovers. The original meal has never been found.

I can remember my mom and dad taking me to exotic, faraway places—and trying to leave me there.

All mothers are champs at giving advice. This little old lady was held up by a rough character with a gun. She wasn't a bit scared: "You should be ashamed of yourself, robbing a poor little lady like me," she protested. "A man your size should be robbing a bank."

Mother's Day is a little confusing in Hollywood. Most kids play it safe out there. They send a card to their current mother, their previous mother, their original mother—and just to make sure, they also deliver one to the leading lady of their father's new picture.

My neighbor said, "I don't know what to get my wife for Mother's Day. First she wanted a mink, then she wanted a silver fox. It was ridiculous—the house is full of animals."

I remember when my dad came home on Mother's Day and glowed, "Guess what I brought home for the one I love best?" Mom said, "Cigars, razor blades, cuff links, and golf clubs."

My friend Myron tells me, "Last year on Mother's Day the whole family got together for a big dinner, and afterward, when Mom started to clean up, I said to her, 'Don't bother with those dishes—today is Mother's Day. Leave them. You can always do them tomorrow!' "

The whole family met at Mother's house on Mother's Day: "What's for dinner?" Pop asked. "Take out!" Mom said. The old man asked, "What kind of take out?" Mom said, "ME!"

Mother noted, "The trouble with getting money as a Mother's Day gift is that you can't take it back and exchange it for something larger!"

This year the card company is out with a new line of greeting cards for Mother's Day. They come in two sizes: regular and unwed.

My wife suggested we dine in some place where we haven't eaten before for Mother's Day. "Good idea," I said. "How about home?"

Years ago my mom told me not to send her any Mother's Day gifts—she didn't want to be reminded.

The new bride gushed to her mother, "My husband is very good to me. He gives me everything I ask for." Mom said, "That merely shows you're not asking enough."

The woman shouted over the phone, "Hello, Mama, I got great news! I just won $10,000 in the state lottery! One of my tickets won!" Her mother said, "That's wonderful, but what did you mean 'one of my tickets'?" The daughter explained, "I bought four and one of them won." "Dummy," said her mother, "why did you need the other three?"

I'm tired of hearing jokes knocking mothers-in-law. I happen to have the greatest mother-in-law in the world— and I'd say that even if she weren't looking over my shoulder as I write this.

He who fights and runs away—will return when his mother-in-law leaves.

In a Peruvian village a donkey kicked to death a peasant's mother-in-law. When she was buried, the whole male population of the village flocked to the church. After the funeral, the priest expressed his joy to the peasant: "Your mother-in-law was liked very much. I have never seen so many people in any church." The peasant said, "They didn't come for the funeral—they came to buy the donkey."

For Mother's-In-Law Day, do something nice for the lady: Take her out to dinner, send her flowers, divorce her daughter.

My mother-in-law is very well informed: She can complain on any subject.

I won't say my mother-in-law's bad—it's just that she's so nearsighted, she nagged a coathanger for an hour.

My pal left his wife because of another woman—her mother.

Statistics prove that Japanese women make the best wives. They care for you, pamper you, feed you—and your mother-in-law lives in Osaka.

My mother-in-law needed a blood transfusion, but we had to give up on the idea. We couldn't find a tiger.

Song title: "Fly Me to the Moon—And Don't Call Me Till Your Mother Leaves."

My neighbor's mother-in-law had just come for a visit. His little son was ecstatic: "Now Daddy can do his trick!" he yelled with glee. "What trick is that?" his grandmother asked. "Well," the boy answered. "Daddy said that if you stayed a week, he'd climb the walls. I never saw anyone do that before!"

Two young college kids were having a slight argument about their relationship: "I don't mind your mother living with us," the guy was saying, "but I do wish she'd wait until we get married."

My mother-in-law should get the meddle of honor.

No man is really successful until his mother-in-law admits it.

Pessimists Versus Optimists

A pessimist nowadays is a man who really knows what's going on. An optimist is a man who hasn't yet read the morning papers.

An optimist is a guy who tells you to cheer up when things are going his way.

Always borrow money from a pessimist: He never expects to be paid back.

An optimist is a guy who attacks a girl, she files a complaint—and he thinks she's trying to continue the relationship.

An optimist is a husband who goes down to the marriage bureau to see if his license has expired.

A toast to the optimist: He doesn't care what happens—as long as it happens to somebody else.

A pessimist is a man who feels all women are bad. An optimist hopes so.

Love is responsible for most of the optimists and marriage for most of the pessimists.

I'll tell you about a real optimist: He got married when he was seventy-five—and then looked for a house near a school.

A real pessimist is never happy unless he's miserable.

An optimist is a guy who expects his wife to help him with the dishes. A pessimist won't let his wife do the dishes because he's afraid she'll drop them and he'll have to buy new ones.

A pessimist is a guy who has a choice between two evils —and takes both.

An optimist does not believe he's unpopular—it's just that his answering machine is.

An optimist is a person who thinks he can borrow money from the bank. A pessimist is one who has tried.

A pessimist says there are thirteen men running for president and that none of them is any good. An optimist agrees, but says, "Look at it this way—at least only one of them can win."

My neighbor carries a little card in his wallet. It says: "I am a pessimist. In case of an accident—I'm not surprised."

"I believe," said the happy one, "that for every single thing you give away, two come back to you." The sad soul said, "That's been my experience. Last January I gave away my daughter and she and her husband came back in March."

Politics and Politicians

The only reason we have elections is to find out if the polls are right. . . . Not that it matters, but if a guy is leading in the polls—you know he is the one taking the poll.

If you fool people to get their money, it's fraud. If you fool people to get their votes—it's politics.

I'll never understand polls. A new one released this month shows that 85 percent of the Americans polled are completely confused about United States foreign policy. Now that's a pretty alarming figure—especially when you consider that the poll was taken at the State Department.

Said the politician: "If you go to the polls and elect me, all your troubles may not be over—but mine will."

A good candidate is one who runs his campaign deeply into debt in the hopes that he'll have a chance to do the same for the entire country.

The Senator says, "To err is human; to blame it on the other guy is politics."

A good man nowadays is hard to find. That's why we have to settle for politicians.

One candidate was presenting his argument before the party's finance committee: "I want 10 million dollars for my campaign," he said. "But your campaign won't cost that much," the chairman protested. The candidate said, "I know that—but in case I lose I want to be able to live comfortably."

Some candidates lose because nobody knows what they've done. Others win for the same reason.

A magician and a politician are the same: They both fool the public. But when a magician does it taxes don't go up.

I like politicians. They're like heros to me—lots of dough and full of baloney.

On the tax form, where it says dependents, can I check off for my senators and congressman?

The guys at the club were discussing their man running for Congress: All agreed that he was born poor and honest but he managed to overcome both difficulties.

With all the troubles in the world today, if Moses came down now, the tablets he would carry would be Anacin.

I know a big shot politico who's about to retire and will be honored with a testimonial probe.

In Washington, D.C., the waitress told me at one restaurant, "Of course congressmen are poor tippers. Do you think they're as careless with their money as they are with ours?"

No wonder the politicians want to fix up our jails: Look how many are winding up there.

There are so many candidates this year—there may not be enough promises to go around.

Politicians used to kiss babies to get elected. Now some politicians wait till the babies are grown.

During a severe winter millions of homeless people will travel to Washington, D.C., to find warmth in congressional hot air.

Under the recently enacted amnesty program, millions of aliens are becoming American citizens. Now they can stop hiding from immigration agents and behave like other Americans—start hiding from the IRS agents.

You rarely see a thin politician. It's because of all those words they have to eat.

On U.S. foreign policy, our dealings are an open book—a checkbook.

What's the difference between Congress and the Boy Scouts? The Boy Scouts have adult leaders.

The trouble with Congress fighting today's inflation is it's a lot like the Mafia fighting crime.

The U.S. Congress is an institution—which is a proper place for some of its members.

Congressional junkets could save us a lot of money—if they were only one-way tickets.

Congress can be so unpredictable. . . . You never know what urgent problem they're not going to do anything about.

A little girl asked her mother whether all fairy tales began with "Once upon a time." "No," replied the mother. "Today most of them begin with 'If I am elected.' "

The teacher told the kid in class: "You'll never grow up to

be president—but with your absentee record, you might make it to the Congress."

It's ridiculous for the Russians to accuse us of spying to find out what's going on in Moscow. We're kept too busy trying to find out what's going on in Washington.

These days, more and more politicians are doing something for some of their former colleagues: They're becoming "pen pals."

Post Office

I can't believe the price of stamps nowadays. . . . I don't know anybody I want to get in touch with that much.

We pay so much to mail a letter or a postcard it costs a lot to lose our mail.

Postage is now so high just mailing a get well card can make you sick.

They say airmail is expensive. I say, you don't have to send it first class—tourist is enough—and you don't have to show it movies.

The truth is, there is nothing wrong with paying what we pay to have a letter delivered from New York to New Jersey: It works out to just a penny a day.

My brother is always defending the post office: "The postman always rings twice—especially if there's postage due."

The post office express service now guarantees same-day service: That means they promise to lose your package the same day you mail it.

Myron says: "With stamps going up, you should see what my girlfriend charges to play post office—and she's not even first class."

Talk about highway robbery. . . . The next time the post office issues a new stamp with a higher rate, I suggest they put Jessie James's picture on it.

I don't mind taking a licking, but for that kind of increase in price, they could at least flavor the backs of the stamps with chocolate, vanilla, or strawberry. If the prices of stamps go even higher—they'll have to flavor them with Valium.

You know when you go to the post office on your lunch hour, and they have only two clerks on duty, even though it's the busiest time of the day? With so many waiting in line you can't even fit in the lobby? Well, with the increase in postal rates, they will be able to do something about all this: They're going to enlarge the lobbies at every post office.

If postal rates don't stop going up, it will be cheaper to go yourself.

The postmaster says they are losing money and may have to raise their rates again. I can't understand why the post office should have a deficit. Look at the way volume has increased—on complaints alone.

I don't want to criticize the P.O., but when was the last time you got a get well card while you were still sick?

If the world is getting smaller and smaller, how come it costs more and more to mail a letter?

They tell me the post office is going to have to eliminate some of its less essential services—like mailbox delivery. They plan to have a large mail truck just dump all the mail in the middle of the street—and you can come and get it.

Sooner or later, everybody gets what's coming to them—unless it's coming by mail.

Doesn't it sometimes seem like the mail service is against

us? Rebate checks take weeks to travel through the mails—but bills always show up the day after they're posted.

Special delivery assures that your mail will have a nice leisurely journey.

I won't say the mails are late—but the flower seeds I ordered arrived as a bouquet.

Our local postmaster is mad at me because I turned in the name of our mailman to the missing persons bureau.

The post office is annoyed at that TV ad claiming the service is slow. The postmaster general sent a letter of complaint to the TV station three weeks ago, and as soon as it arrives, all hell will break loose.

One actor in Hollywood was complaining about the inefficient postal system in Los Angeles: "I'm not saying the mail in Hollywood is slow, but I just got my invitation to Elizabeth Taylor's first wedding."

The U.S. Postal Service is nothing to write home about, but I finally found a way to get back at my postman for slow service: I mailed him his Christmas gift.

A female letter carrier was fired for having sex with males on her postal route. It's nice to know that at least someone in the post office delivers.

The post office mail service was even mentioned in the Bible: "The Lord made every creeping thing."

Old postmen never die—they just lose their zip.

This gorgeous girl invited me to come and play post office—but I forgot her zip code.

The post office has a new method for sorting mail: It's called "Hit and miss."

Priority Mail: The first to get lost. First Class Mail: Guaranteed to be delivered within one week—but not necessarily to the right address.

My cousin was retiring after thirty years in the post office. The boss asked, "Have you learned anything after thirty years with us?" My cousin said, "Don't mail my last paycheck."

I really like air mail. It gives me a chance to travel around the world vicariously. For instance, I once sent a letter to a friend in Canada. She never got it; but, when it was returned to me six months later it was postmarked England, France, Italy, Australia, Japan.

The post office is having big problems with deliveries, and they're spreading. I know a letter carrier whose wife is in her twelfth month.

I don't want to say the mails are slow, but if Paul Revere had been a letter carrier, we'd now be known as the fifty *colonies*.

My grandfather wrote to the White House to complain and he just got back a reply—signed by Franklin Delano Roosevelt.

The post office says all problems will be solved with the nine-digit zip code, which will pinpoint exactly where we are now. Now all we need is a zip code that pinpoints exactly where our mail is.

Remember the mailman's creed: Neither rain, nor snow, nor sleet shall prevent the mail from being returned to sender.

There's a new system where you can vote by mail. That's good—except by the time the letter is delivered, the candidate is too old to serve.

The postal service's credo, updated: Neither snow, nor rain, nor gloom of night stays these couriers from the swift completion of their appointed rounds, so there must be some other reason.

Preppies

Preppies are born—they are not made. Basic requirements for preppieism are money, connections, position, lineage, country home, and money and connections. And if you have money and connections, you can forget the position, lineage, and country home.

Preppies do not believe in the common man because they have never seen one.

I know a preppie mommy on an economy kick who washed her own diamonds.

How do preppie families travel? They arrive on the *Mayflower* and depart in a Rolls Corniche.

The only thing that saved the girl from flunking her classes was the fact that she was fluent in wealthy parents.

There was so much boozing at my friend's son's prep school, the only thing he passed was *out*—but he got an A in Frozen Daiquiris.

My neighbor told me, "I think my son is home from prep school." I asked, "How do you know?" He said, "Well, I haven't had a letter asking for money in three weeks—and my car is missing."

One girl wrote her mom from prep school: "There is a lot of kissing and necking going on here and I don't like to be left out of it. Is it okay to remove the braces from my teeth?"

Another preppie girl wrote her mom: "It's only fair to tell you that I have already done it. All I want is your consent."

The definition of a debutante: A girl with a million-dollar smile: She only smiles at millionaires.

The preppie's ambition: To marry a rich girl who is too proud to allow her husband to work.

It takes the wool from the sheep and the bank account from one father to clothe the average preppie.

How long does a preppie spend in finishing school? As soon as she finds a man, she's finished.

Definition of a preppie: A human gimme pig.

A preppie's idea of heaven is dating the nymphomaniac daughter of the owner of a chain of liquor stores.

Then there was the mommy who was very worried about her daughter attending Vassar, who, after reading *Everything You Always Wanted to Know about Sex but Were Afraid to Ask*, wrote to the author to suggest four new chapters.

A real party girl is a debutante who came out five years ago and hasn't been home since.

Presidents

Jimmy Carter gave us plenty of laughs. In fact, he was the laughingstock of the White House.

I'm not too sure about George Washington's wit. . . . I only know he's the only chief of state who didn't blame the previous administration for his troubles.

JFK threw one-liners better than any stand-up comic: "When they call a candidate a favorite son—it's the greatest unfinished sentence in history."

JFK on Barry Goldwater: "He's standing on his record—so nobody can see it." On Senator Eugene McCarthy: "I like the straightforward way he dodges all those issues." On Joey Adams: "He knows a lot—he just can't think of it."

President Jimmy Carter was asked, "How about the powerful interests that control you?" He said, "Leave my wife out of this."

Said Richard Nixon about Carter: "The president is delivering a lot of speeches in the Rose Garden—and where he stands, it's never grown so good before."

Abraham Lincoln: "A woman is the only thing I am afraid of that I know will not hurt me."

FDR's advice to speakers: "Be sincere, be brief, be seated."

Ronald Reagan: "I don't want to make an issue of my age—but I did once have a pet dinosaur."

Theodore Roosevelt: "I think there is only one quality worse than hardness of heart and that's softness of head."

LBJ: "If there is ever a price on your head—take it."

Prostitutes

The old saying, never mix busines with pleasure does not apply to the business of pleasure.

Ever since Eve gave Adam the apple, there has been a misunderstanding between the sexes about gifts.

The prostitute says, "You can call me mercenary or call me madam, but as I always tell my customers, just call me anytime."

Everything is put so nicely in England: A call girl is known as a maid to order.

A German call girl sounds so ominous. . . . When she calls—you listen.

Is an Eskimo hooker called a frostitute?

My friend was picked up by a prostitute. When they got to her room he was amazed by the college pennants and diplomas ornamenting the walls. "Are those yours?" he asked. She said, "Sure, I graduated from Penn State, I have a Masters from UCLA. I took my Ph.D. at Princeton." He said, "But how did a girl like you ever get into a profession like this?" She said, "I don't know—just lucky, I guess."

One girl approached an exec and said, "Please give, sir, to take a wayward girl off the street." He asked, "How much?" She smiled. "It depends on how long you want to keep her off it."

This man-about-town was cruising in his Bentley when he stopped beside a very attractive young thing and invited her to take a ride. As she got in, she slyly informed him she was a witch and could turn him into anything she wished. "Go ahead and try," he smiled. She leaned against him and whispered in his ear—and sure enough, he turned into a motel.

Irving was showing his out-of-town pal around the city and pointing out the beauties: "That's Helen—twenty dollars—and that's Betty—fifty—and the redhead is Gloria—eighty dollars." His pal said, "My God, aren't there any nice, respectable girls in this town?" Irving said, "Sure, but you couldn't afford their rates."

Proverbs and Other Sayings

A man is known by the company he thinks nobody knows he's keeping.

A bird in the hand is bad table manners.

Remember, it's always darkest before the light bill is paid.

The old believe everything, the middle aged suspect everything, the young know everything.

One way for husbands to get the last word—is to apologize.

The trouble with the rat race is that even if you win you're still a rat.

A smart girl is one who knows how to play tennis, piano, and dumb.

No man is lonely while eating spaghetti—it takes so much attention.

I saw one picture so dirty—you get arrested just for reading the marquee.

I don't know if drafting women is right—but it would make induction physicals more interesting.

As you go through life, trust absolutely no one except yourself, and when you play solitaire, cut the deck first.

We should be thankful for the fools who have lived and are now living in the world. Had it not been for them, the rest of us might not have succeeded.

An acquaintance is a person whom we know well enough to borrow from, but not well enough to lend to.

If efficiency experts are so smart—how come they're always working for somebody else?

There's one nice thing about being a kleptomaniac: You can always take something for it.

An unlucky patient is one who gets cavities in his false teeth.

A chrysanthemum by any other name would be easier to spell.

Let a smile be your umbrella—or your face will rust.

Better late than audited.

If at first you don't succeed—failure may be your thing!

Early to bed and early to rise is a sure sign you're fed up with TV.

A friend in need—is a pest.

Whatsoever a man sews—will rip.

Wife swapping is one thing I'm against: It's too much of a letdown when you get your real one back.

If you ever need a friend—buy a dog.

An American is a person who isn't afraid to criticize the president—but is always polite to traffic cops.

Psychiatrists

Psychiatry is very helpful—especially to psychiatrists.

My friend was put under the care of a noted Park Avenue shrink. "How soon will I be cured?" he asked. The doc said, "As soon as you run out of money."

The psychiatrist had this sign up in his office: YOUR FINANCIAL OBLIGATION DOES NOT END WITH SUICIDE.

"You can't win," Myron told me. "My shrink told me to talk

freely. After my monologue was over, he charged me $100."

To me, psychology is the science that tells you what you already know, in words you can't understand.

A man was telling his doctor about his frenzied attempts at slumber: "Last night I dreamt I was the only man in a nudist colony." The doc asked, "How did you sleep?" "Fine," said the patient, "but I didn't get any rest."

The woman entered and asked, "Are you the crazy doctor?" He said, "Well, madam, I am a psychiatrist." She said, "Good, I'm very nervous and have to see you—but first, how much do you charge?" He said, "Fifty dollars an hour." She hollered, "Fifty dollars? Good-bye—that crazy I'm not!"

My aunt told me about her psychiatrist: "I'm not too sure about him," she says. "During my last visit he insisted we try nude therapy. *I* was fully dressed and *he* was nude."

I'm not too sure my psychiatrist knows what he's doing. Rumor has it he won his diploma in a craps game.

"Now tell me why you feel your parents rejected you?" the shrink asked my neighbor. "Well, for one thing, there were those times when I would come home from school, and they weren't home!" The doc said, "Did it ever occur to you that they might be out taking a walk or doing errands?" "Yeah, but nobody takes the furniture with them when they go for a walk."

Henny Youngman goes to the psychiatrist. He says, "Doc, I have this terrible feeling that everybody's trying to take advantage of me!" The psychiatrist responds, "Relax, Mr. Youngman. It's a common thing. Everybody thinks people are trying to take advantage of them." Youngman sighs, "Doc, that's such a relief! How much do I owe you?" The psychiatrist answers, "How much have you got?"

A psychiatrist never has to worry about things—as long as other people do.

A shrink is a person who will listen to you as long as you don't make sense.

Whoever said, "A penny for your thoughts"—never had to pay for psychoanalysis.

The psychiatrist said to the Internal Revenue agent on the couch: "Nonsense! The whole world isn't against you. The people of the United States, perhaps, but not the whole world."

The man visited the doctor and told him: "You must help me. I have my entire ceiling and all the walls of my bedroom covered with pictures of Joan Collins, Cher, and Dolly Parton." The shrink said, "I'd like to help you, but I don't understand what your problem is?" The patient said, "My problem is that I sleep on my stomach!"

You go to a psychiatrist when you're slightly cracked—and keep going until you're completely broke.

Doctor Rose said to his patient, "If you think you're walking out of here cured after only three sessions—you're crazy."

The man said, "After six years and $30,000 worth of analysis, I finally realized what my trouble was: If I had the $30,000 in the first place—I wouldn't have needed the analysis."

"Lie down on the couch," the woman's psychiatrist said. She answered, "I'd rather not—that's how all my trouble started!"

The pretty little thing told the shrink, "I've been misbehaving and my conscience is bothering me." The doc said, "And you want something to strengthen your willpower?" "No—something to weaken my conscience."

My neighbor paid his psychoanalyst $50 to be cured of an inferiority complex. The same day he was fined $100 for talking back to a traffic cop.

I told my shrink, "I'm always forgetting things—what should I do?" The doc said, "Pay me in advance."

Sign in psychiatrist's office: IF YOU HAVE TROUBLES COME IN AND TELL US ABOUT THEM. IF NOT, COME IN AND TELL US HOW YOU DO IT.

Two psychiatrists meet at a convention. One says, "Charlie, I've got to see you about my inferiority complex." The other says, "But you're a psychiatrist!" The first says, "I know—but I'm not charging enough."

A psychiatrist was telling his colleague about a patient who believed in voodoo and black magic. "He doesn't realize that all that mumbo jumbo is ridiculous. Voodoo is just a lot of superstition." "You told him that, of course?" the colleague asked. "Oh, no, not I," said the doctor. "Do you think I want him to put a curse on me?"

The patient said to the shrink: "It's a long, long story. . . . If only I had the money to tell you."

The patient lying on the couch said to the shrink: "When you say I should forget the past—does that include the money I owe you?"

I went to a doctor for a ringing noise in my head and he cured me. Now I've got an unlisted head.

Puns

One day two old ladies went for a tramp in the woods— but he got away.

When the principal asked the teacher how long she planned to teach school, she replied, "From here to maternity."

The call girl recorded her daily activities in a loose-life notebook.

If your daughter lived with a fellow without the benefit of clergy, would you call the guy your sin-in-law?

Did you hear about the Swedish wife who walked out on her husband? She left his bed and smorgasbord.

Old accountants never die—they just lose their balance.

I asked the vice president if he plays an instrument. He said, "How's second fiddle?"

My cousin said, "Did *we* throw a big party in our basement last night!" I asked, "Was fat Uncle Charlie there?" He said, "Was he? He was the big party we threw in our basement!"

The waiter at the White House raves about his job: "I love to set a president."

There was a family of high-class potatoes who sent their daughter to the finest schools. She came home one day and announced to her parents she was quitting college to get married. She proudly told them she had met and fallen in love with that nationally famous newscaster, Dan Spud. Her mother shrieked, "My God, girl. After all that we have done for you, how could you marry a common tater?"

The woman about to be married for the eighth time explained, "I guess I'm just a sucker for a rite."

Two actors met at Sardi's: It was an "I" for an "I."

If your nose runs and your feet smell, you know you are built upside down.

Did I tell you that the drunk went to China to Taiwan on?

Have you heard about the lady of the evening who got a taxi license and is now known as "The Happy Hacker"?

They were driving down the road, and the little boy had been looking at all the signs: "Gee," he cried, "there sure are a lot of bullboards!"

When some local politician walked into the club, the band played "Here Comes the Bribe."

Men with money to burn have started many a girl playing with fire.

Sign at the entrance of a nudist's colony: PLEASE BARE WITH US.

The first nudist convention received little coverage.

This eighty-year-old woman has become quite a frivolous girl: "I'm seeing six gentlemen every day," she writes. "In the morning Will Power helps me out of bed, then I go to see John. Later Charley Horse comes by. When he leaves, Arthur Ritis shows up and stays the rest of the day, and goes from joint to joint. I enjoy a brief session with Jack Daniels at dinner, and after such a busy day, I'm glad to go to bed with Ben Gay!"

Rock music is frequently played by those who are stoned.

With traffic the way it is—it seems that the city is getting too big for its bridges.

Adam and Eve had their first serious spat over who wore the plants in the family.

Miniskirts are getting higher every day: The police say "the thigh is the limit."

The governor told me that because he was once signed to play for a major league baseball team, and often speaks at high school and college sports banquets, he is frequently introduced as an athletic supporter.

Those with money or access to same are usually loved principally for their purse-enality.

My flat-chested sister called to tell me she just bought a new bra: "This is the real decoy."

Definition of a diet: Girth control.

A lady sent this letter to the newspaper editor: "I am lonely and have had no attention for months. Please answer by return male."

Safety experts say all car passengers should be belted.

My friend tells me about a guy who goes to see a psychiatrist: "Doctor, doctor, you've got to help me. Every night I have a horrible dream—I dream I'm an Indian teepee. Other nights I go to sleep and I have the nightmare that I'm a wigwam." The doc says, "Some nights you dream you're a teepee and other nights you dream you're a wigwam?" "That's right!" "Your problem is obvious—you're too tents."

A politician is a guy who makes an issue of himself.

The rich old guy may have married the young gal to carry on the family name—but is he heir conditioned?

A career girl's mind moves her ahead—while a chorus girl's mind moves her behind.

I understand that many chess players have love affairs in Czechoslovakia: They love Czech mates.

The out-of-work stripper had no acts to grind.

A high school paper informed its readers that their football coach was up and around again "after being laid up for a week with a bad coed."

My wife would make a very good soccer goalie—I haven't scored in months.

My wife says I'm bisexual—I do it twice a month.

My brother says, "When people ask a bachelor like me what my philosophy on marriage is, I just tell them it's basically an institution that separates the men from the joys."

Fireproof is what you are when you marry the boss's daughter.

Then there was the vacationing tabby cat who wrote to her girlfriend: "Having a wonderful Tom—wish you were here."

A harried woman bought a sheet of stamps in a small post office and began licking them to stick onto a stack of letters. "Will you help me lick these?" she asked the clerk. "Can't," he replied. "Why not?" she asked. "I don't have a licker license," he said.

A young couple approached the desk in a big hotel. "We've just been married," the young man explained, "but we forgot to make reservations. Could you give us a suite for the night?" "Certainly," replied the clerk. "Would you like the bridal?" "Oh, no thanks," said the young man. "Now that we're married we're going to stop horsing around!"

In Russia, when the general secretary wants attention, he just snaps his fingers: I guess you could call him "The Red Snapper."

Rednecks

It's difficult to recognize a redneck—he usually covers it with a hood.

I just bought the world's thinnest book: *The History of Redneck Culture*.

What is smarter than a smart redneck? A dumb hillbilly.

Why do haircuts for rednecks cost eight dollars? The charge is two dollars per corner.

This announcement just came over the air: "A tornado ripped through redneck territory in West Virginia and caused $6 million in improvements."

An old farmer and his wife were leaning on their pigsty when the old lady wistfully murmured, "Tomorrow's our golden wedding anniversary, John. Let's kill the pig." The farmer pondered the suggestion, removed a stray straw from his sleeve, and wearily replied, "What's the use of murdering the pig for what happened fifty years ago?"

A southern gentleman is a redneck with money in the bank.

The old mountain man was watching the storekeeper unwrap a shipment of brightly colored men's pajamas. "What's that?" he asked. "Pajamas," replied the store- keeper. "What are they for?" "You wear them at night," the storekeeper explained. "Would you like to buy a pair?" "Nope," said the mountain man. "Don't go no place at night except to bed."

Two hillbillies were chatting in a bar: "Ain't it a shame about Suzie losing her mind?" one asked. The other replied, "No wonder. She worked in the same house with us for years and then she found out we wuz gettin' paid."

Two farmers' wives were discussing the problems of getting their husbands up in time for work. "How do you git Herb outta bed in the mornin'?" asked Myrtle. "Well," replied Olga, "ah jes open the bedroom door and let the cat in." Myrtle asked, "Does that git him up?" "Darn right," Olga said. "He sleeps with the dog."

Religion

"Please, God," the man prayed, "you know me. I'm always praying to you, and yet I have had nothing but misery, bad luck, and despair. Look at the butcher next door. He's never prayed in his life, and he has nothing but prosperity, health, and joy. How come a believer like me is always in trouble, and he is doing so well?" A voice boomed from beyond, "Because the butcher doesn't bug me, that's why!"

There are a lot of things to be said in favor of religion: The priests so far have the lowest divorce rate.

I know one New Yorker who's so religious he wears stained glass contacts.

The priest was lecturing to his audience that Jezebel was more to be pitied than censured—we should pray for her. One listener shouted out, "I've been praying for her for years, but I never got her!"

Here are some tasty jokes to set before the prince: God called together his writers. "Gentlemen, I have a big show coming up next week on Mount Sinai and I need some material." "How about: Thou shalt not steal!" one of them volunteered. "Thou shalt not kill!" suggested another. "Thou shalt not—" "Wait!" thundered the Lord. "How many times have I told you I can't use one-liners!"

Brown suddenly got religious and was being examined by the rabbi before being fully accepted into the faith. "You have renounced sin, I'm sure?" the rabbi asked. Brown said, "Yes, sir." The man of the cloth asked, "You'll be honest and fair to all?" Brown said, "Of course." The rabbi asked, "You understand that means paying all your debts?" Brown said, "Now, hold on, Rabbi, that's out of line—you're talking business, not religion!"

Jones swore more than any member of the congregation. The parson took him aside on Sunday and said, "Every time you swear you must give ten dollars to the nearest stranger—that will cure you." As Jones left the preacher he stubbed his toe and silently handed ten dollars to a woman just entering the church. "Okay," she whispered, "but can you wait till after the services?"

Two fellows opened a butcher shop and prospered. Then a preacher came to town, and one of the butchers was saved. On Thanksgiving he tried to persuade his partner to accept salvation also, but it was to no avail. "Why not, Sam?" asked the born-again guy. "Listen, Charlie," the other butcher said. "If I get religion too, who's going to weigh the turkeys?"

After this deacon delivered his exciting sermon about loving your neighbor as yourself, one congregant asked him privately, "Do you love *your* neighbor?" The deacon replied, "I try to—but she won't let me."

The priest explained, "There's a time and place for everything. For instance, saying 'But enough about me—let's talk about you!' is fine at a cocktail party—but in a confession box, not so good!"

Most people have some sort of religion. At least they know what church they're staying away from.

No matter how many new translations of the Bible come out, people still sin the same way.

"He may preach against gambling and cheating," one parishioner admitted, "but I have nothing but praise for our new minister." His neighbor agreed: "I noticed that when the collection plate was passed."

After the services, Myron remarked to his friend, "Did you hear Roberts snoring in church this morning?" "Yes I did—he woke up me."

The rich old couple was sitting in church, when the collection plate came around. "Don't put in more than a dollar," advised the lady. "Look, Prunella," said her husband, "Andrew Carnegie gave over half a million for his seat in heaven; John D. Rockefeller gave over a million. Where the hell do you think I'll sit for a dollar?"

The Italian kid stayed out of school on Chanukuh. The next day the teacher said, "Why did you stay out of school on the holiday? You're not Jewish." The boy replied, "Yes, Teacher—but I'm in sympathy with the movement."

The youngster was praying: "Please, God, I don't want to

go to heaven if my piano teacher is going to be there—and please put vitamins in candy instead of spinach."

The minister was explaining the facts of life to his daughter. The youngster listened attentively as her father told her about the birds and bees, then asked, "Does God know about this?"

The Sunday school girl asked her friend, "Do you really think there's a devil?" The other said, "It'll probably turn out like Santa Claus—it'll probably be my father."

Listen, I'm for Santa Claus. . . . Any guy who drops into your house only once a year—and doesn't want to drink, eat, or stay over—could be my friend for life.

Two churches were on either side of a street. The marquee on one, a liberal church, announced: THERE AIN'T NO HELL. The other one retorted: THE HELL THERE AIN'T.

A church marquee had this legend: YOU THINK IT'S HOT HERE!

One minister I know has on his calling card: "Let me knock the hell out of you!"

In a small village church, a poor widow put one dollar in the collection plate, twice her usual offering. The pastor noticed and asked why. She said, "I'm thankful that my grandchildren are visiting." Two weeks later she put a five-dollar bill in the plate and explained, "They just left."

The rabbi told me he has very strict morals: He would rather not perform a wedding ceremony. I asked, "Why? What has that got to do with morals?" He explained, "My conscience will not let me take part in a game of chance."

Too many people who occasionally go to church expect a million-dollar answer to a one-dollar contribution.

I believe in the Bible all the way: I sure respect Noah for building the Ark to preserve the species and put two of everything on board—but why did he have to include mosquitos, roaches, fleas, and Communists?

There's a definite return to religion in this country. A recent poll showed that 60 percent of all Americans believe in miracles: Half of them are churchgoers and the others put their faith in the lottery.

The Three Wise Men were on their way to Bethlehem. Suddenly, one of them ground his camel to a halt: "Now listen, fellows," he said to the other two. "Remember, no mentioning how much we paid for the gifts."

Las Vegas is the most religious city in the world: At any hour you can walk into a casino and hear someone say, "Oh, my God!"

I've got a friend who's Catholic and whose mother is an atheist: When he goes to confession he brings his lawyer along.

Humor is a divine quality, and God has the greatest sense of humor of all. He must have, otherwise he wouldn't have made so many politicians.

The minister was discussing with some politicians what it must be like in heaven: "One thing you can be sure of—we will have a good rest. No graft, bribes, fraud, lying." One pol interrupted, "Of course not—that's not where our politicians have gone."

God heals—and the doctor takes the fees.

Union officials have only one thing against God: He worked a six-day week.

If Moses had been a committee, we would have had eighty-nine commandments instead of ten.

The first thing today's motorist prays for when he gets to church on Sunday morning is a place to park the car.

A Baptist church got rid of unwanted cars in their parking lot after they erected this sign: NO PARKING—VIOLATORS WILL BE BAPTIZED.

The preacher was telling his flock about a biblical character who had a thousand wives and concubines and fed them all ambrosia. "Never mind what he fed *them,*" a guy yelled from the back of the congregation. "What did *He* eat?"

"Jane," the Sunday school Bible teacher asked, "tell the class, who was the first man?" She cried, "Oh, please, not even my mother knows!"

Father Bob was having dinner with Rabbi Mann: "Come on," said Father Bob, "when are you going to let yourself have some ham?" The rabbi said, "At your wedding!"

Most people hate to think they're missing out on anything. A recent bulletin from the Bible Society mentioned that there are now 143 officially recognized sins. Since then, thousands of letters from all over the world have poured in, asking for a copy of the complete list.

The minister asked, "Do you know where little boys and girls go when they do bad things?" The bad boy answered, "Sure—in the back of the churchyard."

I've got news for you: I read the last page of the Bible, and it's all going to turn out okay.

I think those TV evangelists are getting a bad rap. Their ministries do bring joy and prosperity into lives—*their* lives. Obviously the main concern of these evangelists is the hereafter: They're here after our money.

The TV minister arrived in New York and was given a beautiful suite at a class hotel. When he walked in the bedroom, he saw this gorgeous redhead sitting on the bed. He called the desk and screamed, "What's the meaning of this outrage? How dare you embarrass me this way? I'm a most distinguished evangelist, and you have the audacity to humiliate me this way? I'm going to sue this hotel for every cent it has!" At this point, the girl got off the bed and started to leave. The minister turned to her and said, "Just a moment, miss, nobody's talking to you!"

One listener called the TV evangelist and asked, "How do you really feel about the ladies?" He said, "Every man should have a girl for love, companionship, and sympathy—preferably at three different addresses."

There are those times in life when it's useless to try to hold a man to anything he says—when he's madly in love, drunk, or a TV evangelist.

"Actually, there's a lot to be said for sin you know," one clergyman said to another. "After all, if it didn't exist, we'd be out of a job."

My wife is so Catholic we can't get fire insurance—too many candles in our house.

Hollywood Catholics are different: They're the only Catholics who give up matzo balls for Lent.

Rich People

I know a guy so rich now that when he flies, his wallet is classified as carry-on luggage. Would you believe, this guy is so wealthy he has a sleep-in banker?

My rich uncle says, "One of the advantages of being rich is that all of your faults are called eccentricities."

The millionaire had to buy another yacht—his first one got wet.

As a youngster, my rich cousin was so loaded, he was the only kid in town with a Rolls Royce tricycle. . . . Who else do you know had a Gucci Christmas tree? . . . Not only does he have a friend at Chase Manhattan—his friend *is* Chase Manhattan: When the bank needs a loan, they bypass the treasury and phone my cousin direct.

Don't knock the rich: When was the last time you were hired by somebody poor?

My neighbor is a man of untold wealth—because he never reports it on his income tax return.

With my neighbor, money is no object. The other day he went for a drive. His gas station attendant said, "Regular or high test?" He hollered, "What regular or high test? Gimme the best—homogenized!"

You can't talk rich without mentioning Texas: One Texas teenager told his father he needed some oil for his hair—so his father bought him Oklahoma. I also know this magnate from Houston who bought an oil well because he was always running out of fluid for his cigarette lighter.

The billionaire was trying to impress his old friend, who wouldn't play along: "I got a stretch limousine with a chauffeur." "So what, quite a few people got limos with chauffeurs." The billionaire continued: "You should see my house: It's got fifty rooms in it." "I've heard of fifty-room houses before." The billionaire kept trying: "I got an eighteen-hole golf course, too." His friend asked, "Inside the house?"

Sure a lot of people have money to burn—why not? It's cheaper than gas!

I've got news for you: There are a lot of rich people around. One Long Island neighborhood I know is so rich the high school mascot is a mink.

There is one rich school I know that is now called Our Lady of the Dow-Jones Average.

Money brings everything to you—especially relatives and girls. "Darling," my uncle said to the pretty little thing, "I don't know how to tell it to you—but I lost all my money. I haven't a cent in the world." She said, "That won't make any difference to me, sweetheart. I'll love you just as much even if I never see you again."

One businessman, already rated a millionaire by his associates, continued slaving sixty hours a week, including weekends, without a vacation. His doctor asked him,

"Why do you work so hard just to make more and more money?" He said, "I'm curious to see if there's some income my wife can't live beyond."

Cynthia was telling us about the amorous old millionaire who asked her to marry him: "I just happened to have the combination that opened his safe: 38-24-36." The old boy asked her, "How do I know you're not marrying me for my money?" She said, "We're both taking a risk. How do I know you won't go broke in a year or so?"

The self-made millionaire was addressing the graduating class at his business school. "All my success in life," he said, "I owe to one thing—pluck, pluck, and more pluck." One kid in the back said, "That's great, sir. But will you please tell us something about *who* to pluck and *how*?"

How easy it is for a man to die rich, if he will but be contented to live miserable.

Riddles

Riddle me these—only I don't want your smart answers, just your smart-ass ones:

Questions

1. Why was the pretty nurse nicknamed appendix?
2. What is the difference between lightning and electricity?
3. Why wasn't the elephant allowed on the airplane?
4. What does a Jewish kid say when he gets bar-mitzvahed in China?
5. How can you tell if a politician is lying?

6. How can you beat the first four races at the track every day?
7. A man was driving a black truck. His lights were not on. The moon was not out. A lady was crossing the street. How did he see her?
8. What's the difference between Congress and a kindergarten?
9. In show business it's take the money and run. What is it in politics?
10. What kind of nut is a guy who goes to see a topless girlie show?
11. What is the best way to see flying saucers?

Answers

1. Because all the doctors wanted to take her out.
2. You don't have to pay for lightning.
3. Because his trunk was too big to fit under the seat.
4. "Today I am a man-darin."
5. His lips are moving.
6. Don't show up till the fifth.
7. It was a bright, sunny day.
8. A kindergarten has adult supervision.
9. In politics it's run and *then* take the money.
10. A chestnut.
11. Pinch the waitress.

Romance and Dating

I asked my friend, "How come every time you go on a date, it's with a fat gal?" He replied, "Well, I'll tell you. To me, a date is fun, and I like a lot of fun."

Any girl can live on love—if he's wealthy.

Is sex dirty? Only if it's done right.

He who loves and runs away—may live to love another day.

Never trust a girl who says she loves you more than anybody else in the world: It proves she's been experimenting.

All the world loves a lover—except the husband.

"Darling," she whispered, "will you still love me after we are married?" He considered this for a moment and then replied, "I think so—I've always been especially fond of married women."

My niece cried, "He is the man for me! He's handsome, he's sexy, he's smart, he's funny, he's strong, he's—" I interrupted, "He's married." She said, "So—nobody's perfect."

This playboy talks about this playgirl: "The first night we met, we exchanged numbers. She gave me her phone number and I gave her my savings account number."

The disco was jammed. On the dance floor, a pretty little redhead said to a young man, "Thank you for the dance." He said, "What dance? I was just pushing my way through to the bar."

My nephew told me, "You know I used to go with this girl until I found out she spent $15,000 a year on dresses." I asked, "So you broke up over that?" He said, "Yeah, now I go out with her dressmaker."

A rather homely young farmer, proposing to his sweetheart, confessed: "I know I'm not much to look at." "That's all right," she said. "You'll be out in the fields most of the time."

A bachelor said he'd visited a computer dating office and listed his specifications: He wanted someone who is on the small side, likes water sports, is gregarious, looks good in formal dress, and says little. . . . He drew a penguin.

I was a judge at a pet show and was instructed to look for obedience, friendliness, loyalty, and good grooming. I told my instructors: Forget the pets—those are the makings of a great girlfriend.

Some people really know how to take the romance out of everything. I recently heard one doctor refer to Cupid as the world's first acupuncturist.

It's probably true that men don't make passes at girls who wear glasses. Often, though, they will make them at girls who drain them.

Russia

I know a Russian comedian, which is not so odd—his whole country is laughable.

Now that my friend is out of the U.S.S.R., he can afford to laugh.

In Russia when you're asked embarrassing questions, you're being interviewed by the KGB. In America, you're being interviewed by TV reporters.

In Russia, when you dial information—you'd better have some.

Here there are talk shows. In Russia they have "don't talk shows."

My Russian friend is happy to be here and loves to compare societies: "In the U.S., it's 'innocent until proven guilty.' In Russia, it's 'guilty until you die.' "

Here you have freedom of speech. You can go up to the president of the United States and say, "I don't like the president of the United States." You can also do the same thing in Russia: You can go up to the party chief and say, "I don't like the president of the United States."

Disneyland is made up of fantasy and fairy tales. The Russians have the same thing: They're called elections.

Only in Russia do they have loose-leaf history books.

My Russian neighbor says, "At home I never wore tennis shoes. They're for running. If you ran in Russia, they'd shoot you."

The slogan for the Russian credit card is "Don't leave home."

The big commercial on Moscow TV is: "You asked for it, you got it—hard labor."

The favorite game in Siberia is hide and stay hidden.

My neighbor got out of Russia in a very unusual way— alive.

People don't know they have comedians there. They do. They're dead, but they're there.

My aunt's husband told me, "I left the U.S.S.R. on Thanksgiving Day. It was July, but any day you leave Russia is Thanksgiving."

A man is sitting in a park in Moscow studying a Hebrew book. A KGB agent comes over and asks, "What's the point of studying Hebrew? You can't go to Israel." The student says he knows that, but they speak Hebrew in heaven. The KGB man says, "Heaven? Maybe you'll go to hell!" The student answers, "Well, I already know Russian."

Russian comedians are from the real Borscht Belt.

Russian comedians must be careful of what jokes they tell. If they say, "Take my wife, please," when they get home—she's gone!

Communism is when the state owns everything. Capitalism is when your wife does.

There are a few nice things about Russia: For example, there are plenty of parking places. Trouble is, they've got nothing to park.

Vacation is the word Americans use to describe going someplace for fun and to get away from it all. The English call it *holiday*. In Russia, it's known as *defecting*.

There is an amusement park in Siberia called Dissidentland: When they take you for a ride, they don't bring you back.

The president asked the Soviet premier if he objected to jokes about himself. The premier said, "No, I like jokes about myself." The president asked, "Are there any such jokes?" The premier said, "Enough to fill three labor camps."

When you think about it, it's no wonder the Reds pass us in some fields: They don't have to spend all their money and time in fighting communism.

Did you read that *Pravda* started a letters-to-the-editor column this year? It's a little different from the *Post*'s version: They publish all beefs, criticisms, and complaints, but you have to give your name, address—and next of kin.

The president says, "We need a man to talk back to the Russians." I know a thousand cab drivers who will do that.

In the Soviet Union, nobody dares throw eggs at the Red officials: If the people had eggs they would eat them.

A Muscovite entered the police station and reported his parrot was missing. "Does your parrot talk?" the officials asked. "Yes," answered the frightened comrade. "But any political opinions he expresses are strictly his own."

This one official explained, "I really do feel toward the U.S.S.R. the way I feel toward my wife—I don't love it, I can't change it, and I can't help dreaming of something better."

Russia is where you are allowed to go anywhere they please.

The last time I was in Moscow, I saw this sign in the synagogue: IN PRAYING HERE—YOU KEEP YOUR EYES CLOSED AT YOUR OWN RISK.

The newspaper *Pravda* is running a contest for the best political joke. First prize is twenty years.

The Moscow University professor told his class that interplanetary junketing was distinctly in the cards: "We will be able to travel to Mars, Pluto, and Venus." One student in the back of the lecture hall raised his hand: "When," he asked, "can we travel to America?"

The prisoner stood before the three judges in Uzbek. ". . . And your punishment is ten years of hard labor in Siberia! Have you anything to say?" The prisoner said, "Comrade Judges, the United States is a terrible, decadent, capitalistic country. It savagely exploits the proletariat. Hunger, racism is everywhere in the land—is that not right?" "Right," the three judges agreed. "So if you want to really punish me—why not send me there?"

The Russians know nothing about interior decorating. Why would anybody with good taste prefer an iron curtain to Venetian blinds?

Russia had a new track star—a fantastic runner. Every day he ran twenty or twenty-five miles—but they caught him and took him back to Russia.

A couple, both ninety years old, recently celebrated their seventieth wedding anniversary in their communist village. A reporter asked, "How did you manage to live so long?" The man replied, "You call this living?'"

Living in my house is like living in Russia: I can say anything I want, provided my wife okays it.

In Russia, two men are talking on the street: "What is your opinion of the recent party resolution?" "Same as yours." "Then I arrest you in the name of the secret police."

What's the difference between the United States and the

Soviet Union? In the United States everybody talks and nobody listens. In the Soviet Union everybody listens and nobody talks.

An American official was playing cards with a Russian diplomat. The Red lost all he had, and offered to stake his wife for 500 rubles. The American thought the price was too high. The Russian reduced it to 200. The Yankee still refused to go along with it. "What would you pay for her?" the Russian finally asked. "Nothing," the American said. "Okay," the diplomat said. "You can have her."

Another Russian diplomat was telling his colleague, ". . . it's a rotten government," when a KGB agent grabbed him and said, "You're under arrest." The diplomat asked, "What for?" "Because you said it's a rotten government." The diplomat protested, "But I never said *what* government." The agent replied, "No good—there is only one rotten government, and you know it!"

Salesmen

A good salesman can handle any situation: The store-owner said, "Did you ever see anything as unsettled as the weather the last few days?" The salesman answered, "Well, there's your bill here!"

Said one traveling salesman to another, "What's the matter, Max, you only had a sandwich for lunch? You on a diet?" "No," said Max. "On commission."

The traveling man and his wife arrived on a combined business and pleasure trip. Tired and hungry from the long journey, the husband ordered a large meal. The wife made some rapid calculations, then complained, "Jim, that adds up to about eight thousand calories." The husband replied, "Who cares? I'll put 'em on my expense account."

This salesman was trying to sell me a computer. "If you're selling these machines way under price, like you say," I told him, "how can you make a living?" The man said, "Simple—we make our money fixing them."

Good salesman? The only orders he takes are from his wife.

The greatest salesman was the one who sold two milking machines to a farmer with one cow and then took the cow as a down payment.

Secretaries

I told my secretary: "You are the nicest. You are not only pretty but you dress well, you're patient and romantic, your manners are perfect—everybody loves you." She said shyly, "Gee, thanks." I said, "And now we will discuss what to do about your typing, spelling, filing, shorthand, punctuation, and ignorance."

I asked one new secretary if she could take dictation. She said she believed in democracy.

I told one new girl, "Always add a column of figures at least three times before you show me the result." The next day she came in with a broad smile. "I added these figures ten times." I said, "Good—I like a girl to be thorough." She said, "And here are the ten answers."

The boss's secretary makes very few mistakes—she never does anything.

The secretary was visited by one of the other secretaries in the hospital. "How are things at the office?" she asked. "You don't have to worry about a thing," the visitor said. "We're all sharing your work: Mae is making coffee, Sarah is doing the crossword puzzles, I'm watching TV, and, oh yes, Mary is making it with the boss."

I had one secretary who worked eight hours and slept eight hours—I had to fire her because they were the same eight hours. My other secretary spent so much time on personal calls, the phone company threatened to take away our commercial listing.

Two big executives were creating an expense account at lunch. One said, "Life is unfair. I've got a business that's gone bad and a secretary that won't."

One big office has a gorgeous secretary who has everything a man could ask for—so they're all asking.

The head of a secretarial school was interviewing a pretty young applicant: "In our classes in shorthand and typing," he said, "we stress accuracy above everything." The girl asked, "What about speed?" He replied, "Well, out of last year's classes, fifteen girls married their employers within the first six months."

This secretary was complaining to a friend, "If it weren't for the good salary, the air conditioning, the swimming pool, the free theater tickets, the four-week vacations, and the generous pension and profit-sharing plans, I swear I'd quit this miserable job."

My last secretary was fired because she lacked experience: All she knew was typing and shorthand.

My neighbor says, "I don't mess with secretaries: If at first I don't succeed, they're fired—that's all."

My uncle says, "My secretary thinks I'm really small-minded because I believe words can be only spelled one way."

At least my secretary's honest. Last week she called in lazy.

One boss was told by his secretary, "If I don't get a raise, I'm going to start wearing long skirts."

Another boss told his secretary, "You've been here two months now, and I'm happy to say that your typing has improved considerably. However, it hasn't gotten so good that you can stop wearing those tight sweaters yet."

The boss yelled at his pretty secretary, "We may have made love a few times, but who said you could be late for work?" She said, "My lawyer."

The secretary confessed to me the other day that she was tired of trying to build a career. "I want to get married— but the trouble is I don't want to hitch up with a mere go-getter. I want an already-got!"

The secretary was bragging about her beautiful allover tan. "How did you get it?" the stenographer asked. "I did everything under the sun," she said happily.

Sex

Everybody goes to doctors, lawyers, psychiatrists for advice. I give it to you without reservation and without knowing what I'm talking about. I have discovered that sex is bad for one—for two, great. I've discovered that a normal man wants only one thing from a woman— companionship. Of course, I'm talking about a very old man. But a man is as old as the woman he feels.

One fan wrote me: "I've been married to the same woman for forty-five years and it's starting to go dull. I know her every move before she makes it." I answered, "Look, pal, *she moves*—don't complain."

One character talked to me about his love life: "I feel bad—I cheated on my wife." I asked, "How many times?" He growled, "How the hell do I know? I'm a lover—not an accountant!"

The beautiful young thing cried to me: "What can I do? Help me—I'm pregnant." I asked, "Who is the father?" She cried, "How should I know—my mother never would let me go steady."

One nice lady writes to ask, "When should parents tell their children about sex?" My anwer: "When they're old enough to understand—and before they're old enough to do what they already did."

The girl asked me, "Do you think a girl has to be an easy mark to be popular with men?" I said, "Well, it will sure keep her from having a lot of enemies."

One girl told me, "I'm against free love." I said, "Would you accept a Diners Club card?"

One nice girl asks, "Where do nice girls meet nice men these days?" I told her, "There are singles clubs all over town and in the Catskills. The girls go to look for husbands—and the husbands go to look for girls."

Women are a problem, but they're the kind of problem I enjoy wrestling with—with no holds barred.

A man told me, "I'm eighty and I just married a girl of twenty. My problem is I'm afraid I won't be able to satisfy her—any suggestions?" "Take in a boarder," I advised. Three months later he called and told me my advice worked: His wife was having a baby. I asked, "What about the boarder?" He said, "She's having a baby too."

Advice to single girls: Never look for a husband—look for a single man.

My friend the lover received this letter: "If good girls go to heaven—where do bad girls go?" The love sage answered, "Anywhere they want."

One sexy Hollywood beauty was giving free advice: "I owe my success to being in the right place at the right time." I said, "Right—in the producer's bedroom when he's there!"

Q: Is it true that behind every successful man there is always a woman?
A: Yes, and usually she catches him.

A friend pleads: "How can I find out what my girl really thinks of me?" "Marry her!" I advised.

Another asked, "With sex so dangerous these days, what do you suggest?" I told him, "It's better to skip the sex entirely and go right to the cigarette."

Q: Why is sex so popular?
A: It has no calories!

The young lady told me: "The man I marry must be bright and colorful and entertaining, yet, when I'm in the mood for peace and quiet, I want him to remain silent. I want him to be up to the minute in sports and politics and the news of the day—and I insist that he stay home nights with me!" I answered, "You don't want a husband—you want a TV set."

The definition of petting and necking is the study of human anatomy in braille.

Sex is everywhere. After three years in the Chicago office of a big insurance company, a girl was transferred to the New York headquarters. The boss called her in on arrival and said, "I hope you like it here. The work will be the same as in Chicago." She said, "Fine, kiss me and let's get started."

The purest definition of fear is the first time you discover that you can't make love a second time. The purest definition of panic is the second time you discover that you can't make love the first time.

These two old farmers wandered into the disco to watch

the convulsions. "Look at 'em dance," one groaned. "If any of my dogs started actin' like that, I'd race 'em off to the vet to be pumped full o' worm powder!"

The spent Romeo was bemoaning the fact that when he retired in a couple of months, he would have only an old-age pension to live on. "My dear," his wife said, "I've got a surprise for you!" She led him to the window and pointed to the row of houses across the street. "Every time we made love," she said, "I put ten cents in the jar. We now own all those houses and we have nothing to worry about." He sighed, "And to think if I had given you all my business, we would have had the pub on the corner as well."

The couple were on their honeymoon at a motel next to a church, where a watchman rang the bell every hour through the night. "Tell you what, darling," the ardent groom said. "Let's make love every time that bell rings." The next morning, pale and exhausted, the groom staggered from the hotel to find the watchman. "Here's some money," he said. "It's yours if you'll only ring that bell every two hours." The watchman answered, "I can't. Early last evening a young lady paid me to ring it every half hour."

Personally, I don't think sex is that important. I much prefer a musical concert. But lately I've begun to notice that if I don't get to a concert for a year and a half, I don't miss it.

"It's good to have sex with a mature woman," my brother suggests. "You take your clothes off, and they wash and iron them."

How can you tell if you're in love? You ask yourself, "Would I mind being destroyed financially by this person?"

The thing that takes up the least amount of time and causes the most amount of trouble is sex.

Courtship is a period when a man pursues a girl who is running toward him.

A girl who says she'll go through anything for a man— usually has his bankbook in mind.

The gold digger advises: "A woman should never chase after a man—unless, of course, he's getting away."

The only difference between love and insanity is in the duration of the disease.

The best gift for Valentine's Day is sex: You can take it on a trip and it doesn't need batteries.

Adam may have had his troubles, but he never had to listen to Eve talk about the other men she could have married.

This blonde actress scoffs at the idea of going to a psychiatrist: "Why should I lie down on a man's couch and then pay him?"

My ex-girlfriend lectures, "A girl can wait for the right man to come along, but in the meantime that still doesn't mean she can't have a wonderful time with all the wrong men."

A man who had been going out with a young woman came to call on her one night carrying a little box in his pocket. At what he judged to be the right time, he pulled out the box, opened it, and showed his beloved an engagement ring with her name engraved inside. "I want you to be my wife," he said. "I don't know how to tell you this," she replied, "but I love another." "Tell me his name!" her suitor demanded. "No, no," cried the woman. "You're looking for a fight!" "I am not," shot back the man. "I just want to sell him this ring."

A man said to his date: "Why don't we go to my apartment—sex is good for relieving arthritis." She said, "But I don't have arthritis." He said, "What's the matter? You don't believe in preventive medicine?"

The disgruntled lass was complaining bitterly to her roommate about last night's blind date: "Not only did the bum lie to me about the size of his yacht," she said, "but he made me do all the rowing."

The seventy-year-old patient explained his predicament to his doctor. He had recently married a gorgeous twenty-

year-old, but, unfortunately, every night at bedtime, when
he and his bride were ready, he would fall asleep. The
doctor wrote out a prescription. The old man said, "You
mean that now I'll be able to—?" The doc said, "No, I'm
afraid I can't do anything about *that*—but now *she'll* fall
asleep too."

My niece doesn't mind if a man loves her and leaves
her—if he leaves her enough.

It's not hard to meet my niece: Just open your wallet and
there she is.

The modern girl has no difficulty keeping the wolf from
the door—she invites him in.

Men don't meet the modern girl—she overtakes them.

In the old days, man's greatest fear was that a woman
would take it to heart; today, his greatest fear is that a
woman will take it to court.

What with all the sex films, adult books, and strip clubs,
the best way to avoid sex is to get married.

The call girl said: "Who says hookers have it easy? How
would you like to get dressed all the time just to go on a
coffee break?"

The hysterical girl called her psychiatrist: "You've got to
help me. I love him. He loves me. We like the same things.
When we're apart we're miserable. I don't know what to
do." The doctor said, "I don't get it. You sound like you're
completely compatible and in love. What's the problem?"
She said, "What's the problem? The problem is what shall
I tell my husband?"

The girl called the sex therapist and said, "Remember
when you told me the way to a man's heart was through
his stomach? Well, last night I found a new route. . . .
Now I need some birth control pills." The doc asked,
"What's his occupation?" The girl said, "Army." "Active
or retired?" "If he wasn't active I wouldn't need these
bloody pills, would I?"

The young man was making love to the model and said, "I don't have a lot of money like my millionaire friend, I can't afford a big diamond like my millionaire friend—but I love you." The doll said, "I love you, too—but tell me more about your millionaire friend."

The blonde bombshell said to her date, "There's something I must get off my chest." "What is it?" he asked. "Your eyes."

I know a gal who is very sanitary-minded—she's trying to take some filthy rich guy to the cleaners.

Then there's the debutante who called up her boyfriend to advise him: "We'll have to postpone our marriage for a little while—I've just eloped with another man."

"Your new boyfriend is somewhat of a loafer," Barbara's dad grumbled. "What does the lad do, anyhow?" She explained, "He inherits."

Susan decided on a vacation in Rome. "Did you pick up any Italian?" her friend asked when she returned. "I'll say I did," she said enthusiastically. "Okay—let me hear you say some words." "I didn't learn any words."

The last remaining bachelor girl in the office came in grinning one morning and began to pass out cigars to everybody. "What's the idea?" they asked. She displayed a diamond ring and cried out, "It's a boy—six feet tall and weighs 190 pounds."

The sexpot's advice: "You've got to take care of yourself: no fatty foods, no liquors, and only one cigarette after you make love—I'm down to two packs a day."

After a wild night, the star said to the pretty little doll, "Do you tell your mother everything you do?" She cried, "Certainly not, my mother couldn't care less—it's my husband who's so darn inquisitive."

Two teenagers were walking home from school and stopped to rest on a park bench. "Jane," he cooed, "I'm groping for words to express my love." She said, "Well, move your hands, John. I ain't got no dictionary there."

On a visit to the zoo, one kid asked his mom, "How do lions make love?" She answered, "I really don't know, dear. Most of your father's friends are Knights of Columbus."

"My darling dearest," sighed the young man, quoting from a picture he saw the night before, "I love you, I worship you, you are the sun and the moon to me—and the stars and all life." She said, "No, please, don't," as she tried to disengage herself. "What's wrong my one and only?" he panted. She said, "I just don't want to get serious." He said, "But wait—who's serious?"

My neighbor was worried about how her little daughter would react to the new sex education program in school. One morning the kid came home and said, "Mommy, guess what? We learned how to make babies today." The mother screamed, "What?" Then calmly she asked, "Tell me, dear, how do you make babies?" The kid said, "Easy—you drop the *y* and add *ies*."

One father was complaining about his son: "I sent my boy to college and he spent four years going to parties, having fun, necking, lovemaking, drinking, and carrying on. It's not that I'm sorry I sent him—I should have gone myself."

After a romantic evening on his couch, the young man said, "Isn't it nice here?" His girl said, "You silly jerk—it's nice anywhere."

The young man joined her at the bar and said, "You look so sad—what's your problem?" She said, "Everything I do is wrong." The boy's eyes lighted up. "Great," he said. "Let's go up to my room."

The eighteen-year-old single girl had just been told by her doctor that she was going to have a baby. "If only I had gone to the movies with my parents that night," she sobbed. "Well, why didn't you?" the doctor asked. "I couldn't," the girl cried. "The film was rated X."

I asked my sister-in-law, "If you came home and found a strange man there, what would you do?" She snapped, "I'd scream 'finders keepers.' "

A man in a record shop was discussing the sexy album covers. "One customer came in mad. He said he'd bought an album a month ago and just discovered there was no record in it."

The young man showed his date a lot of love and affection: He took her to a drive-in movie and let her peek into the other cars.

"Was your father very shy?" "Shy? My mother told me that if he hadn't been so shy I'd be five years older now."

The problem with extramarital sex is that you have to be married to have it.

You can learn plenty about sex at the movies—that is, if you don't let the picture disturb you.

Help keep prostitutes off the streets: Take them to your apartment.

There will be sex after death—we just won't be able to feel it.

"Did you get a nice Valentine from your fella?" I asked one secretary. She confided, "I've broken up with him. He keeps begging me to make love to him—pleading—and I keep refusing, explaining that I'm saving myself until I get married." I said, "But you just said you've broken up with him." She said, "Yes, I did that last month—but the sex-crazy nut has phoned me every week since, asking 'Are you married yet?' "

Sex over fifty-five can be dangerous: Always pull over to the side of the freeway.

The girl at the singles bar said to the handsome man sitting next to her: "They say that people with opposite characteristics make the best marriages." He said, "That's why I'm looking for a girl with money."

A maid in a wealthy home, an unmarried girl of nineteen, tearfully told her mistress that she was pregnant. Anxious to keep the girl and to help her through her distress, the couple agreed to adopt the illegitimate infant. Next year, same situation, same solution. A couple of years later, ditto. Finally, the maid quit. "I'm sorry," she explained, "but I can't work in a home where there are so many children."

I respond to most appeals—but my favorite charity is still the sex drive.

A woman's best beauty aid is a nearsighted man.

A thing of beauty keeps you broke forever.

It's good to be a woman—you don't have to worry about getting men pregnant.

Too much of a good thing is wonderful.

The ends justify the jeans.

I lived through the sexual revolution and never even got wounded.

Chaste makes waste.

A fox is a wolf who sends flowers.

I know a woman so loose:
 At school she was voted the girl most likely to concede . . .
 She could hardly wait until she got married. In fact, she didn't . . .
 She's the kind of pushover you can make—even if you play your cards wrong . . .
 She has a slight impediment in her speech: She can't say no . . .
 That fur coat does a lot for her—but then, she did a lot for it.

You know why the Garden of Eden was called Paradise? It's because Adam was a man, Eve was a woman, and the headache hadn't been invented yet.

This guy asked his wife if she'd like to go to a nudist camp. She said: "I'd like to go, but I have nothing to wear."

You know the hardest thing to do in a nudist camp? To keep looking in a person's face while talking to them!

My niece told me, "I once went steady with an undertaker's son, until I found out he just wanted me for my body."

Whoever put Bibles in hotel rooms missed the point. When a man's alone with a woman in a hotel room, whatever he's praying for, he's already got!

My friend told me, "What a date I had last night! Wow! I took this great-looking broad up to my apartment to see my etchings and it worked! She bought three of them."

One guy told the clerk, "I'd like a size 7¼ bra for my wife." The clerk asked how he measured. He said, "With my hat."

Worrying about the past is like trying to make birth control pills retroactive.

My doctor told my wife and I that we should enjoy sex every night. Now we'll never see each other.

One twin came home one morning after staying out all night and bragged to her sister, "Well, kid, we're not identical twins anymore."

Just think what a drive-in would be called if there were nothing on the screen.

When a guy asks a gal if she has a parking space he could use, he's not talking about his car: He's talking about his shoes.

I've about had it with women undressing me with their eyes. What's wrong with their hands?

Nobody knows what to give her as a gift: What do you give to the girl who's had everybody?

My sister believes: "Some women think men are animals, and maybe they're right. A man can be meek as a lamb, brave as a tiger, and have the courage of a lion. But the minute he meets a pretty girl, he becomes a jackass."

Kissing is an expression of affection that gets two people so close together they can't see anything wrong with each other.

A friend of mine married one of those flat-chested girls for her brains. When he gets horny he hollers, "Quick, honey, say something smart."

My neighbor confides: "On the subject of birth control, my husband and I believe the simpler the better. Our idea of birth control is to just turn the lights on."

The big executive painted for diversion. He asked a young lady of his acquaintance to pose for him in the nude, insisting, "Everybody is doing it." She said, "Sorry—I'm not a model." He said, "That's okay—I'm not an artist."

In this country, you're allowed to buy almost anything. If you need a shirt you have a right to buy it, but if you need sex, you don't. What's more important, sex or a shirt?

One thing that never went over big at the nudist camp was the masquerade ball, because even though the guys wore masks, somehow the gals were able to identify them.

Some girls are music lovers—others love without it.

When the young sheik was bar mitzvahed, he inherited his father's harem. "I know what to do," he announced. "But where the hell do I begin?"

Harry ran into his old friend Joe, who said, "It's been a long time—I hear you got married." Harry replied, "Yes I did. I have two children—Practice, the oldest boy, and Jimmy, who is two years younger." Joe said, "That's great, but I never heard the name Practice. Who is he named after?" Harry replied, "Actually, nobody. You see, he was born a year before we got married."

It is better to have loved and lost, than to have paid for it and liked it.

If pornography relieves sexual frustration, why aren't cookbooks given to the hungry?

My girlfriend has got sex on the brain: I only love her for her mind.

One man said to another: "I hear your wife had a mirror installed over your bed because she likes to watch herself laugh."

With the peek-a-boo dresses, the see-through blouses, and the mini skirts—there is no longer any such thing as a blind date.

Two little girls were talking about religious knowledge. "I'm past Original Sin," boasted the first one. "That's nothing," answered the other. "I'm beyond Redemption."

He said to his girl, "Come a little closer, my love. I'm going to make you melt in my arms." She answered, "No, thanks. I'm not that soft and you're not that hot."

The eighty-year-old was vacationing with another octogenarian. During their stay they both met some ladies younger than themselves, and decided to get married in a double ceremony. Following the wedding night, they are both in their rocking chairs. One says, "You know, I'd better see a doctor." The other says, "Why?" "Well," the first says, "I couldn't consummate the marriage." "Oh," says the second, "I'd better see a psychiatrist." "Why?" says the first. "I didn't give it a thought."

One fella told me he dated a pair of Siamese twins. I asked if he had a good time. He said, "Yes and no."

A man went to see the doctor complaining that he could think of nothing but girls. "You have to stop that," the doctor said, "or you'll lose your hearing." "Is that so?" asked the patient. "What did you say?" asked the doctor.

The battle of the sexes will never be won by either side: There is too much fraternizing with the enemy.

I never go to pornographic films—I object to seeing

someone have more fun in an hour than I had in a lifetime.

Kissing a girl is like opening a bottle of olives: If you get one, the rest come easy.

Signs

At a fire hydrant: PARK NOW—PAY LATER.

In the window of an auto store: COME IN AND HAVE FUN WITH OUR PARTS.

Behind the bar at "Fortune Gardens": NOT RESPONSIBLE IF OUR BARTENDER'S OPINIONS CONFLICT WITH YOUR ANALYST'S.

Sign on the gate of a new factory on Long Island: MEN WANTED TO WORK ON NUCLEAR-FISSIONABLE ISOTOPE COUNTERS AND THREE-PHASE PHOTOSYNTHESIZERS. *NO EXPERIENCE NECESSARY.*

Sign in a brassiere shop: WE FIX FLATS.

Sign in bar: IF YOU ARE OVER 80 AND ACCOMPANIED BY YOUR PARENTS WE WILL CASH YOUR CHECK.

Bumper stickers:
HONK IF YOU LOVE QUIET.
DRIVE CAREFULLY—WE NEED EVERY TAXPAYER WE CAN GET.
PUTTING YOUR SHOULDER TO THE WHEEL—IS A DANGEROUS WAY TO DRIVE.
TWO HEADS ARE BETTER THAN ONE—EXCEPT IN A HEAD-ON COLLISION.
KEEP AMERICA BEAUTIFUL—EAT A BEER CAN!
WIFE SWAPPING IS THE SUBURBS' ANSWER TO BINGO.

Sign in IRS office: IN GOD WE TRUST—EVERYONE ELSE WE AUDIT.

One reducing salon advertises: REAR TODAY—GONE TOMORROW.

Sign on a diner: DON'T MAKE FUN OF OUR COFFEE—YOU TOO MIGHT BE OLD AND WEAK SOME DAY.

Sign on one of our sanitation-removal trucks: OUR GUARANTEE! IF YOU ARE NOT SATISFIED WITH OUR METHODS—YOU WILL RECEIVE DOUBLE YOUR GARBAGE BACK.

Sign on one road upstate: MAIN HIGHWAY OPEN FOR TRAFFIC—WHILE DETOUR IS BEING REPAVED.

Outside the town of Comfort, Texas, which happens to be between the villages of Alice and Louise, a motel has this invitation: SLEEP IN COMFORT BETWEEN ALICE AND LOUISE.

On the wall of a large business office: THOSE WHO ARE UNDERPAID WILL BE THE LAST TO BE FIRED.

One union official posted this sign: IT WOULD BE A CINCH TO LIVE TO A RIPE OLD AGE—IF WE DIDN'T HAVE TO WORK SO HARD PROVIDING FOR IT.

In the window of a Washington, D.C., laundry: WE DO NOT TEAR YOUR CLOTHES WITH MACHINERY—WE DO IT CAREFULLY BY HAND.

One man had this card on his windshield: NOTICE TO THIEVES—THIS CAR HAS ALREADY BEEN STOLEN.

Sign on store window: OUR GOING-OUT-OF-BUSINESS SALE WAS SUCH A SUCCESS, WE'RE HAVING ANOTHER ONE NEXT WEEK.

A beauty shop proclaims: WE CAN GIVE YOU THE NEW LOOK IF YOU STILL HAVE THE OLD PARTS.

A sign in a slenderizing palace: LET US TAKE YOU IN SO THE BOYS WILL TAKE YOU OUT.

This note was on the desk of a bank manager: YOU GET A FRIEND—IF YOU CAN COME UP WITH THE CASH.

Sign in a singles bar: MEN, NO SHIRTS—NO SERVE; WOMEN, NO SHIRTS—NO CHECK.

Sign in a Hollywood jewelry store: WEDDING RINGS FOR RENT.

Sign in a women's shop: SEE-THROUGH BLOUSES FOR THE GIRL WHO HAS EVERYTHING.

Pawnshop: PLEASE SEE ME AT YOUR EARLIEST INCONVENIENCE.

In the window of a restaurant: WE HONOR DINER'S CLUB, CARTE BLANCHE, AMERICAN EXPRESS, AND MONEY.

A cafeteria has this notice on the wall: EFFICIENT, COURTEOUS, FRIENDLY, PROMPT, SELF-SERVICE.

This sign on a church: REMEMBER THAT DETROIT IS NOT THE ONLY PLACE THAT THE MAKER CAN RECALL HIS PRODUCT.

An advertisement for donkey rides in Thailand: WOULD YOU LIKE TO RIDE ON YOUR OWN ASS?

Notice in a Parisian cocktail lounge: LADIES ARE REQUESTED NOT TO HAVE CHILDREN IN THE BAR.

In Dublin, Ireland, this sign was displayed prominently in Murphy's restaurant: MURPHY'S LAW—DON'T MESS WITH MRS. MURPHY.

This poor soul saw a sign on an escalator at the railroad station: DOGS MUST BE CARRIED ON THE ESCALATOR. He started looking around desperately, mumbling, "Now, where the hell am I going to find a dog at this hour of the night?"

For Sale sign on a posh condo: ANY REASONABLE OFFER WILL BE REFUSED.

There is a sign in the window of a clothing store in San Francisco reading, GOING OUT OF BUSINESS SALE. Underneath, in smaller letters, is an addendum: WE RESERVE THE RIGHT TO STAY IN BUSINESS IF THIS SALE IS A SUCCESS.

On the other coast, there is this sign displayed in the show window of a shop on Broadway: DO NOT BE FOOLED BY IMITATORS —WE HAVE BEEN GOING OUT OF BUSINESS IN THIS LOCATION SINCE 1950.

Big sign in the office of a Wall Street brokerage house: IT WOULD BE A WELCOME CHANGE TO SEE A HORSE'S HEAD AROUND HERE ON OCCASION.

Sign at farm: EGGS LAID WHILE YOU WAIT.

Sign in the no smoking section of a midtown restaurant: IF YOU SIT HERE WITH OTHER PATRONS, PLEASE BUTT OUT.

Sign in supermarket: NOBODY UNDER $21 ADMITTED.

This sign on the wall at the German circus: NEVER PLAY LEAPFROG WITH A UNICORN.

The traffic court judge canceled the fifty-dollar ticket against the man who said he completely misunderstood the sign where he left his car. It read, FINE FOR PARKING.

The sign in the back of the diner said: SO YOU LIKE HOMEMADE BREAD? SO YOU LIKE HOMEMADE BISCUITS? SO YOU LIKE HOMEMADE PIES? THEN GO HOME!

There's a sign in a small town: 30 DAYS HATH SEPTEMBER, APRIL, JUNE, AND NOVEMBER—AND ANYONE EXCEEDING OUR SPEED LIMIT.

Sign on a church bulletin: ON THURSDAY THERE WILL BE A MEETING OF THE LITTLE MOTHERS CLUB. ALL WISHING TO BECOME LITTLE MOTHERS WILL MEET THE MINISTER IN HIS STUDY.

Sign in the window of a ladies shoe store: FRENCH HEELS— IDEAL FOR STREET WALKING.

Sign in the window of a vacant shop: WE UNDERSOLD EVERYBODY.

Sign in an obstetrician's office: WE DELIVER 24 HOURS A DAY.

Sign in a bar: PLEASE DON'T DRINK ON AN EMPTY WALLET.

Sign for a travel agency: DO US A FAVOR AND GO AWAY.

Notice posted in a hotel in Utica, New York: IN CASES OF ILLNESS, LIFT YOUR RECEIVER AND ASK FOR THE HOUSE PHYSICIAN. WHILE AWAITING HIS ARRIVAL, YOU MAY HAVE THE MAID ON THE FLOOR.

Small Towns and Farms

My friend tells me the two happiest days of his life were the days he bought the house in the country—and the day he sold the house in the country.

Living in the country is great if you're one of those freaks who like health and trees and fresh air—and yawning.

I'm a city boy—I even like pollution. . . . At least you can't see the insects.

The biggest change when you move to a small town is the banks. In New York they have gigantic financial institutions. Do you know what the name of the bank in Dullsville is? Chuck's Saving and Loan. And they all have tellers that are sixteen-year-old girls with names like Wendy and Fifi and Cookie. Tell me, are you going to entrust your life savings to a girl named Cookie? I was driving through the town and stopped at the bank and asked the girl to change a twenty. She said, "Do you have anything smaller?"

People in small towns think different. One woman came home after three years in New York and told her mom, "My boyfriend and I have been living together for two years." Mom sniffed. "Hmmm—I wouldn't even think of *driving* without a license."

I placed a call from Utah to an aunt who lives in a small town in Iowa. After I gave my aunt's number to the Utah operator the local Iowa operator came on the line. "I'll ring now," she said, "but I don't think they're home—their car is gone."

Small towns are okay with me—it's just that once you've seen the cannon in the park there's nothing to do. I was in this one town so small the local hooker was the community chest. And dull? If it wasn't for mouth-to-mouth resuscitation there wouldn't be any romance at all. Dull? The mayor went to a gypsy fortune teller, who read his lifeline and in the middle got bored and turned on the TV. One good thing—they don't have crime in the streets. . . . Well, let me clarify that. They got crime: What they don't have is streets.

I will not knock the little villages—some of the greatest men of all time have come out of there. Abe Lincoln wasn't exactly born in a log condo. And that little town of Bethlehem will always be proud of the great star they gave birth to.

I know a town so dull they print the newspaper there three weeks in advance.

I know a town so small the fire department uses a water pistol. That town is so small they only have one fire hydrant—and they didn't get that until the mayor bought a dog. A big time there is to go downtown and watch the parking meter expire. They just named my uncle fire chief. They had to. They're using his garden hose. You know some towns have a Godfather? Well, my uncle's couldn't afford a Godfather—so they had a second cousin.

Some of our presidential candidates come from small towns. How small? So small that not only did they never have a presidential candidate, but they never even had a voter.

This one town is so small, the milkman is a cow, and the mayor is an Elk—a real elk.

Another town I know is so small:
    The dentist's office is the public library . . .
    The local theater is a couple who hate each other and keep the windows open . . .
    They had to close the zoo because the cat died . . .

The only protection the bank has is one guy standing at
the door with bad breath . . .
They had a dust storm and nobody knew it because
there was nothing to blow away . . .
The town spinster and the local hooker are the same
person . . .
The main street goes through a car wash.

Small? The twenty-four-hour diner closes at noon.

My uncle lives in an even smaller place: They don't exactly
have a taxi service—they have a guy with a large skateboard. And you know how big cities have professional call
girls? This town has to get along with volunteers. The
town clock is a wristwatch. And they couldn't teach the
parrot to say "Polly want a cracker," because there was no
one to give it to her. A stranger visited and asked my
uncle, "Does this town have any nightlife?" My uncle
said, "Yes, but she's ill today."

My cousin's another one for small towns. In his:
Howard Johnson's has only one flavor . . .
The tallest building is a Fotomat . . .
The mayor's kid has a piggy bank—it's a real pig . . .
They had to fire the dogcatcher—they caught the
dog . . .
Their idea of a traffic jam is three people in one car . . .
Formal wear is a T-shirt.

There's a town so small that they don't have gossip,
because it would either have to be about the person who
was telling or the one who was listening. Small? There
was nobody to watch the July 4th parade, because everybody in town was in the parade.

A farm is a four-letter word meaning a piece of land where
if you get up early enough and work hard enough you will
make a fortune—if you strike oil on it.

The hillbilly woman told me: "I come from farm country—
real farm country—where a woman is considered liberated
if she stops after eight kids."

Some kind of record was set in marital affairs when a rich hillbilly died last month and left his estate in trust for his wife: She can't touch any of it until she's fourteen.

Smoking

Cigarettes Anonymous is a new organization: When you feel like smoking, you dial a number and hear a minute of coughing.

People who give up smoking have the same problem as the newcomers in the nudist camp: They don't know what to do with their hands.

The best way to stop smoking is to use wet matches.

Talk about a progressive society. I know one public school that has a smoking and nonsmoking section for first graders.

My father never knew from Surgeons General or Surgeons Corporal. He never said much about it being good for us or bad for us. All he ever said was if he ever caught us smoking, *he* would be hazardous to our health.

The young graduate cornered his girl in the backseat of the car and was amorously trying his hand at her. She kept resisting and finally shrieked, "Myron, I don't know what's come over you! You've always been so restrained and gentlemanly." He said, "Yes, I know, but I just can't help it—I'm trying to give up smoking!"

The government puts health warnings on cigarettes. Why don't they put them on bombs?

In some areas smoking is a felony. Mugging is okay, but cigarettes and cigars are out.

There's a filling station that displays a big sign saying: NO SMOKING. YOUR LIFE MAY NOT BE WORTH MUCH—BUT GASOLINE IS.

Psychiatrists are great to help you stop the smoking habit: The sessions cost so much you can't afford to buy cigarettes anymore.

The romantic young man said to the pretty little girl at the singles bar, "Do you mind if I kiss your hand?" She said, "Not at all—but don't burn your nose on my cigarette."

The sign in the motel said, DO NOT SMOKE IN BED WITHOUT UMBRELLA—EXTRA-SENSITIVE SPRINKLING SYSTEM.

What's the big deal about giving up smoking? I've done it a thousand times.

I don't like the idea of the government telling you what's no good for you: First it's smoking—what if sex is next?

Doctors tell you if you quit smoking you'll be able to taste food. I know one guy who took the advice and quit smoking completely: "Now," he said, "I can really taste food—and I find I've been eating a lot of things I don't like."

"You and your diets," the patient gasped to his doctor. "I cut out sweets, I cut out starches. That I didn't mind! But you limited me to one cigar a day. I never smoked before—and that damn cigar a day nearly killed me!"

Reformed smoker: "I haven't smoked in three years, eight months and ten days—and I never miss it or think about it."

Society People

I've always been interested in society. That's because in my old neighborhood, we never had any. In my part of town:

The post office delivered warrants in the mail marked "occupant" . . .

The most popular form of transportation was the stretcher . . .

There was a sign in the local hotel: WASHINGTON WOULDN'T SLEEP HERE . . .

When you made a reservation at the restaurant, you requested the "non-shooting" section . . .

The garbage trucks didn't pick up—they delivered.

I know a young socialite who wears a riding habit just to pitch horseshoes. The only thing the rich scum ever did for a living was read his father's will.

Another wealthy lad was boasting to me about his family tree: "My family traces its ancestry back to Charlemagne." I said, "I suppose you'll be telling me next that your ancestors were in the ark with Noah." He said, "Indeed no—my people had a boat of their own."

Most society snobs like to live in the suburbs. That's a community in which a man will lend you his wife—but not his golf clubs.

Society is not a dirty word to me. Some of those guys are pretty classy: I know one guy so rich, he even goes to a drive-in movie in a taxi. I can understand why he has a car with an unlisted number, but a glass-covered golf course is too much. He has music in all his elevators—live bands. He even owns a split-level Chrysler.

These society characters are all trying to top each other:

One bought his son a bicycle with whitewall tires. Another bought his daughter an air conditioned baby carriage. One big man is proud of his little girl, who is selling Girl Scout croissants. And how about the class guy who has *TV Guide* in hardcover? Don't you think his four-room Cadillac is a bit ostentatious?

One chic snob decided to take a job for kicks—but he insisted on an unlisted social security number.

Two older society gals, poor but snobbish, were talking about a matrimonial prospect. "He's got plenty of money," one said, "but he's too old to be termed eligible." The other said, "Dahling, he's too eligible to be termed old."

Then there's the most fashionable lady of them all: If she was going to shoot her husband—she'd wear a hunting outfit.

A snob is one whose grandfather made money and who therefore refuses to associate with persons who have made it themselves.

A very aristocratic Boston family was shocked to hear that one of the daughters had become a call girl in New York. As they sat in council to discuss the disgrace, old Aunt Amelia broke the silence: "How terribly disgusting," she thundered, "that one of our family should have to work!"

A society snob is a person who craves equality—but only with his superiors.

The distinguished stuffed shirt was lecturing at the country club to a roomful of stuffed shorts: "Those X-rated movies are disgraceful. I saw one last night that included sexual perversion of every kind, every vulgarity. It was a disgrace to the human eye." He concluded, "And now, ladies, will there be any questions?" In unison, three women shouted, "Where is it playing?"

Mrs. Vanderschwartz was showing off as usual: "I have all my diamonds cleaned with caviar juice, my rubies with strictly imported wine, my emeralds with the finest brandy from Spain, and my sapphires with fresh milk from baby goats." Mrs. Snobhead interrupted: "When *my* jewels get dirty—I throw them away." She's such a snob, she won't ride in the same car with her chauffeur.

This haughty socialite died and arrived at the gates of heaven. "Welcome," said St. Peter. "Come right in." The snob sneered, "I will not! Any place where a perfect stranger can get in without a reservation is not my idea of heaven."

You can't keep a good snob down: Even when he's broke he's puttin' on the Ritz.

I know one character who can't afford air conditioning, but he doesn't want his friends to know. So he drives around on the hottest days with his car windows closed—and sweats off ten pounds every summer.

Two women met at the chic restaurant: "Sylvia, what have you done to your hair?" one asked. "It looks like a wig." The other said, "It is a wig." "Isn't that marvelous," said the first. "I never would have guessed."

Sons

He was only a traffic cop's son—but he preferred the red light district.

He was only a salesman's son—but he was always looking for free samples.

He was only a football player's son—but he made a pass at anybody.

He was only a TV evangelist's son—maybe that's why he believed so much in loving thy neighbor.

He was only a tennis player's son—but did he try to score.

He was only a jockey's son—but he tried to get every gal in the saddle.

He was only a farmer's son—but could he throw the bull.

He was only a banker's son—but he gambled so much even his cash bounced.

He was only an explorer's son—but he tried to go too far with the girls.

He was only a baseball manager's son—but he struck out with every girl he met.

He was only an accountant's son—but he played with all the right figures.

He was only a sanitation man's son—but he tried to pick up anything that moved.

He was only a violinist's son—but he tried to pluck every G string.

He was only a chambermaid's son—but he was a devil between the sheets.

He was only a lawyer's son—but he tried to break every girl's will.

He was only a stockbroker's son—but he tried to sell every girl short.

He was only a comedian's son—but only his lovemaking was laughable.

He was only an actor's son—but every time he looked in the mirror he took a bow.

He was only an obstetrician's son—but with a girl he couldn't deliver.

He was only a union leader's son—but he put plenty of girls in labor.

He was only a judge's son—but he could never pass a bar.

He was only a politician's son—but he lied, cheated, and stole on his own.

Sports

I'm not exactly athletic: I get winded turning on the TV set.

How can you tell your wife is fed up with Monday Night Football? When she strips, comes in the den, stands in front of the TV set, and announces, "Play me or trade me."

Did you hear about the football lineman whose coach told him to put on a clean pair of shorts every day? By the sixth day he couldn't get his pants on over them.

Why do ball players smoke marijuana? They like to spend their afternoons and evenings on grass.

Skiing is best when you have lots of white snow and plenty of Blue Cross.

People go to ski lodges to find romance. My cousin tells me, "I met a girl and we ended up in bed: We both were in traction."

My friend told me, "I met a girl at a ski lodge and it was a case of opposites being attracted to each other: My cast was on my left leg, hers was on her right leg."

The national pastime in Tahiti is making love. Us silly fools, we picked baseball.

I'd never ski. I do not participate in any sport with ambulances at the bottom of a hill.

My neighbor's wife was bragging, "My uncle has a gold medal for swimming, a silver cup for golfing, and a solid gold watch for high jumping." I said, "He must be a great athlete." She said, "No—he owns a hock shop."

Do you know what seven-foot basketball players do in their off time? They go to the movies and sit in front of you.

Fish may be dumb, but no one has ever seen one buy $500 worth of equipment to hook a man.

Bob told me, "I'm thinking of giving up golf—I can't even break ninety when I cheat."

Bob asked his priest, "Will I sin if I play golf on Sunday?" The father answered, "The way you play, it's a sin to play any day."

Bob says, "I wear Arnold Palmer shirts, Arnold Palmer shoes, and Arnold Palmer clubs—and I play like Betsy Palmer."

Bob explains, "It's not that I cheat with golf—I play for my health, and a low score makes me feel better."

Subways

With so many vigilantes now riding the subways, the transit authority is getting letters from muggers asking for safer working conditions.

Today a group of liberal lawyers began lobbying for a law that would require subway riders to carry at least $100—so muggers could make a decent living.

These days you really have to watch out for muggers. You know what a mugger is? A guy who takes your money without having to get elected.

The other day two muggers shot each other in a case of mistaken identity: Each mugger thought the other was a vigilante.

I took the subway once: It was so crowded I couldn't even

put my hand in my pocket—somebody else's hand was already there.

A lot of people don't think New York is a friendly city. That's not true. Where else would a mugger knock you down, take your wallet, and then tell you to have a nice day?

Some Hollywood stars are planning to entertain our fighting forces this next Christmas. I know a subway in New York that would love to have them.

Some people think our criminal justice system is slow. Maybe—but the criminal usually receives justice before the victim.

Not all muggers work in subways. A number of gunmen held up one of our big banks. They herded all the men into one vault and slammed the door. The girls were taken by another mugger into a private office and ordered to lie down on the floor. The girls meekly started to lie down on their backs. "Turn over!" the mugger yelled. "This is a stickup—not a directors' meeting."

Did you know that the subways are mentioned in the Bible: "And the Lord created all manner of creeping things."

I asked the station guard at Forty-second Street, "What's the best way to get to Brooklyn?" So he called me a cab.

The mayor is in favor of police being stationed in subways: "It has been a big help: Up until today, not one train has been stolen."

Summer

With school out, the teachers are very happy to hand their Valium over to the parents.

The water shortage has helped this summer: Bars are now serving Scotch and milk, and prisoners are being given bread and wine.

You know it's really hot when you wake up in the morning to a tingling sensation and then you realize your water bed is perking.

The drought is going to kill off a lot of good sex for the creative young marrieds: Instead of a water bed, they'll have to use the old-fashioned mattress.

Now there's a new slogan: "Be patriotic—bathe with a friend." The drought is so bad, armored cars are now delivering bottled water.

It's vacation time: Everybody goes to the beach for the same reason—hoping to see a body in worse shape than theirs. That's why *I* like to go to the beach: It makes everybody else so happy.

There may not be anything new under the sun but there's a lot more of it showing on the beach.

It was so hot in New York, the tough guys were tossing men in the harbor stuffed in seersucker sacks.

It was so hot, instead of carrying a torch, the Statue of Liberty was holding a glass of iced tea.

I get sunburned easily. Whenever I lie in the sun, I can just hear the excited voices of hundreds of mosquitoes exclaiming: "Oh, boy, a barbecue!"

My neighbor told me he's having a great vacation this

year. He bought a new car and put all his kids in the back-seat—and he's taking a cruise.

My nephew told me, "Money is pretty tight this year—about all we can afford for a vacation is a roll of film, some suntan lotion, and maybe a couple of nights in the Laundromat."

They say if you take a European vacation it shows you've got money. Wrong—it shows you *had* money.

One reason I'm glad I'm not an Arab: How'd you like to be tooling down the highway and have your camel boil over?

My neighbor says he likes hot weather: He keeps hoping it will thaw out his wife.

Hey, don't slave over a hot stove in weather like this. Do it the easy way: Rush home and toss a couple of TV dinners on the sidewalk.

Summertime is the greatest for the nice long weekend motor trips—one day driving and two days folding the road maps.

Please make this a safe summer. Riding on the parkway is like Russian Roulette: You never know which driver is loaded.

I was lucky on my trip last summer: They had the highway open while the detour was being fixed.

The nice thing about going on a summer trip is after it's over you're still reminded of your memories for years to come—usually right around the first of each month.

On our last trip we stopped at the Hilton, the Interconti-nental, and a lot more hotels whose names I'd like to tell you, but at the moment, those towels are still in the laundry.

My wife likes to take home a souvenir whenever we vacation. Other people invite friends over to see the slides of their trip—we invite them over to see our ashtrays!

Have you ever noticed, when *you* visit a relative, it's because you want family ties—but when relatives spend their vacations at *your* house, it's because they're free-loading bums?

Two ladies were relaxing at the pool: "How about a cocktail before dinner?" one suggested. "It's vacation time." The other said, "No, thanks, I never drink." "Why not?" "Well, in front of my children, I don't think it's right, and when I'm away from my children—who needs it?"

Taxes

The only fallacy in raising taxes to reduce the federal debt is that it increases our own.

Congress is worried about lowering taxes because it could establish a dangerous principle: The right of the people to keep their own money.

A fair tax structure is one that gives every taxpayer an equal opportunity to cheat.

Let's face it, nowadays, America's favorite pastime is tax evasion.

A Wall Street bookshop is doing big business with the sale of a new book telling you how to save 90 percent on your income tax: It's packaged with a one-way plane ticket to Fiji.

I blame it all on the IRS. . . . Income tax has made more liars out of the American people than has golf.

Who is Congress to tell me what I can deduct for charity?

I put six of my wife's relatives down under contributions—I defy the government to prove they're *not* an organized charity.

Listen, my accountant can come up with so many extra deductions, you'll wind up with enough money left over to post bail.

I did some figuring. We can soon balance the federal budget if we close twenty-seven states.

A communist government won't let you make a lot of money. A democratic government will let you make all you want—but they won't let you keep it.

Now that the tax reform bill has gone through, we are no longer treated unfairly by the old tax laws—we're treated unfairly by the new tax laws.

To control the budget deficit, the Congress wants to increase taxes on cigarettes and alcohol. We might even be able to *balance* the budget if more people had bad habits.

The Congress can balance the budget, they tell me, if smokers will pay $300 a pack for cigarettes. That should drive you to drink, and then we can put a higher tax on booze.

The new tax laws are like a do-it-yourself mugging.

I've got nothing against the new tax laws: It's just that every time my ship comes in—the government unloads it.

I think the new tax laws deserve a lot of credit: They've brought poverty within the reach of all of us.

There are no atheists in the IRS waiting rooms. Let us bow our heads and pay.

The Internal Revenue Service is the nearest thing to a Chinese dinner: No matter how much you gave them, a year later they're hungry again.

In filing your income tax return, make sure you let an accountant instead of your conscience be your guide.

Taxation without representation was tyranny, but it was a lot cheaper.

Only in a democracy have the citizens complete freedom in deciding how to pay their taxes—by check, cash, or money order.

If crime could be taxed, there would be no need for other taxes.

When the meek inherit the earth, they will have very little left after paying inheritance, capital gains, and other taxes.

The only person who gets paid for sticking his nose in other people's business is the tax collector.

Some taxpayers close their eyes, some stop their ears, some shut their mouths, but all pay through the nose.

The way taxes are going these days, a fellow has to be unemployed to make a living.

My neighbor told me, "Last year I saved so much money on taxes, my wife wants us to go to Europe, I want us to go to Africa—and the government wants us to go to Leavenworth."

Fifty percent of Americans file their income tax—the other 50 percent chisel it.

There are dozens of books about how to make out your income taxes—but none of them has a happy ending.

Don't get excited about any promised tax cuts—it's like a mugger giving you back carfare.

Remember, before sealing your IRS envelope, be sure you've enclosed your Social Security number, all W-2 forms, and an arm and a leg.

The American public owes a lot to the IRS—ulcers, nausea, shingles . . . .

As far as we're concerned, members of the Internal Revenue Service are just pickpockets with taxes.

My CPA has this sign on his desk: TELLING THE TRUTH WILL INVARIABLY CONFUSE THE IRS.

I asked a well-known novelist to tell me his greatest work of fiction. He said, "My 1986 income tax return."

I just received my tax form today. . . . Well, so much for my New Year's resolutions about not swearing.

My uncle told me, "I love reading mysteries—I can hardly wait to get my new tax forms."

My uncle says, "I think the IRS ought to serve coffee and doughnuts. The Red Cross does when they take your blood."

My accountant was lecturing: "It's April 15—when the money supply gets out of hand: Out of your hand and into the government's."

I just paid my taxes and now I know what IRS stands for: Internal Robbery Service. Hiring an accountant can save you a lot of money on your taxes, and you'll need it—to pay your accountant. Watching an accountant fill out your income tax is always a fascinating experience. It's like putting your savings on hold. I have my taxes done by a very considerate, a very compassionate, fella: He's the only accountant I know with a recovery room.

There will always be two classes of people who don't like to pay income taxes: men and women.

Income taxes could be a lot worse—suppose we had to pay on what we think we're worth.

You've got to admit the government's shrewd: They've got this thing called withholding taxes—a sneaky way of getting at your paycheck before your wife does.

I really don't mind paying taxes. The way I look at it is if I didn't spend my money on taxes, I'd probably just squander it away on foolish luxuries like groceries, rent, electricity . . . .

I'm proud to be an American taxpayer, but to tell the truth, I could be just as proud for half the money.

No wonder newborn babies cry. They've got nothing to eat, no clothes—and they already owe the government about $2,000.

The businessman said, "I want my last will and testament to contain a provision that after my death, my remains are to be cremated." His lawyer asked, "And what do you want done with the ashes?" The businessman said, "I want them sent to the IRS with a notice reading, 'Now you've got it all.'"

Listen, the way taxes are today, you may as well marry for love.

I just decided—I'm sending my entire income to Washington. Who can afford taxes?

When I went up to the tax department, I really let them have it—every dollar I had.

It's very confusing to be an American. The "Star-Spangled Banner" tells us it's the land of the free. The IRS tells us, "Forget it!"

My neighbor tells me, "I had good news and bad news today. The good news is, I got a phone call and a deep, throbbing, sensuous voice said, 'Your place or mine?' The bad news is, it was an auditor from the IRS."

A fool and his money are soon parted—the rest of us wait to be taxed.

The way to get rich is to cover up with something that's low priced, habit forming, and tax deductible.

My brother screamed at the tax guy, "You mean that after paying taxes all these years I can't list the government as a dependent?"

I hope you have a good accountant. An accountant is a man hired to explain that you didn't make the money you did.

My accountant is a man who solves a problem you didn't know you had in a manner you don't understand.

Speaking of taxes, everybody is worried about entertainment expenses. The government wants you to keep a diary, so when I went out with some people the other night, I marked everything down: "One hundred dollars for food, forty dollars for champagne, twenty dollars for tips . . . ." The government disallowed it. They found out I was a guest.

There was a time when this country didn't have an income tax. I think it was known as the Garden of Eden.

I'm always worried about our marriage around tax time: My wife always lists our relationship for a depreciation allowance.

We always complain about the Ten Commandments like they were something new. There were internal revenue services back in biblical times. You remember Moses came down from Mount Sinai with two tablets? One was the Ten Commandments—the other was an expense account.

Listen, even the president has to file an income tax return. Can you imagine the IRS asking the president questions about his return? "Tell me, Mr. President—do you have any liabilities?" "Yes, I do—the Congress."

I never worry about the future. High interest rates have taught me how to live within my income—and high taxes have taught me how to live without my income. But, listen, don't get me wrong. I think it's a privilege to pay income taxes. It's just that sometimes I get the idea I'm definitely overprivileged!

You've got to hand it to the tax people. . . . If you don't they'll come and get it.

This guy is in trouble now: He deducted $5,000 because he had water in his basement—then they found out he lives in a houseboat.

I feel like writing a letter to the income tax bureau and telling them I can no longer afford their service.

One thing about my tax man—he's the type who could swim safely through shark-infested waters. No doubt he'd be given professional courtesy.

If the average citizen gets robbed once in a year it's called a crime wave. If he gets robbed every day of the year it's called government.

It wasn't until I was called for an audit by the IRS that I heard my accountant worked his way through college performing in clubs as a juggler.

I hear talk about lowering taxes. I hope they lower them down enough so we can pay them.

The working man's big problem is that his paycheck comes minus tax—and his bills come plus tax.

My Uncle Sam is beginning to cost me as much as my wife.

What an honest guy! On his 1040, he reported half his salary as unearned income. It's hard to believe this country was founded partly to avoid paying taxes.

I lied on my income tax last year—I listed myself as head of the household.

My accountants pledge that if I'm audited, they'll stop by and feed my dog until I get paroled.

The income tax guys must love poor people—they're creating so many of them.

I know a terrific accountant: He's available twenty-four hours a day. One phone call and the warden brings him to the phone.

The capitalist system is the best in the world. Where else could you make enough to owe so much?

The IRS has a new easy payment plan: 100 percent down and nothing per month.

America should be a very clean place. Every day the average taxpayer gets taken to the cleaners.

This year the government claims the tax forms will be very simple: "Even a five-year-old can understand them"—providing he's a CPA.

Taxis

I think cabbies are very helpful—they'll take you anyplace *they* want to go.

I was in one taxi where the driver skillfully avoided four pedestrians in a row. "If you hit 'em," he explained, "you've got to fill out a report."

At school, if you couldn't find the shortest distance between two points—you became a cab driver.

Rain is what makes flowers appear and taxis disappear. In fact, the off-duty lights on Manhattan cabs are wired to go on whenever they are touched by a drop of rain.

All things come to him who waits for a taxi on a rainy day—except a taxi.

Taxi drivers have the uncanny knack for knowing when people are late for work: That's when they pass them by every time.

The pretty lady gave the cabbie an address outside of town and asked him to stop in a park. She invited him to the backseat, then said, "I'm really a prostitute and I have to charge you fifty dollars." He paid her and they made love. Later, he sat motionless behind the wheel. "Aren't we leaving?" asked the hooker. He said, "Not yet—I'm really a cab driver and the fare back is fifty dollars."

I like cab drivers. I find if you do exactly what they want, you have no problems. Want to light a cigarette? The driver's allergic. Want change? He has none. Want a receipt? He just gave away his last one.

Cab meters go faster than the cabs. In fact, taxis are getting so expensive it's cheaper to be mugged and wait for an ambulance.

I went to a gypsy fortune teller who predicted I was going to take a long trip. An hour later I was in a taxi going crosstown.

Did you ever get in one of those traffic jams? I was in one so bad, it's the first time I was ever passed by an abandoned car.

My cabbie hit the car in front of him three times. I screamed at him. He said, "Sorry, my windshield is covered with safety stickers—I couldn't see a thing!"

Do you want to frustrate your cab driver? Tell him to take you to his garage.

At a New York bar, a Texan was bragging about the Dallas Cowboys. The bartender said to him, "Okay, so they're great, but here in New York City, we have great cowboys too; they're modern, they're on wheels. We call them the New York cab drivers."

A pedestrian was struck down by a taxi and dragged about twenty feet. He was carried to the sidewalk and an ambulance was summoned. A police car arrived and the officer asked the victim if he had gotten the license number of the cab. The victim said he had. "Let's have it," the cop said, starting to write. The victim shook his head. "Please," he said. "Leave me out of it. I don't want to get involved!"

It's a shame that the people who really know how to run this country are too busy driving taxis for a living.

Telephones

They say the breakup of the telephone company into dozens of parts has brought warmth into your home—and I believe it. I get hot every time I see my phone bill.

Anybody who believes this country has free speech—must not be paying his telephone bill.

They claim they cut up AT&T so it would be easier for everybody. The next time I have a full day with nothing to do, I'll have enough time to get out my phone bill and read it from beginning to end.

And the rate increases are something. . . . You now pay for everything separately: the wires, the buttons, the telephone, the operator's laundry.

I just got an obscene phone call from AT&T. They want me to pay my bill.

My friend lost a quarter in a pay phone and asked the operator to refund it. "Give me your name and address," the operator said, "and we'll mail you a refund." My friend declined this logic and pushed the coin return button once more. A rush of coins settled down the chute, and the operator, realizing what was going on, said, "Please put them back." My friend ended the connection: "If you'll just give me your name and address . . . ."

Car phones make you think the person in the car is the busiest guy in town. The truth is, if the guy was so busy, he'd be at work instead of riding around gabbing on the phone.

Having a car phone could be great in a crisis—like if you're in the backseat with your girl at a drive-in movie and need to place an emergency call to Dr. Ruth.

Telephone prices are like babies: They get changed pretty often.

It's true that money talks—but these days only Arabs can afford to speak on the phone.

It's not surprising to find that they have to raise the phone rates: Somebody has to pay for those Out of Order signs on the phone booths.

Those street phones are like people employed by the government—only one in three works.

Progress works both ways. In the old days you could dial wrong numbers only locally. Now you can dial them all over the world—and wrong numbers will cost you twice as much.

When the telephone operators finish lunch, they don't call it going back to work—it's more like returning to the scene of the crime.

I still remember that blue Monday in 1929 when the holders of the gilt-edged AT&T stock were ready for the big jump. I remember putting a dime in the coin telephone slot and a voice said, "God bless you, sir."

I think this direct dialing is wonderful. The other day I made an overseas call. I dialed 1-0-285-369-842796-4397-1-8295—and you know what I wound up with? A blister.

Now, for the first time, you can reach long distance wrong numbers without operator assistance.

People frequently complain about the services they receive from the telephone company. One man called to find out the number of information. The operator told him he'd have to dial information.

Even the athiests have a number to call when they're in need. It's the same as "Dial-a-Prayer." The only difference is no one answers.

Alexander Graham Bell transmitted his first telephone message to his assistant in the next room: "Mr. Watson, come here, I want you!" "Who is calling?" Watson asked.

If there had been a teenager around the house, Alex never would have bothered.

We've come a long way. Those push-button phones are great time-savers. Today I got three wrong numbers in the time it usually takes me to get one.

I installed my own phone. It works great except every time somebody calls, the burglar alarm goes off—and I have to ring the doorbell to get a dial tone.

I've got one of those long distance services where you have to dial twenty-seven numbers. By the time you finally get through to the people you're calling—they've moved.

Now I save a lot of money on long distance service: I wait for my friends to call *me*.

I asked the phone company to start sending my bill in Arabic. I figured why the hell not? I don't understand what I'm paying for anyway.

Listen, if you were a creative TV producer, you could make your phone bill into a mini series.

Did I tell you that AT&T may merge with Playboy? Now you will be able to reach out and touch something worthwhile.

The voice on the other end said, "I'd like to talk with your wife." I said, "She's out right now—do you want to leave a message?" The voice said, "Yes." I waited, and said again, "Do you want to leave a message?" The voice asked, "Are you a recording?" I said, "No." He said, "I'm sorry—I was waiting for you to beep."

Now, with the breakup of the phone company, there is so much confusion, an operator called *me* for directory assistance.

My neighbor showed up at a party with a bandaged nose. I asked what happened. He said, "It's the telephone got it broken; I called a friend at three in the morning because the rates are cheaper. When he got out of bed and answered the phone I said, 'Guess who?' " I asked, "So how did you get your nose broken?" "He guessed who."

The phone company had better be careful about raising the rates. There are very few conversations worth the money now.

One friend showed up at my party minus an appendix. I said, "I didn't know you had appendicitis." He said, "I didn't, but I had to run into my doctor's office to use his phone—and how could I leave without buying something?"

One company is selling a new toll-free 800 service for only a dollar a month. And it works like every other 800 number. Your customers can call it from anywhere, toll-free, seven days a week, twenty-four hours a day—and get a busy signal.

When they split up the phone company, they said everybody's bills would be smaller. And they are . . . but they send you five of them a month!

The man who said talk is cheap never gave his teenage daughters their own phones.

Television

TV is a wonderful thing. You meet so many new people—mostly repairmen.

I just met the town's richest man—a television repairman who moonlights as an air conditioner repairman.

In my opinion the greatest spectacular of the year was my TV repairman's bill.

A good commercial is what makes you think you've longed all your life for a thing you've never heard of before. Let's be honest about it. What four out of five doctors really prefer they couldn't show on television!

TV is so bad I can hardly wait for next year's political programs.

Cable TV is performing a great service—getting nudity off the theater screen and back into the home where it belongs.

I'm now enjoying television more than ever. I have a six-foot screen—it's Chinese, and I have it in front of my TV set.

When I was growing up, we didn't have a TV set, so we bored a hole in our neighbor's apartment and watched wrestling every night—until we found our neighbor didn't have a TV set either.

I love watching old movies on TV, but some of those movies on late-night television are too old to be kept up that late.

People tell me they enjoy TV because it takes them away from the frustrations of real life. I enjoy real life because it takes me away from television.

The word is being spread about a new TV soap opera. The plot centers around an unfaithful wife, a drug addict, a student anarchist planning on bombing the White House, a dirty old man, and a corrupt public official. It will be called, "Just Plain Folks."

Say, if there's a ban on bombs—how come so many of them got on TV this season?

Some of the quiz shows and game shows on TV are getting ridiculous. I know a nine-year-old kid who had to get married because he won a honeymoon vacation for two in Hawaii.

TV is education. It teaches you how much you can put up with.

Reading maketh a well-rounded person. So doth watching TV with potato chips and a six-pack of beer.

Television has gotten so bad—kids are doing their homework.

When I was a kid you could see two pictures for a dime in any theater. Now it costs you $500 for a TV set, and what do you get? The same two pictures.

Texas

Ever since December 29, 1845, when Texas was kind enough to annex the U.S.A., they have refused to put *small* in their dictionaries.

Big is a little word in Texas. They start with *tremendous, fantabulous, expansive, gigantic*—and then they get larger.

Did you hear about the loaded Dallas farmer who was so rich he bought his dog a little boy?

One banker from Houston chided his son, "I heard you asking a man just now what state he was from. If a man is from Texas, he'll tell you; if he's not, there's no use embarrassing him."

A friend was admiring a Texan's new sports car. "And is it air conditioned?" he asked. "No," replied the oil man, "but I always keep a couple of cold ones in the refrigerator."

I know a Texan who has two Cadillacs—one for red lights, and the other for green.

And how about the Dallas Cowboy who hated wearing glasses, so all his cars have prescription windshields.

This Dallas oilman had a bankroll so big he had to have it put on microfilm before he could stuff it in his pocket. A Houston playgirl seated herself next to him in the bar. Soon they were talking business. In the middle of it all, she asked the chap in his early millions, "Pardon me, how much did you say your name was?"

Traffic

New York City is one big gridlock: A traffic sign on Fifth Avenue says: NO STOPPING—NO STANDING—NO PARKING—NO KIDDING.

Our one-way streets help. On a one-way street the motorist is bumped from the rear only.

The warning sign on upper Broadway says: BEWARE OF CHILDREN GOING TO AND FROM SCHOOL—ESPECIALLY IF THEY ARE DRIVING CARS.

The new laws warn you to drive carefully: "The life you save may belong to a pedestrian on his way to remove his car from the parking place you're looking for."

The main trouble with the straight and narrow path is—there's no place to park.

The only place where you can park as long as you want to—you don't want to.

This guy was stopped so often by traffic cops, they finally gave him a season ticket.

The police are really cracking down on bad drivers. I know one guy who got fifty traffic tickets. He used to drive one of those fancy foreign sports cars, but the cops finally caught up with him. Not only did they take away his driver's license, they even deported his car.

Listen, the judgment of a traffic cop is not always right—but his customers are always wrong.

I was out driving one afternoon, when a traffic policeman pulled me over to the side. "Hey," the cop yelled. "Do you know you were doing sixty miles an hour?" I answered, "That's ridiculous, officer. I'm not even on the road an hour."

I'm such a lousy driver—would you believe I got two tickets on my written exam?

One way to solve the traffic problem in New York would be to keep all the cars that are not paid for off the streets.

When a New Yorker is in a hurry, he doesn't take a taxi, he walks.

A cab driver picked up a passenger who wore a hearing aid. He said, "I guess just about all of us have something the matter. Take me, for instance. . . . I can hardly see!"

UFOs

Suddenly we have lots of new reports of UFO sightings. "What's new about it?" my brother asks. "All I have to do is come home loaded one night and you never saw so many unidentified flying objects thrown at me—and my wife never misses."

A Martian landed in New York and found he had broken one of the little wheels on his spaceship. That night, while passing the deli, he noticed some bagels in the window. "I'd like to buy some of those wheels," he told the manager. "Those aren't wheels," he was told. "They're bagels—you eat them." The manager sliced a bagel in half and offered it to him. After chewing a bite, the Martian beamed, "Hey, this is great—it should be good with cream cheese and lox."

Two UFOnicks come to Brooklyn and land on an apartment house in Flatbush. They see all the TV antennae, and one says, "Hey, dig the beautiful broads!"

A spaceship from Mars tried to land in New York City but

couldn't find a parking place—so the ship moved to New Jersey.

A spaceman brought his contraption down in Atlantic City, just as a slot machine player hit the jackpot. As the shower of silver dollars poured out noisily, the Martian patted the machine and said, "Buddy, you'd better do something about that cold."

The visitor from outer space was kissing and hugging a traffic signal, when it quickly changed from GO to STOP. The visitor snickered, "What do you expect? Earth women are all teases."

If you think the space program is expensive now—just wait till the astronauts union is formed and they start charging by the mile.

"Your mission on earth," said the moon boss to the explorers, "will be to capture two earthlings and bring them back alive." The moon men zipped down to earth and brought back two gasoline pumps. "Great," said the moon boss. "You accomplished your mission—we'll breed them and soon there will be slaves for all." The captain of the spaceship interrupted, "You're all nuts. Can't you see they brought back two male pumps?"

An earthnik landed on Mars and saw a large crowd around one store. There was a machine in the window that was delivering babies. Every time this Martian pressed a button, a newborn baby arrived. "What kind of thing is this?" he asked one onlooker. "That's our baby machine. Don't you make babies like that on earth?" The earthnik said, "Are you kidding? On earth we use a completely different method: A couple gets married, goes on a honeymoon, and nine months later there is a baby." The spaceman said, "Up here—that's how we make trucks."

Ugly People

I asked my friend why he picked the ugliest girl in town for his wife. "The beauty of marrying a homely girl," he explained, "is that in twenty years, you know she'll be pretty as ever."

My neighbor asked her older sister, "How come you're marrying this man? He's so old and wrinkled!" My sister said, "Yeah—but so's his money."

If you're not pretty, cultivate your voice: At least you'll look better on the telephone.

Like I said to my neighbor, "You have beautiful children—thank God your wife cheats."

Two men met at a cocktail party, and as they stood talking, one glanced across the room and remarked, "Get a load of that ugly broad—a nose like a pomegranate, walks like a cow, and a backside to match." The other guy said, "Hey, that's my wife." The first guy said, "Oh—I'm sorry!" The husband said, "*You're* sorry!"

After one week of marital bliss a wife asked her husband, "Will you love me when I'm old and wrinkled?" He said, "Of course I do!"

The shorties use their height to advantage: They walk under turnstiles. If they're superstitious they walk under black cats.

The baldies have it made: They don't need barbers—they comb their head with a twirl and they are proud that they have a beautiful head of skin.

I'm tired of all those beauty pageants like Miss Universe, Miss America, Miss Bagel—how about a contest for the ugliest beast on the block? How about a Miss Ugly contest? Like my neighbor: She has Early American features—she looks like a buffalo. The only person who ever asked her to get married was her mother. . . . A peeping Tom reached into her window and pulled *down* the shade.

A sure winner in the men's division is the guy who sent his picture to the lonely hearts club. They not only sent it back, they touched it up first. They returned it with the explanation that they were lonely—not desperate. . . . When his girl kisses him she closes her eyes—she *has* to! . . . He was an ugly baby. He used to go to parties and play spin the bottle, where if you didn't want to kiss anybody, you had to give them a quarter. Would you believe by the time this guy was twelve, he owned his own home?

The contestants for the Miss Ugly contest are coming in by the thousands. . . . I like the very religious one: People look at her and say, "Oh, God!". . . Men look at her and dress her with their eyes. . . . She got her nose from her father—he's a plastic surgeon. . . . At one time this girl was considered an ugly duckling. Now she's not considered at all. . . . I'll tell you one thing: This girl makes a fortune—by renting herself out for Halloween parties.

Another girl is so ugly:
　　She's proud of the fact that the police put her picture in all the jails in the country to discourage sex offenders . . .
　　The only man who thinks she's a ten is her shoe salesman . . .
　　When she walks into a bank they turn off the camera . . .
　　She spends hours at the beauty parlor just for estimates.

She is so ugly, her passport pictures come out nice.

My doctor made me a deal. He'll take out my appendix—if I'll take out his daughter.

My uncle is not too pretty. Customs made him put

somebody else's picture on his passport. He's got the kind of face that grows on you—if you're an ape.

First prize goes to my friend Charlie: If you really believe man is made in the image of God—one look at him would make you an atheist. His photographs do him an injustice—they look like him.

My sister laments, "You've heard of body language? I have nothing to say."

A man told his drinking buddy, who had been badly beaten: "I think you were pretty stupid to call that guy's girlfriend ugly, Ralph." "I didn't call her ugly," Ralph said. "I just asked if she was allowed on the furniture."

United Nations

Every time there's trouble in the world, somebody calls the U.N., and the U.N. is finally doing something about it—they're getting an unlisted number.

We have to be careful cutting back foreign aid to the third world nations. They need our aid to buy Soviet weapons.

The delegates at the U.N. read an eye chart looking for a hidden meaning.

Diplomacy is the art of saying "Nice doggie" until you have time to pick up a rock.

The art of diplomacy is to say nothing, especially when you're speaking.

I asked the diplomat, "What's your favorite color?" He said, "Plaid."

A diplomat is one who thinks twice before saying nothing.

I have come to the conclusion that one useless man is called a disgrace, two are called a law firm, and three or more are called the U.N.

Diplomacy is the ability to take something and act as though you are giving it away.

A real diplomat is one who can cut his neighbor's throat without having his neighbor notice it.

I asked one U.S. diplomat how he felt working in the U.N. He said, "It's okay—except that there are too many foreigners."

The secretary of the U.N. said to the American ambassador one morning: "I have checked all the cables, newspapers, and TV—there is no trouble in the world. What will we do?" The American ambassador consoled him: "Don't worry, something will happen. I have faith in human nature."

Someone who saw a camel for the first time exclaimed: This must be a horse designed by a U.N. committee!

Four U.N. diplomats meet a gorgeous blonde at a reception at the U.N. The Frenchman kisses her hand. The Englishman shakes her hand. The American puts his arms around her. . . . The Russian cables home for instructions.

The U.N. was started after World War II to make everybody act like friends. So far they're all acting like relatives.

The U.N. says it wants all the countries in the world to live as one big family. If you want to take my family as an example—they've succeeded.

The best way to describe the U.N. is to compare it to an ex-girlfriend of mine: All the parts are there but they just can't get together.

Diplomatic language has a hundred ways of saying nothing but no way of saying something.

The U.N. keeps the peace, all right. In all the years of its existence, there has never been a war in the U.N. building.

A true diplomat is always ready to lay down *your* life for *his* country.

A typical American is somebody who feuds with his neighbors, argues with his employees, disagrees with minority groups, yells at his family—and can't understand why the people at the United Nations can't get along with each other.

A diplomat is a person who can tell you to go to hell in such a way that you actually look forward to the trip.

The best definition of a diplomat is the story about two men meeting in a bar when the subject of Green Bay, Wisconsin, came up. The first guy said, "It's a real nice place." The other said, "What's nice about it? Only things ever come out of Green Bay are the Packers and ugly prostitutes." The first said, "Hold it, you punk. My wife comes from Green Bay." The other replied, "Oh, does she? What position does she play?"

A diplomat must learn to yawn without opening his mouth.

Diplomacy is the art of letting someone have your way.

A good diplomat never stands between a dog and a hydrant.

One thing about those foreign delegates, they are all sincere—whether they mean it or not.

An optimist believes that at the U.N. every man is as honest as the next guy. A pessimist believes the same thing.

The U.N. had an art exhibition. I admired one abstract painting. I looked at it from all angles, and I must admit it's the best picture of the U.N. I ever saw: No matter which way you look at it—it doesn't make sense.

The credo of the U.N.: "I regret that I have but one lie to give for my country."

A lot of diplomats will do anything to help their country—except shut up.

The trouble is, the world is getting smaller—the Near East is too near, and the Far East isn't far enough.

The U.N. is a strange world. A man gets up, speaks for an hour, and nobody listens to him—but as soon as he sits down, everybody disagrees with him.

Vacations and Travel

Let's face it: Vacations aren't any fun unless you can go someplace you can't afford.

A European vacation is a great equalizer. People come back from them just as broke as their neighbors who couldn't afford to go.

A well-organized vacation is having your two weeks run out before your traveler's checks do.

Vacation is a time when you get away from being cooped up with your wife and kids in a tiny apartment, and spend two weeks with them cooped up in a tiny motel room.

My wife and I are making vacation plans. She decides where to go and I decide how to pay for it. We're saving a fortune on our trip to China this year—we're not going.

Over 30 million Americans will go camping this summer. They'll also go camping this winter—they can't afford to pay rent.

Two women were meowing at lunch: "I was talking to Sylvia the other day about vacation plans, and she tells me that you aren't going to Paris this summer." The other lady said, "No—that was last year. This year we're not going to Rome."

Two of my friends just got back from a wild cruise. The highest ranking officer aboard ship was the wine steward.

One thing I've learned about vacationing by car: The clean restrooms are all locked. . . . It's always great to get back home. At my age real security is knowing that the bathroom is in the same place every night.

One motel on the road was murder. Nothing free. I even had to rent a pen to sign the register.

My neighbor told me, "I was looking for a place to board the dog while I'm on vacation, and one kennel offers air conditioning, gourmet food, and lots of petting and affection. I was so impressed, I'm sending the dog on vacation and I'm staying at the kennel."

Vacation: That's a system whereby people who are merely tired become exhausted!

What I like about a vacation is it fills your year. If you take your vacation in August, you get your pictures back in September, your bills back in October, your health back in November, and your luggage back in December.

If you look like your passport photo, you aren't well enough to travel.

There's a book that tells you where to go on your vacation: It's called a checkbook.

What most Americans would like is a dollar that will go a long way—but won't go very fast.

My neighbor told me: "We just got back from Europe. We spent most of our time studying ruins—our budget."

The girl was visiting Alaska, met a man, and married him after a very brief acquaintance. I asked her how come their courtship was so short. She explained, "When it was dark enough to park, it was too cold—and when it was warm enough, it was too light."

My neighbor told me he's going to the usual place for his summer vacation—to a bank for a loan.

The husband said, "I can hardly wait for our vacation." The wife agreed, "It will be good to get away." He said, "Yeah! Forget about rising utility bills and house payments." She said, "Forget about the way food prices are going up." He: "Forget about Social Security rates and property taxes." She: "Forget about gas prices and air fare." He: "Forget about the vacation!"

Two expectant fathers were nervously pacing the floor of the maternity ward waiting room. "What tough luck," one grumbled. "This had to happen on my vacation." The other groaned, "What the hell are you complaining about? I'm on my honeymoon!"

My friend spent two weeks fishing at an expensive resort and didn't get a bite, but on the last day of his vacation, he caught one fish. "See that fish?" he said to a bystander. "It cost me a thousand dollars." The man said, "Ain't you lucky that you didn't catch two."

A couple I know decided to spend their vacation at a nudist camp. "What are you going to do there?" I asked. She said, "Oh, I guess it's a good way to air our differences."

It's hard to settle down when you return from vacation. It's even harder to settle up.

There's increasing need for three-week vacations: They would give your postcards time to reach home before you do.

The man who said you can't take it with you never saw a camper truck packed for a vacation.

My neighbor told me, "We're thinking about separate vacations this year. My wife could go to Canada, the kids could go to Disneyland—and I could go bankrupt."

Nobody remembers exactly when we lost control of the economy—but it might have been when we discovered that fifty weeks of work couldn't pay for a two-week vacation.

There are certain basic rules of travel you should be aware

of. Like, when they say you should travel light, they mean your suitcase—not your wallet.

Husbands are like traveler's checks: You can't leave home without them.

Last year we discovered a vacation spot that was convenient, comfortable, relaxing, informal, and priced right— it's called the living room.

A man and wife walked into a hotel in Vermont and asked the desk clerk, "Do you take children?" The clerk replied, "No, we take only cash and credit cards."

My vacation plans are very simple: My boss tells me when I can go, and my wife tells me where.

All the trouble in the Garden of Eden started when Eve bit into a piece of fruit. I had the same problem in Mexico.

In Afghanistan, Mullah was crying because his donkey died. His neighbors roasted him, "Mullah, it's not nice you should grieve more for your donkey than your wife who died last summer." He answered, "When my wife died you consoled me that you would find me a younger and prettier wife—but so far no one has suggested finding another donkey."

In Saudi Arabia, after a violent sandstorm had disrupted service, this sign appeared in telephone booths: UNTIL FURTHER NOTICE PLEASE LIMIT CALLS TO FOUR WIVES.

What do Poland and the United States have in common? In the U.S. they will not accept zlotys when you go to buy something. In Poland they will accept zlotys, but there's nothing to buy.

Wall Street

Wall Street is on the up side. They've even relaxed security and taken the locks off the upper floor windows.

The stock market is jumping all around. I've been poor before and I've been rich before, but never in the same day.

You've got to look at the positive side of Wall Street; like, the sound, secure investments of today are the tax losses of tomorrow.

Stocks no longer provide for your old age, but they do hasten its arrival.

My stockbroker is a golf nut. One day he called me and said, "Guess what? I just broke eighty!" I said, "I know— I'm one of them."

I don't want to criticize my broker's recommendations, but Wall Street just voted him Man of the Year—1929!

The stock market has its own unique system of checks and balances: For every nut selling, there's another nut buying.

I had a big talk with my broker yesterday and I feel much better about the market. We set up a calculated, all-encompassing program designed to reach certain invest-ment goals during the next five years—like getting even.

Do you think this means anything? My broker has stopped wearing his crash helmet!

My neighbor was reading the stock market report and said to his wife: "Remember that stock I was going to retire on at 55? Well, my retirement age is now 350!"

Then there's the sad story of the Wall Street broker whose migraine just split two for one.

I know you can't take it with you, but the way things are going, I think my stocks will get there before I do.

My broker has been wrong so many times he's been offered a job as a government economist.

One guy buys a hundred shares at 10; the stock goes up to 20 and he wants to sell. The broker says, "This stock is now a better buy at 20 than it was at 10." The guy says, "Gee, if I had only waited."

My stocks aren't listed on the business pages anymore. I now find them in the obituary column.

My broker is a professional consultant. That's a guy who knows fifty ways to make love—but can't get a girl.

I don't want to say my brokerage firm has a closed mind— but the company suggestion box is a garbage disposal.

The minister was counseling a young stockbroker: "You know, the Lord works in mysterious ways." The broker said, "I know that, Reverend, but when he plays the market, is there some method he uses?"

You can always tell when prosperity has come back to Wall Street: You look on a window ledge and see more pigeons than brokers.

I saw a very disturbing sign in the financial center: It said, THE BUCK DROPS HERE.

They sure make a lot of money on Wall Street. Down there, if your income isn't in six figures—you qualify for food stamps.

I asked my uncle, "If your broker keeps losing your money, why do you stay with him?" He said, "I never have to worry about taxes."

A stock market investor is someone who is alert, informed, attuned to the economic heartbeat of America—and cries a lot.

Wall Street is the only place you can take a bath without

water. Forget about the prayer in school—what we need is a prayer in the stock market.

The stock market has made everybody money mad: I'm mad because they took my money away.

What's the difference between a rich man and a poor man? A rich man has a wallet crammed with bills. A poor man has a wallet crammed with bills, too—unpaid ones.

The stock market has really caused inflation. Even barbers have to charge more now—the faces are longer.

My neighbor cried to me: "My financial situation is now fluid—everything's going down the drain!"

Frankly, I've stopped accepting calls from my broker. I kept getting obscene prices.

After ten years in the business, my brother has learned to do one thing very well—apologize.

Actually, I'm not sure what's going on in the market today, but my broker just moved his office to a crap table in Atlantic City.

I don't know if it's true—but I hear they're moving the Wailing Wall from Israel to Wall Street.

Life has become much more sophisticated. Years ago it was ghosts and goblins and monsters and witches that scared you. Now it's the Dow-Jones Average.

They say the institutions are getting back in the market. What bothers me is Bellevue is an institution—and so is Leavenworth.

Because of oil, the Arabs have most of their wealth in the ground. Because of the stock market, so do we.

Two New York Stock Exchange officers were comparing notes one morning: "Boy, I wish I had a secretary like Klein's got," said one. "Why?" asked his friend. "Do you think she fools around?" The first said, "Are you serious? Last week she made the NYSE's most active list."

I take a philosophical view of things. Like, if God had intended us to be rich, he never would have given us the stock market.

My mother taught me never to get mixed up with bad company—so did the stock market.

The only difference between the current stock market and the *Titanic* is that the *Titanic* had a band.

My broker called me and said, "I think you should buy a thousand shares of X company." I asked, "Why should I buy them?" He said, "Because it's the only way I can sell mine."

The ninety-five-year-old multimillionaire was still looking to make more. He met with his financial advisor, who told him excitedly, "I just found out about an investment I can make for you which will double your money in five years!" The old man screamed, "Five years? Are you kidding? At my age, I don't even buy green bananas!"

What a country! Where else can you see somebody invest in the stock market with a welfare check.

Even now my broker called with a "hot tip." He's not worried. He got out of the market a month ago—and they are still looking for him.

I have an incompetent broker: He jumped out of a basement window.

The more you visit your stockbroker today—the more you'll visit your pawnbroker tomorrow.

Winter

Cold? This morning I tried to brush my hair and it broke! I'll tell you how cold it is. Did you notice three statues of joggers in the park this morning? Well, they're not statues.

I love New York no matter how cold it gets. At least we've got something to talk about. In Hawaii, where the weather is the same all year round, how do they start a conversation?

My boss isn't taking chances today: He came to work all wrapped up in his electric blanket. I'm still trying to find out where he got that 3½-mile extension cord!

Last night we all gathered around the living room fire. It was such fun—I'm even thinking of putting in a fireplace.

This weather doesn't bother the politicians: They know how to cover up. In fact, it was so cold in Washington, the pols had their hands in their pockets.

How about this weather? Do you realize this is the first snow job in weeks that hasn't come from Washington? Well, at least we should have a hot air mass moving in from there—now that Congress is back in session.

As a special winter feature, one pastor preached on the Eleventh Commandment: "Thou shalt not take the Lord's name in vain when trying to start your car."

Not only has the iceman cometh—I think he has decided to stayeth.

But let's look at the positive side of this weather. Do you realize that any day of the week you can go out to the beach and find a parking place?

My superintendent gave me some bad news: It's supposed to drop to 5-below tonight. The good news is he is finally fixing my air conditioner.

It was so cold I had to drink a six-pack of Prestone.

It was so cold, before she could say "I'm not that kind of girl"—she was.

It was so cold—they had to chip me out of my waterbed.

You think you've got problems? I've got a frozen zipper!

This weather is a wonderful experience for anyone who has ever wanted to live inside a Good Humor truck.

I was so cold only my heartburn kept me warm.

I awoke to find two feet of ice in my bed—both of them belonging to my wife.

I can't believe my electric bill—I'm going to have to keep my thermostat at no more than 62 dollars a day.

A realtor has decided to put up condo igloos: He promises central refrigeration.

It's so cold they're putting thermal underwear on the Statue of Liberty.

This is the time of the year for skiing, or as orthopedic surgeons call it—the busy season.

When you're zooming down a ski slope, there are two things you must never lose: Your composure and your Blue Cross card.

I went to one ski resort that had three slopes: beginners, intermediate, and call-an-ambulance.

It's so cold, even my neighbor's wife is acting frigid.

Women and Women's Lib

Would you believe women still want equal rights? What do they mean equal? Women who want to be equal to men lack ambition.

A group of women's libbers was demonstrating outside the White House as the president was about to leave. One woman cried out, "Free women!" The prez hollered back, "Marvelous—do you deliver?"

A career woman is one who would rather go out and take orders than stay home and be boss.

Marriage is a lot like the U.S. Constitution: A man begins by laying down the law to his wife—and ends up accepting all her amendments.

My neighbor's wife cries: "If you do housework for $200 a week, that's domestic service. If you do it for nothing—that's matrimony."

Listen, anyone who believes a woman's place is in the kitchen—hasn't tasted my wife's cooking.

When my mother married my father a promise was made to love, honor, and obey. And my mother did her very best to make sure my dad kept that promise.

A women's libber says, "We cannot reduce women to equality—equality is a step down to most women."

Women's lib came up with a very interesting argument. They say, if God was satisfied with Adam, how come he made Eve so different?

My aunt says, "When it comes to taxes, women are equal."

If it's true that men are such beasts—this must account for the fact that most women are animal lovers.

To a smart girl men are no problem—they're the answer.

Sex appeal is 50 percent what you've got and 50 percent what people think you've got.

Women are a problem—but they're the kind of problem I enjoy wrestling with.

That no two women are exactly alike is proven by the fact that when two members of the gentle sex feel sorry for each other, the chances are one has a baby and the other hasn't.

My niece tells me, "What's the hang-up about whether we're supposed to dress for men or women? With me, it's simple: I dress for women and undress for men."

My aunt claims: "A woman is like a tea bag: You never know her strength until you drop her in hot water."

They caution pregnant women not to drink alcohol. It may harm the baby. I think it's ironic: If it wasn't for alcohol most women wouldn't be that way.

I'm always attracted to older women—they don't slap as hard.

My sister said about her stockbroker: "If it weren't for his money—he wouldn't have any personality at all."

My sister again: "Love is more important than money: I intend to wait until the right millionaire comes along. I'll wear my long low-cut gown—I'll show them a thing or two."

A woman's age is like the speedometer on a used car: You know it's been set back—but you don't know how much.

If there hadn't been women we'd still be squatting in a cave eating raw meat. We made civilization in order to impress our girlfriends.

My neighbor: "Women's lib sure has changed our way of thinking. I used to believe that old maxim, Never send a boy to do a man's job. Today you'd better send a woman!"

I won't say some of today's women dress scantily, but I know a doctor who went crazy trying to vaccinate one woman in a place where it wouldn't show.

The lady put a gun in the doctor's ribs: "Crime doesn't pay," he lectured her. She answered, "Well, neither does housework, buster, so hand over your wallet."

My aunt claims: "Nowadays, if a woman says she sits around all day talking to her plants, it could mean her electronic plant in Pennsylvania and her textile plant in New York."

My niece says her husband gave her a household hint on what to do with her old clothes: "Wear them."

My sister cried to me: "With my face-lift, my only shock was finding that the one underneath looked even worse."

One mother I know has a real problem. She has two daughters: One is mad at her because she won't let her wear a bra yet—and the other is mad because she won't let her throw hers away.

Women's lib means opening the door for a lady and standing aside so she can rush in and take the job you're after.

Generally speaking, I think a woman's mind is cleaner than a man's. It has to be—she changes it more often.

My aunt: "I'm a firm believer in loyalty. I think when a woman reaches an age she likes, she should stick with it."

Frankly, I think no woman is likely ever to be elected president. They never reach the legally required age!

"I'm joining the women's lib movement," my aunt told me. "I want to get married and not have to work anymore."

I think women are better at math. Only a woman will divide her age by two, double the price of her dress, triple her husband's salary, and add five years to the age of her best friend.

The first girl asked, "Wouldn't you like to be liberated?"

The second girl said, "No, I'd much rather be captured."

My aunt claims: "There are two kinds of male chauvinists—those who think men are superior to women and those who think women are inferior to men."

My sister reminds us: "Just desserts—that's a man marrying a woman because he wants someone to cook and keep house, and then discovering she married him for the same reason."

My sister-in-law has a one-sided opinion: "It has been said that women are more irritable than men. Maybe so, but the reason for this is probably that men are more irritating."

Listen to my sister: "The reason that few females play golf is that we women have more important things to lie about."

Worst Jokes

She: "The baby has swallowed the matches." He: "Here, use my lighter."

The day after the bank robbery, the teller phoned the man and said, "Your pictures are ready."

"I'm glad I wasn't born in France," my friend said. "Why?" I asked. "I can't speak French."

The doctor opened the window wide and said, "Stick your tongue out the window." I said, "What for?" He said, "I'm mad at my neighbors!"

Last night I ordered a whole meal in French, and even the waiter was surprised—it was a Chinese restaurant.

They showed real old movies on the plane. The pilot wouldn't get on—he had already seen the picture.

A duck, a frog, and a skunk wanted to go to the movies. The admission was one dollar. Which one of the three couldn't afford it? The skunk. Why? The duck had a bill, the frog had a greenback, but the skunk had only a scent.

The nice lady said to the young man, "Are you the brave little boy who jumped into the icy river and saved my boy from going over that horrible waterfall?" "Yes I am, ma'am, I sure am." "What did you do with his mittens?"

My neighbor told me, "My pioneer great-grandfather went west in a covered wagon. He was a rugged man— but he died after having his ears pierced." I asked, "How could he die from having his ears pierced." My neighbor explained, "They were pierced by an Indian's arrow!"

Another neighbor told me, "My brother just opened a shop." I asked, "How's he getting on?" He said, "Not very well—it wasn't his shop."

The penalty for bigamy is two mothers-in-law.

My uncle's cat committed suicide—shot herself in the head nine times.

What would you do if you were alone in a jungle and an elephant charged you? Pay him!

Who knows if it's true: Benjamin Franklin's wife was responsible for his famous discovery. When he told her he was going to try to harness the electricity of lightning, she cried: "Go fly a kite!"